# THE AMERICAN WEST

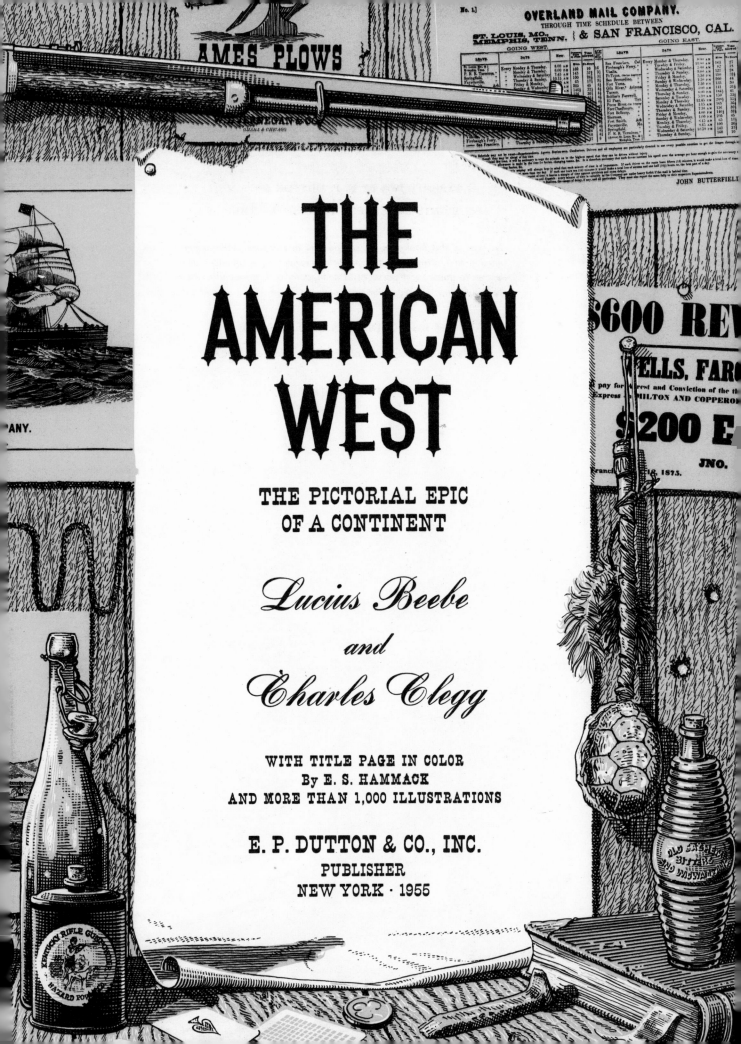

# THE AMERICAN WEST

## THE PICTORIAL EPIC OF A CONTINENT

*Lucius Beebe*

and

*Charles Clegg*

WITH TITLE PAGE IN COLOR
By E. S. HAMMACK
AND MORE THAN 1,000 ILLUSTRATIONS

E. P. DUTTON & CO., INC.
PUBLISHER
NEW YORK · 1955

# ACKNOWLEDGMENTS

FOR THEIR MANY courteous offices of assistance in the preparation of this book, the authors are indebted to Miss Ina Aulls of the Western Collection, the Denver Public Library; Mrs. Rogers Parratt of the California Historical Society; Irene Simpson of the History Room, Wells Fargo Bank & Union Trust Company of San Francisco; Dr. Duncan Emrich of the Library of Congress and Paul Vanderbilt of the same institution; to Stewart Holbrook for pictures and informative data on the Northwest of which he is the acknowledged and studious custodian; the Kansas State Historical Society at Topeka; the Santa Fe, Southern Pacific, Union Pacific and Great Northern Railroads; to Louis Hill, Joseph Henry Jackson; to John Barr Tompkins of the Bancroft Library of the University of California; Mrs. Clara Beatty of the Nevada State Historical Society and Grahame Hardy of Carson City; to Dr. Robert Taft of Kansas; Bernard De Voto of Cambridge, Massachusetts; to Robert Richards of Virginia City for expert assistance in layout and makeup; the *Deseret News* Press of Salt Lake; Alvin Harlow; Culver Service and Brown Brothers. Should this tally of obligations omit any who have helped in the assembly of this picture chronicle, it is hoped the credit lines will correct the deficiency.

# TABLE OF CONTENTS

# Foreword

THE STUDENT, amateur or collector of the pictorial record of the Old West in published form has available to him what is probably a greater variety of art forms than has ever been devoted to any major theme or preoccupation of history.

Without going into the technique of their reproduction, pictorial historians of the West discovered a market for their products in an age when all pictured representation of people and things was through the agency of human artistry, guided by human capacity for such matters and inhibited by human fallibility. In the very height of the vogue of the American West, when its depiction by sketch artists and painters was issued in lithographic form or engravings, the photographic camera came into being as a popular instrument of record and a few years later the half-tone engraving supplied detail in printed reproduction where hitherto only line drawings had been available to multiplication on a vast and popular scale.

Because of this transition the Old West was depicted by contemporaries in a multiplicity of forms which have captured and preserved almost every aspect of its color, animation, motion and personality. Their variety will probably never again be duplicated if only because the technique and professional *expertise* of the staff artist of the illustrated periodicals of the nineteenth century and the medium in which he worked have wholly been supplanted by photographs. In a number of ways which must be apparent to every perceptive intelligence, the selective range of the artist gave him an immeasurable advantage over the mere photographer. Conversely, the photographic plate supplied a measure of indisputable authenticity of record never altogether characteristic of the pictorial artist.

For their inclusion in this volume of a considerable number of pictures of an unquiet, even profane, nature, the authors make no least apology. The subject itself was eminently unquiet and equally profane. If it has not occurred to previous anthologists of Western pictures to include material culled from the files of the *Police Gazette* along with classic examples of Bodmer, Catlin and Remington, we think it was a notable oversight on their part rather than any great discovery on ours. The hurrah and disorderly conduct that was admittedly characteristic of the time and place may be said to find more appropriate expression in periodicals that could never be described as devotional reading than in *Harper's Monthly* or even *Leslie's*. The barbershop clientele of nineteenth century America got what was perhaps a better notion of life in Laramie or Abilene, and certainly a more lively one, than the patrons of the Boston Athenaeum in Beacon Street.

The thing that is important, aside from their explicit atmosphere of tumult and wayward charm, about these pictures is that they are the quintessential representation of the Wild West the way all the rest of the world including the American East wanted and believed it to be. They are the stuff of folklore.

Then, too, there is more than one authenticated example of Western persons and institutions that were modified in favor of what they learned about themselves in print. This obviously doesn't apply to the original pioneers, since it is doubtful if Kit Carson or Jim Bridger or Peter Skene Ogden ever saw their names, much less their pictures, in the public prints during their lifetimes. But Buffalo Bill Cody, first created out of whole cloth in the imagination of Ned Buntline, in time came perfectly to impersonate the altogether fictitious character of the Buntline stories. Wild Bill Hickok was undoubtedly influenced by his own press notices, and a remarkably large part of an entire Western generation came, in varying degree to be sure, to believe in its own publicity and to act the way it was expected to act, which was largely "up."

If the Long Hunters were immune from the effects of a publicity or notoriety which did not in their time exist, a later generation, particularly the bad men, peace officers and gamblers of the Southwest, learned how tough or wicked or valiant or romantic they were in the periodical press and works of semifiction and, being obliging fellows who wanted to please, they set out to live up to their billing. Thus the fact and folklore, the basic character and the assumed characteristics of the Old West became hopelessly involved before the end of the century which is the concern of this book.

Lastly, and like Boston in the old adage, the West was not so much a geographic locale as a state of mind. Bernard De Voto has pointed out that today's resident of Scottsbluff, Nebraska, doesn't consider himself a true Westerner, no matter what his habit of thought or person, because the Wyoming border and hence the authentic West is located a few miles nearer the Pacific than his home. The West of the nineteenth century was successively Kentucky, the Western Reserve, the trans-Mississippi and Kansas, and it finally met itself coming east out of California with the discovery of silver in Nevada.

When the nineteenth century dawned no white American was a Westerner in the sense the word came to assume in the age of Stetson hats and Colt's six guns. Anyone was a participant in the great legend of the Western continent who wanted to be, and that included a number of British milords, sons of Boston merchants in the China trade and Irish paddies from County Mayo.

This book is the pictorial record of as many aspects of the West in the nineteenth century as its authors could come by. In a few cases illustrations which have appeared in their previous books devoted to parallel matters have been included. The pictures seemed essential to both volumes. This book is dedicated to the attention of all amateurs of the Matter of the American West who believe that it was largely a cheerful saga of people going places they wanted most to be and getting things they wanted most to get and who accepted the risks as they accepted the satisfactions.

The Mormons, as they faced into the ineffable, the golden West sang:

> "And should we die before our journey's through,
> Happy Day, all is well."

The Argonaut and the Forty-niner sang:

> "Oh, Susanna, don't you cry for me."

In the last great accounting there is no need for tears for either of them. All was well.

LUCIUS BEEBE
CHARLES CLEGG

*Virginia City, Nevada, 1955*

Most wasteful of all were the hunters who slaughtered the buffalo for their hides, who annihilated the once universal animals in a few short years of wholesale destruction.

# I

## *The Long Hunters*

### Before the Gold Seekers, the City Builders or the Homesteaders, the West Belonged to the Hunters for Furs, the Hunters of the Buffalo

THE LONG HUNTERS and the Mountain Men were pretty much the same thing: operatives in the fur trade in the Rocky Mountain regions of the West in the opening decades of the nineteenth century.

They were the starred performers in the great drama and at times melodrama of exploring the Old West and at least commencing the opening up of its limitless regions to later exploitation by other seekers: land speculators, gold rush participants, railroad projects, cattle grazing, ranching and city building. Before any of these could come in safety or, in fact, at all, the Mountain Men sought out the way and made some sort of record of it available to their successors. Neither the Argonauts to California, the followers of the Oregon Trail nor the later discoverers of Santa Fe and Colorado were, in the essential meaning of the word, pioneers. The Long Hunters had been there before them. When Captain John Charles Frémont first set out for the Far West in 1842 he selected as his guide a Mountain Man who had followed the Columbia to its mouth and known the passes of the Cascades a full decade before that time—Kit Carson. The Long Hunters knew all there was to know—plenty—about the West from the Great Plains of Colorado and Wyoming all the way to Walla Walla and Fort Vancouver, but to the south the Wasatch Range and the margin of Great Salt Lake were the practical limits of their hunting grounds.

Most of the dramatis personae who appeared on this continental stage fell conveniently into four groups, from one to another of which they occasionally moved in shifting allegiances but whose essential framework remained the same as long as the mountain fur trade lasted.

They were the American Fur Company, the vast trust organized by John Jacob Astor, the Rocky Mountain Fur Company, known as "the Opposition," the Hudson's Bay Company, a chartered British monopoly which had merged early in the game with its own most powerful opposition, the Northwest Company, and the independent operators or free hunters. These are the categories of Mountain Men as set up by Bernard De Voto, and any man would be a fool to try to improve on him.

Executive head of the American Fur Company was Ramsey Crooks, and his principal field director, Kenneth McKenzie, "King of the Missouri." Notables in fringed buckskin who owned loyalty to "the Company" were Lucien Fontanelle, Andrew Drips, Jim Beckwourth and Etienne Provost.

Neither the buffalo hunters of Kansas and Texas nor the miscellany of other shooters depicted in the pages that follow were properly Mountain Men or Long Hunters and in this respect the title of the chapter is in error. They have been included among greater Bahrams and their betters as a matter of editorial convenience.

# A Name for American Immortality: Kit Carson

"I TOOK YE FOR AN INJUN!"

Greatest of all the Long Hunters who made the West their back yard in the 1830's was Kit Carson (*above*), of whom Stewart Holbrook says that not even Dan'l Boone was so much on the move throughout a long and restless life. Before the Oregon Trail was an established highway to the Northwest Carson knew the Columbia River and the Pacific Coast. A small man physically, as is suggested by the putative sketch of him in the Rockies at the left, Carson was inexhaustable. Selected to take the news of California's surrender to the Bear Flag Republic, he made the 3,000-mile trip to Washington, much of it through territory swarming with hostile Apaches, in record time. During the Civil War the Union managed to get Kit into a general's suit with gold braid to serve on the frontier against the Indians, who thought it might be a good time to retake the entire West from the whites, but soon he was back again in fringed buckskins hanging around the saloons at Taos. When he at last fell ill at Fort Lyon, he lay on his buffalo robe and demanded his pipe and a man's dinner. Warned they would kill him, Carson said: "No matter. Bring me some fust rate doin's, a buffler steak, my pipe and a big bowl of coffee." He ate two pounds of meat, smoked a satisfying pipe and died. The greatest of all the Long Hunters was given a funeral with a general's honors and buried, as he had wished, at Taos.

Kit Carson was a notable hater of Indians and killed his first redskin when he was sixteen by drilling him through the head at seventy-five yards to the admiration of everyone present. Selected to guide John Charles Frémont to California on the expedition which was eventually to lead to the annexation of California, Carson's men were surrounded by hostile Modocs near Klamath Lake (*above*) and threatened with complete extinction by overwhelming numbers. Alone, Carson circled the besiegers, killing a man every few minutes, until they believed they and not Frémont were surrounded and beat a hasty retreat. Nothing made the day for Carson like killing an Indian or two before breakfast and he did it regularly. Below: fur traders of Carson's time are shown attacked by hostiles on the Missouri.

# Beaver Brought The Mountain Men To Wyoming

The caption on this unsigned action drawing when it appeared in the *Police News* read, "Old Jeff Sampson's Winchester Doing Christian Work," and purported to show life on the frontier, presumably near Fort Union, forty years previous. In the lower drawing Captain John Charles Frémont of the Topographic Engineers of the U.S. Army, flanked by bearded trappers, is shown addressing a group of chiefs on the subject of hunting rights at Fort Laramie in the year 1842.

FORT LARAMIE, OUTPOST AND MEETING PLACE FOR THE LONG HUNTERS

Fort Laramie in eastern Wyoming at the junction of Laramie Creek and the Platte River was the regional seat of the American Fur Company and, excepting only Bent's Fort on the Arkansas, the most important meeting point in all the mountain trade. Fort Laramie originally had been built by the Rocky Mountain Fur Company and named Fort William for Bill Sublette but passed into the hands of the Astorians and eventually to the federal government as a military outpost of importance. Built to a hollow square, Laramie's walls were fifteen-foot-thick adobe with heavily fortified blockhouses at each corner and a vast courtyard for trading within. Almost everyone headed West, including Francis Parkman bound for Oregon, stopped here. The inner portion of Fort Laramie is sketched here by Alfred Jacob Miller, while below a group of Astorians encounter a group of Hudson's Bay retainers for a conference over trapping rights.

## NEVADA IN 1880 WAS STILL WILD IN MANY WAYS

At Carson City, Nevada, itself named for the greatest Long Hunter of them all, Swiss John, a sheepherder, was reported in the eighties as beating off a lynx with the hook affixed to the stump of one of his arms. Wildcats still frequent the eastern slopes of the Sierra, where Carson is located in Eagle Valley, and occasionally carry off small domestic animals. Swiss John has, however, been replaced by Basque François, as the typical Nevada sheepherder. At Minden, south of Carson City, Basque is as commonly spoken on the street as French in Montreal and restaurants list Basque dishes for their patrons.

## OBSTACLE TO RICHES

Paul Frenzeny drew this picture of a tableau in Colorado and called it "The Dangers of Prospecting—A Scene in the Rocky Mountains," and the episode it recounts must have been a commonplace among the gold seekers of the time. The grizzly depicted by Frenzeny wasn't hunted for meat, but small black bears (*below*) showed up in Eastern markets regularly at Christmas time for many years.

# Hunting Bear Was in the Great Tradition of the West

Frenzeny and Tavernier drew both these scenes of bear hunting in the Rockies, a sport which attracted large numbers of well-heeled visitors from the East and England every season. The Mountain Men delighted in grizzly lore and never allowed Joe Meek to forget the time when he and his partner Hawkins were surprised by a maddened bear they thought they had killed, but had only wounded, before going swimming. The bear chased them, naked and weaponless, for miles across the prairie. Meek was known to kill grizzlies with a hatchet, but mostly a rifle was deemed safer.

# Shooting Buffalo Was the Classic Sport of the Plains

## KILLING BUFFALO REQUIRED LITTLE SKILL

Professional buffalo hunters, killing for meat and hides, sometimes rode into a herd (*above*) and moved with it, shooting, across the plains. If the herd could be made to stand, however, it was better to shoot from a fixed position which made loading and firing easier and faster. Visitors from the East often stopped off at the railroad towns of Kansas and Wyoming and drove out to hunt with a guide and hired rig, as shown below.

## BUFFALO WERE THE SOURCE OF LIFE ON THE PLAINS

Until the coming of the white hunters, buffalo were the Indian's main source of life from meat and hides. Mounted on horseback the Indians rode fearlessly into the vast herds, as shown above by George Catlin, but on occasion, as sketched below by W. M. Cary, they would follow the animals into the Missouri River and, while they were swimming and helpless, cut their throats with hunting knives. The Indians seldom killed for sport and viewed with horror and indignation the miscellaneous slaughter which accompanied the white man as he invaded the plains states.

## GO BUFFALO, STARVE INDIAN

The plains buffalo of the West were divided into four great herds that ranged seasonally from the Canadian border to the Colorado River in Texas and were known as the Northern, Republican, Arkansas and Texas herds. When legislation protecting the Texas herd was proposed, General Phil Sheridan, in charge of Indian fighting at the time, hastened to Austin to protest. "The buffalo hunters have done more in two years to settle the vexed Indian question than the entire U.S. Army has done in ten years," he said. "They are destroying the Indians' commissary. Send them powder and lead if you will, but for the sake of lasting peace let them kill, skin and sell until the buffalo are exterminated."

It is improbable that the artist who drew the above sketch entitled "Making for a Tree" was familiar with buffalo, as they seldom attacked a man so, but the lower scene, "A Narrow Escape," was a commonplace if a hunter was thrown from his horse before a stampeding herd.

UNION PACIFIC RAILROAD

## SHOOTING FROM THE CARS WAS COMMONPLACE

Shooting up the herds from the cars of the Kansas Pacific and Union Pacific railroads, both of which ran through the heart of the buffalo lands, hastened the total destruction of the species. The above drawing, although the artist knew neither buffalo nor steam locomotives, typifies the slaughter from the cars. Curing hides and bones, drawn below by Frenzeny and Tavernier, was a considerable industry in Kansas, Arkansas and Texas until the disappearance of the Arkansas and Texas herds. President Grant was, apparently, of General Sheridan's mind in the matter of protecting the buffalo and hence feeding the Indians, since he pigeonholed a bill outlawing hide hunting in Indian Territory.

# The Coming of the White Hunters Doomed the Buffalo

## THE HERDS WERE HEADED FOR EXTINCTION

The oddly Tirolean appearance of these buffalo hunters depicted in a German periodical of the seventies is, however, authenticated by the drawing of Seth Kinman, an old hand at plains hunting, which appeared from the pen of an artist on the scene. Below is reproduced Theodore Davis's celebrated study of the slaughter of buffalo on the Great Plains. During the period between 1872 and 1874 the railroads of the West hauled 1,379,000 buffalo hides to market, 6,752,000 pounds of meat and 32,000,000 pounds of bones, and General Nelson Miles asserted that in the same period 4,300,000 animals had been killed on the Arkansas River alone.

## THE HUNTERS AND HUNTED
## REVERSED THEIR ROLES IN TURN

The Long Hunters of the thirties who went far beyond the Rockies in search of beaver plews waged unremitting guerrilla warfare with the Indians. Most of the great hunters and Mountain Men prided themselves on their prowess in killing off redskins and such notables in the fur trade as Bill Sublette, Joe Meek, Kit Carson, Jim Bridger, Lucien Fontanelle and Etienne Provost had long since lost count of the number of notches which their gunstocks were entitled to. Occasionally, however, the Mountain Men were themselves the hunted and had to take to the streams to hide their tracks, as suggested by W. M. Cary's "Water Leaves No Trail." Water for the wagon trains and for the groups of Long Hunters crossing the plains was also necessary for drinking purposes of man and beast and when Frederic Remington drew the lower illustration of plainsmen discovering a water hole, he simply entitled it "Water."

## VENISON FOR SUPPER

Shooting deer meat for the market never approached the murderous dimension of the killing of the buffalo if for no other reason than that the deer never traveled in vast herds and were uncommonly wary of men. In the tall timber of Colorado huntsmen often built platforms in the spruce trees and shot the deer at night as they came down from the hills for water. The venison thus obtained brought fancy prices, in the hard money of the time, when sent to market in Chicago and New York for the holiday trade. The upper drawing by Charles Graham occupied a cover of *Harper's* in 1886; the lower is by Schuyler Baldwin.

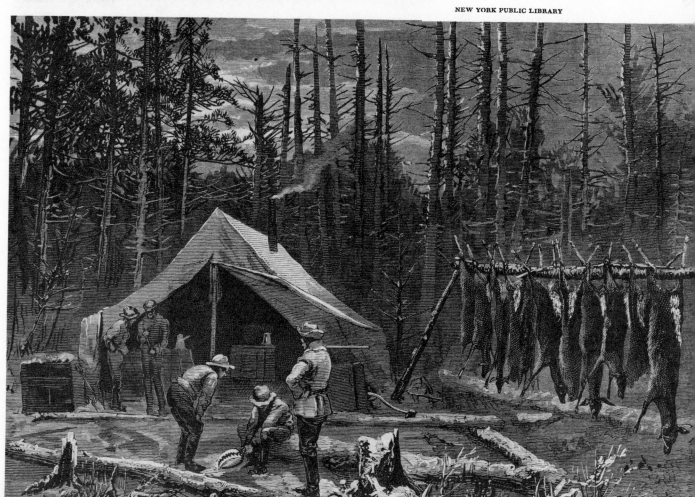

Hunting the swift antelope attracted many artists, including W. M. Cary (*above*), who depicted a hunter attracting them by waving his legs in the air, and Frenzeny and Tavernier (*below*), whose "Shooting Antelope from a Railroad Train in Colorado" is a classic.

## EVERYONE LOOKED WESTWARD

In 1883 *Harper's* made gentle fun of English milords who swarmed through Colorado in the attire of the frontier with this drawing and the caption reading:

"And who, pray, may this be? Buffalo Bill or some bold frontier leader?"

"Why, no, not a bit of it. This is simply Lord Reginald Snigsworth, who has come over to the States to shoot large game."

The sketch below is from *Harper's* at the time of the Centennial Exposition at Philadelphia where the replica of a hunter's camp in the Rocky Mountains was one of the most popular exhibits. Throughout the entire decade of the seventies the eyes of America were turned toward the West so newly opened to everyone through the agency of the Pacific Railroad.

Before the coming of steam and the paddlewheel, flatboats, keelboats and rafts bore a Westering nation over Western waters to the fulfillment of the Western dream.

## II

### *The Gateway to the Land*

#### For Nearly a Century the Mississippi and the Ohio Were Highways to Continental Destiny, the Means of Access to the Waiting Land

**T**HE GEOGRAPHIC FACT of the Mississippi River existed long before it achieved tangible importance in the social and economic pattern of American life. Beginning, however, with the Louisiana Purchase, by the terms of which the United States secured from Napoleon title to all the land, much of it undefined and most of it unexplored, between the Mississippi and the Rocky Mountains, the river itself together with its tributaries and connecting waterways came to assume a dominant position in the destinies of the American West. It was the key to a vast territorial acquisition which in a single transaction doubled the size of the United States in North America and which was, with the course of time, to contribute thirteen states almost in their entirety to the Union.

The ink was scarcely dry on the bill of sale for Louisiana, as the entire region west of the Mississippi was known, before commerce, for the first time freed from fear of confiscation or oppressive duties by foreign governments, began swarming on the Ohio and Mississippi in a race for the richly profitable market of New Orleans.

From 1803 until the completion of the Pacific Railroad almost seven decades later, the Mississippi and other navigable rivers of the inland continent were the most important single fact in the story of the West.

Until the coming of the steam packet and, decreasingly, for some years after it, two types of water-borne craft dominated river commerce: the flatboat and the keelboat. The flatboat was in many cases simply an unwieldy float of joined timbers supporting crude shelters for the protection of passengers and merchandise from the elements. When it reached its destination at Natchez or New Orleans the passengers debarked, the crew disbanded to return north via the perilous Natchez Trace and the craft itself was broken up and sold for lumber.

The keelboat was more elaborate in its structure and was built to survive an indefinite number of trips both up and down the river before being dismantled. Its wooden keel made it available to steering and twenty-foot wooden sweeps each manned by two members of the crew aided its progress. Sometimes keelboats carried a crew of 100, were 100 feet long and required a month for the round trip from Pittsburgh to Cincinnati. Living quarters for passengers contained separate apartments, heating equipment, beds and other rudimentary comforts for families bound downriver to colonize Louisiana and Texas, who traveled with their servants, livestock, farm equipment and complete domestic economy under a single roof much as Western immigrants were to travel in immigrant cars aboard the railroads in later years.

Coeval with the rush of river traffic to New Orleans there began an even more dramatic and eventually far more important continental movement westward by waterway. In 1803 President Jefferson asked Congress for an appropriation to finance an expedition headed by Captain Meriwether Lewis and Lieutenant James Clark which was to make its way to the headwaters of the Missouri and hence overland with the eventual goal of Oregon and the Pacific, an almost incredible feat of exploration which was to show the world the way to the vast and wealthy American Northwest.

Two years later Lieutenant Zebulon Pike explored the headwaters of the Mississippi and then turned westward to the Shining Mountains of Colorado. The rising fashion of beaver hats for gentlemen in England and the eastern United States was to send the fur trade, the Mountain Men and the Long Hunters in his footsteps in an endless succession of pioneers and adventurers whose rear guard was to merge with the forerunners of prospectors for precious metals, forming a continuity of Westward movement that was not to end until California was joined to the Union and Manifest Destiny was an accomplished fact.

For nearly seventy years, and longer in the remote regions as yet impervious to the railroad, the opening of the American West was to be achieved on the surface of rivers which to its farthest distances drained the continent.

Steam navigation came to the Mississippi in 1811 and its ultimate expression, the glittering river steamers of the period just before the Civil War, will live as a legend of wonderment in the American consciousness forever. More than aboard any other vehicle until the coming of the steamcars, the nation rode the river steamers of the Mississippi to far horizons and glorious destinies. Their freight was the American dream and the dream was the West. No dream has ever been realized through an agency of more stately grandeur.

ENGLAND PROMISED SANCTUARY

During the Civil War, as the fortunes of the South faltered and blockade loomed, many Southerners of means, fearing Northern invasion and victory, sent their families to England or the continent. Here Theodore B. Davis shows them embarking at New Orleans during the dark days of the struggle.

In 1873 the high point of navigation of the Missouri was Fort Benton, Montana, almost as far west as Salt Lake City, which will give some notion of the navigable distances on that mighty river. Here is the steamer *De Smet* unloading at Fort Benton in that year; an appreciable portion of its cargo is reassuringly in barrel form.

Here, perhaps aboard the *De Smet* itself, are the cattle of homesteaders westbound with their owners to the vast grazing lands of Montana.

When a Montana wheat rancher in the days before Jim Hill's Great Northern Railroad had a cargo ready for shipment east, he stacked it on the bank of the Missouri and signaled the first down boat by waving a flag at its pilot.

## "FOR DE LAWD'S SAKE"

Polite Victorian standards of conduct permitted few diversions on shipboard save gambling and drinking for the gentlemen and almost any encounter on the river served to break the tedium of the voyage. Passing steamers were hailed with waving handkerchiefs and the landscape reviewed with spyglasses. At the right is a Negro family dispossessed by floods who clamor to be taken aboard as deck passengers on the down trip to New Orleans.

THREE PICTURES: AUTHORS' COLLECTION

## "A-N-Y P-A-P-E-R-S?"

On Sundays, if there were a clergyman aboard, toddies and whist were temporarily banished from the men's lounge (*above*) and divine services were held. This, of course, was in the best Western tradition, since elsewhere on the frontier saloons were frequently used for church services. At the right a pair of boatmen row out to the steamer channel to beg for newspapers, the *St. Louis Post-Dispatch* if the vessel were downbound, the *Picayune* if she hailed from New Orleans.

# GRANDEUR TEMPERED BY MONOTONY

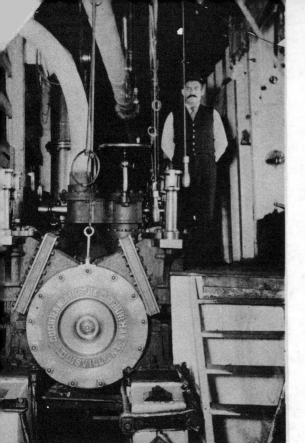

At the left is one of the few extant photographs of the engine room of an old time river packet, probably taken after the turn of the century. Oliver Evans, an early mechanical genius of the nineteenth century, was responsible for the high-pressure engine which soon came into almost universal vogue, although a few steamboat owners still advertised low-pressure boilers as a supposed safety factor. Below is shown the salon of the steamer *Grand Republic,* built in 1876 and destined to be one of the last floating palaces of its extremely ornate and luxurious type. The *décor* followed fastidious Victorian standards with miles of Turkey carpet and ornate gingerbread woodwork wherever it was possible to put it. Staterooms lined the two sides of the salon, the public nature of their approach being an almost certain preventative of illicit amour by their occupants. At mealtimes a shoal of servants transformed the long drawing room into a capacious restaurant while the passengers, temporarily dispossessed, promenaded the decks or sought their apartments to perfect their toilette. Commentators and travelers alike joined in praising the perfections of luxury of the great Mississippi packets but deplored the tedium of the journey itself.

John Durkin

## THE RIVER ONCE KNEW SPACIOUS DAYS AND WAYS

The above photograph shows the cabin of the *Grand Republic* in the seventies just as the steamcars were beginning to eat into the water-borne traffic of the Mississippi. It shows the rococo grandeur of design of the grand salons of the period and the polite attire of the passengers. It is from the collection of Captain Frederick Way, Jr., of Sewickly, Pennsylvania. On the page opposite is the levee at New Orleans on a fine morning in 1875 just as one of the great packets from St. Louis has pulled in, reflecting the life and movement of the river at its highest peak.

## BOILER EXPLOSIONS WERE INVARIABLY FEARFUL

The fearful overcrowding, especially of excursion steamers and on special runs, indicated by the above drawing, which was taken from a photograph, suggests one reason for the high rate of fatality in steamer accidents on the Mississippi. In 1870 on the occasion of a *Saengerfest* in Cincinnati no fewer than 50,000 persons were transported to the picnic grounds on ten steamers, each making two trips. When the boilers let go (*below*) or fire swept the vessel it was inevitable that a frightful toll of lives should result. The extreme violence of boiler explosions coupled with the grievous nature of the injuries they inflicted made an unfavorable impression on the public mind even in excess of that created by the train wrecks which at the same period were becoming a national scandal.

## DEATH RODE THE *GOLDEN CITY* AT NIGHT

As often as not catastrophes on the riverways took place at night when the sudden awakening of the passengers, the imperfect illumination and nature of the hour lent added terror. When the *Golden City* burned below Memphis in 1882 scores of passengers were trapped in their staterooms and died there.

### FIRE ON THE WATERS

ut of control and blazing from em to stern, the *Golden City* was e funeral pyre of more than 200 it drifted down the river. Barge- en along the shore and owners of nall boats saved scores of swim- ers from the water, but the dis- ter was one of the more dramatic its decade and hastened reforms steamboat inspection and navi- ation. After such holocausts and recks the shores of the river often rned up bodies of victims for eeks afterward and no complete cord of the deaths was ever avail- le in hundreds of such catastro- es. Sailing lists of cabin passen- rs were only imperfectly kept and e names of deck passengers, crew, ustabouts and casuals were never own.

## FIRE WAS THE COMMON END OF EVEN THE PROUDEST

Whether they perished massed in fiery holocaust involving half a score of vessels, such as the great conflagration in St. Louis in 1856, or collided and burnèd in pairs in the open river as was the case a decade later with the steamers shown below on the Ohio, the greater number of the inland river packets of the classic age of steamboat navigation were destroyed by fire. Once ablaze, it was virtually impossible to extinguish them and crew and passengers lost little time in attempting to check the flames. Saving themselves was difficult enough and often impossible.

## GHOSTS ALONG
## THE RIVERBANK

Although by mid-twentieth century time and the river have obliterated such tragic landmarks, the banks of the Mississippi, Ohio and other inland waterways were for many years strewn with the skeletons, as above, or in some cases the entire superstructures of steamers lost to mischance. In the first forty years of steam on the rivers nearly 600 vessels were lost by explosion, snagging, collision, fire or a combination of all of them, and after 1850 when the Mississippi became actually congested with traffic the incidence rose incredibly. The melancholy scene at the bottom of the page shows the remains of the steamer *Mississippi*, snagged and abandoned in a bayou of the lower river, and was drawn by Charles Graham for *Harper's* in 1888. For many years boilers, smokestacks, pilothouses and other fragmentary remains of once proud carriers along the riverbanks served as navigational landmarks for Mississippi pilots. In some cases they actually guided pilots who had been involved in the original accident.

## FLAME BY NIGHT AND SMOKE BY DAY

Fire, the classic peril of the river, was everywhere. Charles Dickens on his tour of America wondered at the close proximity of the furnaces to vast sources of potential combustion and concluded that it was wonderful there weren't even more steamboat fires. All the structural furniture of river packets from keel to Texas was wood, usually tinder dry from southern wind and sun. Highly combustible fuel was kept in great store adjacent to the boiler room. Much of the cargo and all the superstructure were inflammable. There was often no metal insulation between the chimneys and the deck around them was habitually charred. Once a fire started it was almost instantly out of control. If the vessel was in motion the draft turned it in a matter of seconds into a blowtorch. If moored at the levee, as shown above in the great fire at Memphis in 1856, it rapidly spread to steamers moored alongside and a general holocaust resulted. So common were such general alarms that the cry "The ships are all afire" was part of the lexicon of river towns. Fire lines and hoses were almost unknown and, in any event, fires usually started in the engine room and would have rendered control of steam pumps impossible had there been any.

Probably the most famous of all river packets in the golden age of Mississippi travel was the *Robert E. Lee,* whose race from New Orleans to St. Louis against the *Natchez* is an American epic. A few years later the *Robert E. Lee* burned to the water-line near Yucatan Plantation in Louisiana, to be mourned in passing as one of the stateliest and most beautiful of all river steamboats of the *post-bellum* years. Its end was drawn for *Leslie's* by Frederick Anderson.

A prime hazard of river navigation was snagging the bottom of a moving steamer on a concealed or partially hidden tree trunk such as the packet in this drawing is avoiding. A bad snag could rip the bottom out of a fast-moving steamer and sink it in a matter of minutes. Often the inrushing waters exploded the boilers before the fires could be drawn. Experienced river pilots sensed the presence of snags by the surface motion of the water in ripples or whirlpools, but when visibility was poor, as at night, they were the terror of the steamer traffic.

## COLLISIONS WERE DRAMATIC BUT NOT OFTEN FATAL

Collisions, although infrequent, were sometimes serious in their consequences and entailed considerable loss of life and property, as in the accident portrayed below when the steamer *Scioto* was rammed and sunk by the *John Lomas* in the Ohio River near Mingo Junction on Fourth of July, 1882. Sharp bends and the narrow width of navigable channels accounted for most collisions and the inability of downbound steamers running with the flow of the river to decelerate their progress accounted for others. As a rule, however, being rammed by another steamer left the navigators of the injured craft time to make shallow water before their vessels sank and so save lives and cargo.

In the recurrent floods which swept the Mississippi Valley before flood control was a science the great river steamers were frequently called on rescue missions. Here F. T. Anderson sketches for *Leslie's* the steamer *Deanada* taking off flooded settlers below Cincinnati.

Old Man River was impartial and when floods impeded river traffic they often inundated the adjacent railroads as well. In this scene William Chandler shows a passenger train of the Jackson Railway taking seas aboard near North Pass, Mississippi.

## THE LOOK OF THE RIVER AS IT SEEMED TO CHARLES GRAHAM

The distinguished staff artist for *Harper's*, Charles Graham, who drew so much of the West of his time, called this scene "The Flood on the Lower Mississippi—Mending a Levee." One of the most distinguished of all artists of the Old West, Graham was a member of the original survey party for the Northern Pacific Railroad and later official artist for the Columbian Exposition in Chicago in 1893. He was also a member of the Bohemian Club in San Francisco and lived until 1911, when many of the faces, scenes and aspects of the frontier he had so faithfully recorded had already passed away.

### TO THE BOATS!

Sometimes in flood seasons homesteaders along the banks of the Mississippi and Ohio placed their cattle and household possessions aboard rafts and were water-borne for the duration.

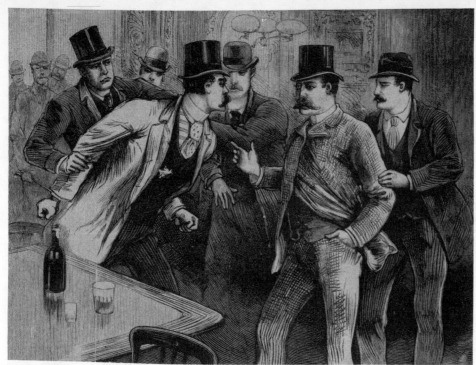

## GAMING WAS SOMETIMES ATTENDED BY TUMULTS

In 1900, if one may believe the *Police Gazette*, a stirring encounter was narrowly avoided when Ned Center, "the swell New Yorker who is the terror of Fifth Avenue dudes," came to near blows with Colonel Mike Duffy, who ran a saloon frequented by the sporting element of New Orleans. Center, an amateur boxer of rare attainments, and Duffy were restrained by friends and later toasted each other at the bar in a magnum of Mumm's Extra. Center returned unblemished to New York, where a short time later he was one of the founders of the celebrated Brook Club, a gentleman's resort with full clubhouse services twenty-four hours a day like the brook that ran on forever. The scene below shows what happened when Colonel Charles Starr, himself an expert professional, detected irregularities in a keno game in St. Charles Avenue.

## THE MISSISSIPPI RIVER GAMBLER HAD PRINCELY WAYS

The amounts of money in play aboard Mississippi packets have always been a matter of dispute. Romantic legend asserts them to have been fabulous, with plantations, family fortunes, slaves and immense sums of currency wagered by travelers and frequent suicides occasioned by their loss to professional sharpers. George Devol, however, a professional gambler with a long career throughout the Old West, wrote in his reminiscences of his river years that such accounts were "pure humbug." "I have grave doubts," he said, "whether a brag of $2,000 has ever been won or lost at cards on the Mississippi." Gaming was nonetheless an accepted institution on the river. Steamer captains hesitated to antagonize even known blacklegs because they were both atmospheric and extremely liberal with the help. Passengers accepted the presence of bad characters as something romantic on a tiresome voyage much as reputable persons accepted bootleggers during prohibition. Despite Devol's testimony, there were probably some games for very substantial sums aboard such richly patronized vessels as the *Robert E. Lee* and *Grand Republic*. Sometimes games became so exciting to the participants that they were continued ashore, as depicted here, at the conclusion of the voyage in the mansions of rich planters at Natchez or St. Louis. In one such princely session Jimmy Fitzgerald, notable in the forties as the best-dressed gambler on the river, lost an expensive wardrobe of forty English suits, four overcoats, his diamond shirt studs, a golden chain a rod long and as big as his little finger and four valuable slaves. Two weeks later, according to Herbert Asbury, he appeared on the gangplank of the *Telegraph* as resplendent as ever complaining that his new boots hadn't arrived from Paris.

A LANDMARK OF RIVER TRAVEL BURNED WITH THE SOUTHERN HOTEL

When in 1877 the Southern Hotel at the corner of Fifth and Elm streets in St. Louis was destroyed by fire, a landmark in the steamboat travel on the Mississippi disappeared forever. The Southern, as its name suggested, was a favored resort of wealthy planters who traveled upriver on business and for their families on their seasonal trips between the cities of the Deep South and such northern resorts as Saratoga Springs, long a favorite with the cotton aristocracy of Louisiana and Mississippi. Of the loss of the Southern a St. Louis paper mourned, "An honored friend has gone from amongst us." Particularly interesting to St. Louisans will be the drawing made after the destruction of the Southern, showing as it does the premises of "Tony Faust's Oyster House Saloon," long one of the great restaurants of the trans-Mississippi. Founded by Anthony R. Faust six years before this picture was made, Faust's was known to its generation as the "Delmonico's of the West" and its fame was national. Its clientele derived from the elite of St. Louis and one of its house specialties, "quail on sauerkraut," was originated by the actor Joseph Jefferson. Long a favorite with theatergoers and actors in the great days of the Road, Faust's was closed in 1916, but its memory is still green in a St. Louis that remembers it with affection.

AUTHORS' COLLECTION

## A MAN FOR BREAKFAST

Political shootings in St. Louis, essentially a Southern city, were not unknown as late as 1882, when Colonel Alonzo Slayback involved himself, fatally as it transpired, with one of the editors of the famed *St. Louis Post-Dispatch*. The editorial writer, John A. Cockerill, had incurred the colonel's displeasure by speaking disrespectfully of a Democratic candidate for office and Slayback, in a towering rage, had called in person on the editor waving a copy of the offending edition and calling on Cockerill to defend himself. In the ensuing reaching for weapons Cockerill was the faster and got two shots into his opponent before Colonel Slayback was so much as able to draw a pepperbox revolver from the tail of his frock coat. The street scene below shows the excitement which greeted the news of the shooting and the crowd which gathered outside the *Post-Dispatch*, whence, leaking bourbon in several places, Colonel Slayback was shortly carried in dying condition. Gunfighting among newspaper editors in the Deep South survived the turn of the century and as late as 1933 the wife of Hodding Carter, a Mississippi editor feuding with Huey Long, followed him to the door one morning calling, "Honey, you've forgotten your shotgun!"

IN THE ST. LOUIS SEVENTIES EDITORS HAD TO BE QUICK ON THE DRAW

### IN THE GREAT DAYS WHEN COTTON WAS KING

By 1883 when this night scene on the New Orleans levee was drawn for *Leslie's* by J. O. Davidson, the "electrical light" was the coming thing, and in the same year crowds gathered to cheer the arrival of a record cargo of 9,226 bales of cotton from upriver aboard the steamer *Henry Frank*.

LIVELY WAS THE LEVEE WHEN THE RIVER TRAFFIC WAS AT FLOOD

Pessimists like Mark Twain began to foresee an end to the river traffic of the Mississippi as early as the eighties, but these fine old time photographs, taken about 1900, show there was still vitality there twenty years later. By this time, however, much of the South's cotton was moving by rail and the predominance of casks in the upper picture would suggest that such unhurried merchandise as resin was the main source of freight revenue.

## THE ICE AGE RETURNED

Fire, explosion and sinking were not the only hazards to which the Mississippi steamers were subject; there was also ice. At the top is a view of the great ice jam at St. Louis which in 1877 destroyed scores of steamers, piling them on the levee and crushing them between giant floes. Below is a scene at Yankton, South Dakota, three years later, when incautious spring shipping moved up the Missouri the first week in May and was caught in a terrible freeze that followed. Dakota townships disappeared, government warehouses at Yankton were destroyed and a 110-foot vessel was floated into the shops there of the North Western Railroad. It was years before the countryside recovered from the damage and much of the shipping on the upper Missouri disappeared, never to be replaced. Everywhere the railroad was making itself felt and everywhere river commerce was in retreat.

## "OF TIME AND THE RIVER"

Between 1848 when the Cincinnati levee had looked as it does above and 1884 when Charles Graham sketched the levee at New Orleans as shown below for *Harper's,* America had come a long way. The continental dream had been realized, the continent spanned by the iron rails and steamcars. By the latter date the United States had found time to build a vast world trade via the ocean lanes, as is suggested by the ocean steamers at New Orleans, where they connected with the traditional river packets of the Mississippi. A cycle had been achieved of life on the river.

Although there were other routes to California the Golden and other agencies of transport, the pioneers who crossed the plains on horseback or with a covered wagon became the symbol of a nation on the march Westward.

# III

## *Manifest Destiny*

### The Compulsions to Continental Limits Set the Faces of America Westward in a National Exodus Like None in the History of the World

N O MORE FELICITOUS PHRASE ever emerged at the right moment to describe what was at once a national state of mind and an inevitable national achievement than "Manifest Destiny."

It was coined in a sentiment expressed by John L. O'Sullivan, editor of the *New York Morning News*, in 1845, when he said, "It is our manifest destiny to overspread and possess the whole of the continent which Providence has given us for the great experiment of liberty."

It expressed what just about everybody, basing their sentiments on the explorations of Zebulon Pike and Lewis and Clark and what was beginning to be known of California, felt about the as yet uncohesive American West. Specifically, what O'Sullivan had reference to was California and Oregon supplemented on a truly continental scale by the possessions of Spanish Mexico, which included all the region between Texas and the Oregon border: in terms of today's geography Arizona, New Mexico, Utah, Nevada and most of Wyoming. It was a territory nearly as great in extent and equally consequential with that acquired forty years previous in the Louisiana Purchase.

At the time O'Sullivan coined his comprehensive phrase, nobody was exactly sure how to go about the realization of its implications. The first step of establishing the United States within the obvious limits of geographic possibilities had been taken in the annexation of Texas. How to go about California?

In 1846, just a year after Manifest Destiny had become currency of the language, the opportunity offered itself to President James K. Polk, the "Young Hickory" from Tennessee who always had an eye to the main chance. A dispute arose over the survey of the Texas-Mexican border and Mexico allowed itself to be euchred into war with fatal consequences.

It cannot be reported that, while events below the Rio Grande were being brought to a satisfactory conclusion, the annexation of California was going forward on a truly heroic scale. The agents of Manifest Destiny were strictly comedians, the chief buffoon of them being Captain John Charles Frémont of the Topographic Engineers and a son-in-law of Senator Thomas Hart Benton, an inspired imperialist known to his generation as "Old Bullion." Frémont, with no specific orders from Washington, still acted under a sort of intangible mandate to seize California for the United States and so prevent an identical but of course dastardly action by the competing British.

This he accomplished by seizing the person and "army" of General Mariano Vallejo, an amiable and sleepy Mexican, at Sonoma. Vallejo's army of eight privates and three officers promptly surrendered and formal terms were dictated by Frémont while Vallejo set out his best California brandy for everyone and wondered what war he was a part of. A Republic of California appeared on paper bearing some traces of wine in the ink, and the wives of two of the conquerors ran up a flag whose device included a bear standing on its hind legs and reaching for something. It was probably the folksiest acquisition of a continental empire in history.

But it served.

Frémont's conquest lost nothing in his telling to his father-in-law by the first available post. His valiant army (thirty-three adventurers) had overcome a strongly fortified enemy garrison—the aforementioned eleven Mexicans, at a metropolis of vast strategic importance—the four adobe houses of Sonoma. The suffering of the American revolutionaries had, according to Frémont, been intense. He did not add that the Spanish brandy hospitably poured by Vallejo packed a mule-size wallop and that the conquerors to a man had grievous hangovers.

Manifest Destiny had now achieved a continental limit, the shore of the Pacific, but the filling in of the vast open spaces between the Missouri and the future site of Market Street, San Francisco, was going to take ponderably longer.

The marked favoritism which Providence had already shown the United States in the acquisition of Texas and California without undue cost or effort continued to show itself with the punctuality that is usually associated only with royalty.

Some great incentive was needed for the population of the West, especially California, a vast compelling urge that should overcome the inclination of a people to stay put and to prove how wrong were the godlike Dan'l Webster and other continental isolationists who saw no good or profit in anything the other side of Dedham, Massachusetts, or, at the farthest, the Great Lakes.

Almost at once the most powerful incentive known to history, idealists to the contrary notwithstanding, appeared in the millrace of Captain John Sutter, an imperial colonizer in his own right, at Coloma. James Marshall, a partner with Sutter in a projected sawmill, thought he saw a glint of gold in the sand at the bottom of the race and picked up a small nugget. This was in January 1848.

It wasn't until April that the news got abroad generally and then the gold rush to the Mother Lode was a purely local affair recruited from San Jose and San Francisco and possessed of overtones of a Spanish picnic or *merienda*. Everyone was friendly; there was lacking the spirit of competition which was shortly to result in stabbing, shooting and lynching as daily occurrences. There were few disputes about claims, since the entire landscape was available to monumenting as far as the eye could reach and the gold was probably more plentiful over the hill anyway.

It wasn't until later in the year when the news got East that all hell was going to break loose. Word got to Washington that autumn and President Polk with what-did-I-tell-you smiles officially announced that gold was available in great abundance in California, and who had been possessed of the shrewdness, foresight, wisdom and discernment to get California for the American people? James K. You-know-who.

The lack of population in the Far West began being remedied just as fast as people in Vermont and Georgia could pack a carpetbag and secure passage on the Erie Canal or the steamcars in the general direction of Westport Landing, Missouri. Those who disliked the prospect of overland travel could, and in great numbers did, book passage to Panama or around the Horn in steamers and sailing vessels. Whichever mode of travel he had selected, everyone shortly wished he had taken the other. No matter; almost all of them got there.

Almost two decades before all these Oh Susanna doings along the southern trails to California, the colonization of Oregon had been under way, largely by agriculturalists and Missourians who have left their mark on the life and thinking of those parts to this very day.

An absurd myth of the region and one which has engaged the horrified attention of professional historians for two full generations is that Marcus Whitman, the missionary later murdered at Walla Walla by Indians who had doubts about the efficacy of his tenets, was responsible for the surge of immigration which in 1843 made it clear to both countries that American sentiment and population were greater in Oregon than the British and secured the territory for the United States.

Until that time there had been some doubt as to sovereignty in Oregon and the Hudson's Bay Company had for many years regarded it as a feudal property held in fief by Dr. John McLoughlin, the company's resident emperor at Fort Vancouver.

The legend holds that Whitman, fearing the machinations of perfidious Albion, hastened to Washington to urge upon President Tyler the recruiting of a vast army of immigrants to march upon the Northwest and toss the treacherous Redcoats into the Columbia River. Whitman didn't go to Washington, he didn't see President Tyler and the wave of immigration was purely coincidental. He went to Boston to ask the moneybags of the Board of Commissioners for Foreign Missions to increase their appropriations for his missions in the Northwest. When he got back the Indians made cat's meat of him and the myth-makers made him a patriot as well as a martyr. Again, no matter. Oregon was snatched from the burning.

While Oregon filled slowly, California was busy doing things on the epic scale for which, like Texas, it has always since been famous. A steady seasonal stream of white-tops was moving out of Independence and Westport each spring and only a few lacked the determination to continue until California was achieved and everyone was a millionaire man just like that.

The Mormons were an exception when they settled in the Great Basin, but at first even they had ideas of empire and charted Deseret to extend as far as the Sierra to the west and south as far as San Bernardino. Only the Recall of 1856 diminished the tide of Mormon immigration beyond Salt Lake and contained the Saints in a tight and solid core of prudence, thrift and self-sufficiency.

All through the fifties the plains of the West were populous with wagon trains creaking slowly Westward despite geography, the elements, Indians and a genius, innate in many of the pilgrims, for doing things wrong. Simultaneously the jungles of Panama teemed with Bostonians and New Yorkers, most of them in silk hats and broadcloth tail coats, heading for Eldorado, and clipper ships from the shipyards of the Mystic and Kennebec were ferrying boatloads of seasick avarice around the headlands of Tierra del Fuego.

By the time the Pacific Railroad was completed in 1869 it could no more concern itself with Manifest Destiny than to put a period to it.

Even Georgia crackers joined the irresistible movement of the nation.

The phrase that was to be the watchword of the eventual continental dimension of the United States originated with John L. O'Sullivan, editor of the *New York Morning News*, in 1845, when he said: "Our manifest destiny is to overspread and to possess the whole of this continent which Providence has given us." It was a dream which had no more resounding advocate than Thomas Hart Benton, sometime editor of the *Missouri Register* and later father-in-law of John Charles Frémont, the swashbuckling adventurer whose comic-opera conquest of California for the United States only briefly anticipated the reality of its absorption. Benton's every legislative activity was to further homesteading in the West, to expedite the enlargement of the ever-advancing frontier.

At the time of O'Sullivan's pronouncement that was to take on the shape of such epic consequences, Horace Greeley's *New York Tribune* was a going concern, but its founder and editor had not yet seen the light in the West which was soon to attract him with such insistence. He was involved in a complex of labor causes, idealistic follies and fatuous philosophic projects the most notable of which was a utopian doctrine known as Fourierism. Greeley first visited the West in 1859, traveling overland via Denver to San Francisco. Everywhere he was received with honorific acclaim for, like his white dust coat and homely ways, the *Tribune* was by now a national institution. Six years after his trip West, Greeley was to become celebrated for another man's remark: "Go west, young man, go west." Actually the sentiment printed in a *Tribune* editorial was quoted from Editor J. L. B. Soule in the *Terre Haute* (Ind.) *Express*, but it might have been Greeley's and he was credited with it forever.

Almost contemporary with O'Sullivan's radiant creation of "manifest destiny" was the speech which Daniel Webster assuredly did not make but which has ever since been attributed to him: "What do we want with the vast worthless area, this region of savages and wild beasts, of deserts, of shifting sands and whirlwinds of dust, of cactus and prairie dogs? To what use could we ever put these great mountain ranges, impenetrable and covered to their base with eternal snow? . . . I will never vote one cent from the Public treasury to place the Pacific coast one inch nearer Boston than it now is." Before he knew the West better, even Frémont inclined to agree with the antiexpansionist sentiments attributed to Webster, although he was shortly to amend his opinion to a fanatic degree. Webster lived to hear the news of California gold before enacting his classic deathbed scene at Marshfield, but its significance was lost upon him.

## !!! THE LATEST FROM THE GOLD FIELDS, THE LATEST !!!

Official news of the discovery of gold in California was slow to reach the East. On August 17 the Military Governor of California had sent dispatches to Washington by official courier and they could have arrived by the then available means of transport in about thirty days. Actually the messenger first went with his diplomatic pouch all the way down the West Coast of South America to Peru before crossing the Isthmus of Panama and going to Jamaica. Eventually he arrived in New Orleans late in November where the word-of-mouth news he carried caused a resounding sensation in the coffeehouses of Bienville Street and the Rue Bourbon although the first formal news report was unaccountably delayed until December 11 for its appearance in the *Weekly Picayune*. It had by then already been printed in Washington and Boston and from then until the eve of the Civil War news from California, as shown in this painting, was the most exciting reading available to millions. The picture, reprinted by permission of the Suffolk Museum of Stony Point, Long Island, shows inhabitants of a Long Island fishing village or seaport reading the latest in the weekly edition of Horace Greeley's *New York Tribune*.

# Guns and Glory in Old Mexico Opened a Highway West

CALIFORNIA HISTORICAL SOCIETY

## CALIFORNIA, HERE WE COME!

Between the region beyond the Mississippi acquired by the Louisiana Purchase and the Pacific lay the vast territory between what is today the Oregon boundary and the Rio Grande, the property of Spanish Mexico. President James K. Polk was agreeable to purchase of California from the Mexican Republic if necessary, but instead the opportunity for a brief and not too sanguinary war gave him the opportunity of seizing it. The Mexican War was in proper fact the first step toward the realization of a continental destiny for the United States. The battles of Resaca de la Palma, Buena Vista and Churubusco opened the way for General Winfield Scott's army, largely composed of Missouri volunteers, to Mexico City and in September of 1847, as depicted above, the victorious forces of the United States paraded through the Grand Plaza of the Mexican capital. The discovery of gold at Sutter's Mill was still a year in the future and California's statehood, three, but the defeat of Mexico assured California to the United States and forces were already at work to cement its advent in enduring form.

## FRÉMONT TOOK OVER MONTEREY WITH THEATRICAL BRAVADO

Even before the Mexican surrender California seethed with ferment and events were taking shape that were to be of enormous consequence to the continental ambitions of President Polk and most of the rest of the United States. In 1846 Captain John Charles Frémont with a disorganized "army" from northern California took over the ancient seaport of Monterey in the name of the Federal government at Washington. Frémont's penchant for gaudy and theatrical gestures in no way abated the importance of his land grab.

A decade after Frémont's melodramatic seizure of Monterey, California was in a fantastic dither of internal expansion. San Francisco had experienced several of the recurrent conflagrations which got it the name of the most combustible city in history. The mines of the Mother Lode were producing a continuous flow of gold, which found its way eastward in the strongboxes of Wells Fargo & Co., which had by now taken over California's expressing lock, stock and barrel from the defunct Adams Express. The state's inland waterways, particularly the broad, placid Sacramento, teemed with profitable commerce. The fast and fashionable *Antelope*, known as "Wells Fargo's Gold Boat" on the San Francisco-Sacramento run, was still a year or so in the future, but the *Rambler* was doing a nice business on the same overnight haul.

# The Forties Seethed with News of Gold and Conquest

Two major excitements dominated the news in the second half of the fifth decade of the nineteenth century in the United States. Coming within two years of each other, the dispatches detailing the victory over Mexico and the discovery of gold in California turned the eyes and imaginations of Americans Westward as nothing had ever done before. In colonizing the then known West from Kentucky to the Great Lakes, American ambitions had hitherto been largely agrarian; now precious metals, vast natural resources and continental conquest entered the picture. Above, Easterners at a county seat are shown reading the news of Buena Vista in the weekly edition of Horace Greeley's *New York Tribune,* an organ generally venerated as holy writ. Below is a sketch of Sutter's Mill at Coloma, the fulminate that exploded the gold rush to California.

## WHEELS ROLLED WESTWARD

Most articulate and influential prophet of the West was Horace Greeley, whose weekly *Tribune* had 100,000 subscribers and an estimated million readers. The *Tribune's* California stories written by Bayard Taylor stirred a nation into movement, activating the stages of Wells Fargo & Co. (*above*) from California to the Missouri and sending the Concords of the Leavenworth & Pike's Peak Express galloping through Old Indianola (*below*) with the mails for San Francisco and the Mother Lode diggings.

# ARGONAUTS AROUND CAPE HORN

A vast majority of the California-bound packets, clippers and, later, steamships actually did go all the way around Cape Horn rather than take advantage of the shorter route through the strait which the Captain General of Spain Ferdinand Magellanes had discovered four centuries earlier on his way to the Great South Sea. Masters were of the mind that the added sea miles involved in turning the Cape were less hazardous to large vessels than the strong tides and currents which made the Straits of Magellan a navigational nightmare. Argonauts who in later years boasted they had "come to Californy 'round the Horn" usually had done so literally. Only a few of the more powerful steamers which followed the clippers essayed the short cut to the ocean Magellan had named the *Mar Pacifico*. The voyage from Boston or New York to the gold fields around Cape Horn might take four months and was seldom accomplished in fewer than 100 days, so that the land and water combination route by way of the Isthmus of Panama was chosen by more urgent and better heeled pilgrims, but all heavy freight and many thousands of passengers went westward in the fifties all the way around South America. The record to that date was set by Donald MacKay's *Flying Cloud* in 1851, which made the New York-San Francisco passage in just under ninety days. At the top of the page: the desolation of Cape Horn from a drawing in *Ballou's Pictorial Drawing Room Companion* in 1850.

Although New England shipbuilding had been a major factor in the economic life of the nation since the second war with England, the great tradition of the clipper ships came into being as an incident to the California gold rush where almost every other consideration was subordinated to speedy passage. No American of the age, not even Captain John Sutter or Horace Greeley, was more surely an instrument of Manifest Destiny than Boston's master shipbuilder Donald MacKay (*below, right*), from whose drawing board there came in 1850 the *Stag Hound*, which was to set the pattern for clipper design that obtained until the final dominance of steam. The shipyards of East Boston (*above*) and along the Mystic (*below*), where MacKay's ships were built for such princely Bostonians as the Perkinses, Forbeses, Shaws, Tudors, Aspinwalls and Trains, saw the launching of MacKay's immortal *Flying Cloud, New World* and *Sovereign of the Seas*.

## ASPECTS OF THE LONG VOYAGE HOME TO CALIFORNIA

The food, even on packets and clippers flying the most respected house flags of the Russells, Delanos, Ammidons, Danas and Coolidges, was notoriously poor and scanty and the artist who depicted the jolly Christmas dinner (*above*) featuring plum duff and eaten by the crew of a California-bound vessel off Acapulco, was probably inspired. Stateroom privacy such as that shown below was only for women or affluent invalids. The Messrs. Howland & Aspinwall's *Golden Gate*, with which the owners had replaced the patriotically foundered *Union*, was scarcely less fortunate than its predecessor and was burned at sea (*below right*) the following year on the Panama run.

The Argonauts headed for the gold fields of the Mother Lode wearing silk top hats from Boston's revered Collins & Fairbanks and clawhammer coats from Brooks Brothers in New York. They brought with them for reading matter such pamphlets as Lansford Hastings's *Emigrants' Guide to Oregon and California* or Simpson's "Three Weeks in the Gold Mines," and absorbed dangerous and misleading misinformation for more than three months at sea. There were more women among the Forty-niners than might be apparent from the chronicles of the time.

Gentlemen from stately mansions in Gramercy Park and graduates fresh from the Harvard Yard fought like street urchins for choice morsels when meals were announced and consumed them with the voracity of galley slaves. The diaries and subsequent memoirs of the Argonauts one and all testified to the revolting food and bad manners on the overcrowded sailing ships that came 'round the Horn. Discomfort, disease and death itself on the long voyage were all discounted in the incurable optimism of the men who followed the vision of the Golden Fleece to Hangtown, to Grass Valley, to Negro Bar.

What staterooms there were were sequestered for the women who dared that formidable voyage on the greatest of all adventures. Amidst their assorted properties of carpetbags, parasols, top hats, Inverness cloaks and discarded stock collars, the menfolk slept on table tops, dreamed of gold nuggets as big as hen's eggs, pockets of easily recoverable wealth as capacious as the wine cellars of the Astor Hotel 6,000 miles away in old New York. When their fortunes were made, in a few weeks at the gold fields at the outside, they would return and drink the Astor cellars dry.

All

Faces

Turned

Westward

Over

The Water

## SAILINGS GALORE

Throughout the fifties the billboards of State Street, Union Street and Commercial Row in downtown Boston were liberally plastered with posters such as that shown above. At the same period Horace Greeley's *New York Daily Tribune*, in an age when the outside front page was still devoted to advertising, bristled with opportunities for Young America to "go West and grow up with the country." Boston and New York were most popular ports of departure with Philadelphia running third.

**NEW YORK HERALD TRIBUNE**

## SHIPPING CROWDED THE SEA LANES

A packet laden with California-bound optimists might drop the pilot off Boston light (*above*) in dead of winter, encounter heat at the Equator which would open its deck seams and rot the food in its holds, again run into blizzards from the Antarctic as it rounded the Horn and repeat the experience all over again on the run to Valparaiso, Acapulco and eventually the Golden Gate. On the return trip eastward in 1851 the ship *Tornado* (*center*) encountered "a most tempestuous passage" which carried away the foremast at the deck and broke the bowsprit off at the knightheads, but its captain, O. W. Mumford, ever-mindful of the best interests of his owners, the New York, Atlantic, Astor, Sun and Mercantile Insurance Companies, refused to shorten sail and brought her into port sixty-five days after the disaster, a distance of 8,000 sea miles. The owners presented Captain Mumford with a silver service "very richly chased and engraved," complete with "solid silver salver or waiter, coffee-pot, tea-pot, sugar dish, creamer and slop bowl." Not all vessels were so lucky. The Messrs. Howland & Aspinwall's steamer *Union*, for example, foundered off the coast of Lower California (*bottom*) on July 5, 1851, with loss of life and property. Commemorative exercises the day previous had incapacitated the crew and her loss was a melancholy monument to patriotic cheer.

## AMENITIES OF TRAVEL WERE FEW AND FAR BETWEEN

Early voyagers across the Isthmus of Panama on their way to California debarked from hired native bongos at either Gorgona or Cruces to make the remainder of the trip to the Pacific on muleback. By this time the more adaptable had shed their ruffled shirts and top hats in favor of tropical attire but still were not familiar with the exigencies of travel by muleback, as is suggested above. A map (*below left*) shows their route and that of the later railroad to Panama City. Some essayed the crossing on the backs of relays of porters called *estriveros,* uncomfortably seated on a plank known as a *tabillo* (*below right*). "My Indian made me up into a bundle of the easiest form to himself," an Argonaut wrote later, "and threw me on his back as a porter does his pack without troubling about my own painful and fatiguing position." Most pilgrims found the native bongos preferable to the *tabillo.*

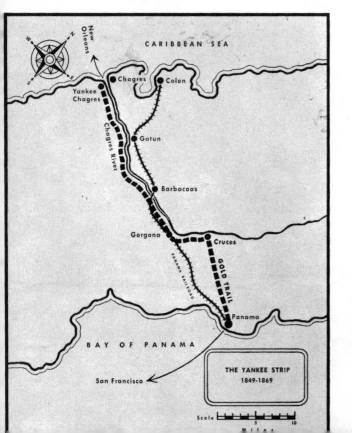

## THE VIGILANTES OF NEW GRANADA

A little-known chapter in the history of the Panama route to the gold fields concerns a group of private gunmen organized as the Vigilantes of New Granada to combat crime on the Isthmus before the coming of the railroad. A group of businessmen headed by Wells Fargo's agents, Hurtado & Bros., imported a Texas gunman named Randy Runnels with unlimited funds and orders to restore order by any means including execution without trial of known criminals. In two nights Runnels and his deputies seized seventy-eight known highwaymen, as shown above, and hanged them from the sea wall at Panama City. Hundreds of others were lynched (*below*) and their bodies left as warning along the jungle trail. In a matter of weeks the Yankee Strip across the Isthmus was free of footpads and a safe highway of commerce and private travel.

Formally attired as for a Sunday stroll on Fifth Avenue, the first Argonauts in search of the Golden Fleece came ashore in New Granada, as Panama was then known, in native boats called bongos. Until the coming of the United States Steamship Company with its piers and other installations at Aspinwall no deep sea vessel could come within a half mile of shore. The pilgrims were eager to make short work of the overland journey across the Isthmus and embark at the other side for the last leg of the long voyage to the Golden Gate. Their city clothes and urban manners put seasoned voyagers in mind of Englishmen away from home who dressed for dinner in the jungle and shaved as often as in London.

The route across the Isthmus before the coming of the railroad was by native bongo up the Chagres River to the village of Gorgona and thence by mule trail twenty-eight miles to Panama City. If water were high it was as far as Cruces by river and then twenty-four miles to the coast. The boatmen chanted strange, monotonous native songs and wild beasts responded from the jungle with savage howls. Contractors for the passage were dishonest, the natives surly unless grossly overpaid. Most Argonauts organized themselves into armed military companies for their own protection during the two days and nights required for the water passage of less than thirty miles.

Late at night on each of the two evenings spent on the water the pilgrims pushed their bongos ashore and sought shelter in crude native hotels which dotted the American Strip between Yankee Chagres, across the bay from Old Chagres, and Panama City. They were served strange native dishes, frijoles and tamales, which had never appeared on the menu at Delmonico's. The night sounds of the jungle terrified the women but the tropic nights were short and in a few hours they were again on the mule road that led to the ancient citadel of Panama.

## CROSSROADS OF EMPIRE

Not until five years after the Isthmian trail across Panama became populous with immigrants bound for California was a modern seaport completed and a railroad built to transport freight and passengers from Aspinwall to Panama City in as many hours as it had once taken days. By 1854 the steamcars of the Panama Railroad were running as far from their Aspinwall terminal as the Culebra or summit station, beyond which the journey was completed on muleback. Life in Aspinwall, named for a Yankee opportunist who became one of the incorporators of the staggeringly wealthy Pacific Mail Steamship Company, was seldom dull. Robberies of gold trains crossing the Isthmus, departure of vast treasure loads to the States and the ever-crescent stream of voyagers California-bound made it very much an outpost of empire.

### BOOM IN ASPINWALL

Aspinwall was still a thriving seaport when, shortly after the Civil War, Lammot Du Pont of Wilmington started manufacturing a new and unpredictable explosive called nitroglycerine to be shipped westward to the deep mines of the Comstock via Panama. The first accidental explosion of the stuff killed Lammot DuPont and did widespread damage to the Delaware countryside. The next was aboard a steamer at the Aspinwall pier, as shown here, and laid the entire waterfront in ruins. When a third blast demolished Wells Fargo's express office in San Francisco an embargo was placed on nitroglycerine until its properties might be more generally understood. Aspinwall wasn't the same for months.

The Panama Railroad, which was placed in operation between Aspinwall on the Atlantic side of the Isthmus and Panama City on the Pacific in 1855, was destined to be the first transcontinental railroad in America, antedating as it did the Pacific Railroad across the Western states by fourteen years. It was also to distinguish itself as the richest short line in the world until the swaggering Virginia & Truckee, serving the Comstock bonanzas of Nevada, came along to give it pointers. Organized with interlocking directorates in the Pacific Mail Steamship Company which connected with it at its western terminal and with the urbane and cultivated Trenor Park, later an ornament of San Francisco's most Corinthian circles, as its president, the cars of the Panama Railroad spanned the forty-eight miles of its main line in approximately four hours. The one-way fare was $25 per passenger while horses were listed in the tariff at $40 and mules at half as much. Hogs could make the trip for a reasonable $2.00, thus anticipating by some years the remark of a railroad executive in the 1930's about a pig not having to change cars to cross the continent. Nearly 200,000 passengers rode the coaches of this primeval railroad in the first four years of its existence and the gross earnings of the company for that period topped $8,000,000.

# RAILROAD ACROSS THE ISTHMUS

So fascinating to railroad men of its time were the operations of the Panama Railroad that a comprehensive history of its financing and engineering sold through several printings and operating executives came from all over the world to pattern their home properties on this wonderful and simple monopoly. Its coaches drew up at wharfside in Aspinwall to receive their cargo, as shown here, with a minimum of time lost, and deposited them in the same way on the dock of the Pacific Mail Company at the other end. Its ticket agents accepted only gold, and gold in bullion form in return constituted a large and profitable part of its freight. Wells Fargo, the universal expressman, imported butter from Vermont for sale in California over the Panama Railroad, a single shipment of this perishable commodity in 1861 running to 713 firkins, all in prime condition when they were opened in San Francisco.

SURVEYING THE FIRST TRANSCONTINENTAL

But if the operations of the Panama Railroad, once it was constructed, were simple, its building was accomplished under terrific hardship. Linesmen engaged in its survey and location worked up to their waists in jungle streams alive with alligators and poisonous snakes and, according to the conservative terms of a contemporary statement, "a large number of laborers died from the effects of the climate and strong drink."

## The Panama Line Was a Road of Country Ways

## PASTORAL WAS
## ITS RIGHT OF WAY

Following the accepted practice of
many larger American railroads of
the day, albeit one which has largely
disappeared in modern times, the
Panama Railroad ran down the middle of the main street of its eastern
terminal of Aspinwall, two contemporary views of which appear on
the page opposite. Its country ways
persisted once beyond the city
limits and its tracks followed an
amiable meander through San
Pablo, Bohio, Frijoles and Gatun
Village in a series of pastoral vi-
gnettes reproduced adjacent. Its
water tanks, in a climate where timber of all sorts is short-lived, were
supported by sturdy masonry, traces
of which are reported still to be
visible, a full century after their construction, overgrown with jungle
creepers and hidden in vegetation
on the banks of the great canal that
in places follows the right of way
where once the steamcars ran.

# New Granada Moved into the Age of Steam

THE PANAMA RAILROAD HAD EVERYTHING

The Panama Railroad possessed all the properties of greater carriers in microcosm. When its westbound daily went into the ditch at Gatun Bridge with appropriate loss of life, the "awful catastrophe" was in due course depicted (*above*) in the illustrated press in New York. More frequently the trains paused (*below*) at Culebra, the summit station, for the refreshment of passengers at the saloons which flourished handy to the right of way.

So great was the success of the Panama Railroad that after a quarter of a century of operation a plan was advocated by Captain James Eads, a notable marine engineer and builder of the first bridge across the Mississippi at St. Louis, that it should be retracked as a trans-Isthmian marine railway. Entire steamships loaded on cradles were to be drawn by two powerful locomotives over twelve tracks from one sea to the other and curves were to be eliminated through the agency of turntables located at strategic points. Nothing came of it.

Treasure chests were transshipped from the cars of the Panama Railroad in dead of night to the side-wheeler *Arizona*, as depicted below. Now and then a case of gold disappeared over the pierside in the darkness. Appropriate hangings next day cured the habit.

# Course of Empire West

## WAGONS OUT OF WESTPORT

Like the log cabin and the little red schoolhouse, the white-topped covered wagon was eventually to take its place as one of the characteristic properties of the American West along with the Concord coach, the buffalo gun and the pioneer newspaper. Stoutly constructed for hauling by oxen, it was usually tightly enough built to float for brief passages like a boat when crossing rivers and of heavy enough planking to turn the low-velocity bullets from Indian guns when used in forting up. The main defect of the covered wagon as it was sold to immigrants at Westport, Independence or Council Bluffs for the journey West was that it was deceptively spacious. Landseekers and colonists bound for California or Oregon loaded it with all sorts of family possessions —Boston rockers, highboys and patent cookstoves made in Malden, Massachusetts, which had to be jettisoned with accompanying heartbreak when the oxen weakened or the terrain became increasingly impervious to travel. In these two sketches, "Crossing Water to Escape a Prairie Fire" and "Thirsty Oxen Stampeding for Water," Remington caught the flavor and essence of covered-wagon travel, at once a hardship and wonderment of freedom and movement which was to become lodged forever in the lexicon, legend and consciousness of the American people.

## DARK THE LEGEND OF THE FOOTLESS DONNERS

Partly because of its macabre details, partly because its tragedy epitomized the hardships of the overland trail to California, the fate of the Donner Party, which encountered catastrophe in the High Sierras almost within sight of its California goal, has become a classic of pioneer times. Three family groups, most notable of which was that of George Donner, a well-to-do farmer from Springfield, Illinois, set out for California with a well-found train comprising three large wagons, twelve yoke of oxen, five horses and a large number of milch cattle. All their household possessions and several thousand dollars with which to start business in California went with them. The number of persons in the train, including two professional teamsters, was twenty-six. Sixteen were children. Forming a microscopic link in the great emigrant wagon chain stretching from Kansas to California, the Donner group achieved Western Nevada without more than average mischance and arrived in Truckee Meadows near today's Reno late in October of 1846. The original Donner group had been joined by others crossing the plains. November is a dangerous season in the Sierra and at the edge of the lake which bears their name, the Donners became bogged down in the first heavy snowfall of the year. Bad judgment, hysteria, starvation and the elements all contributed to the disintegration which followed. An element of the party, leaving all excess equipment behind, started out on foot, as shown here, for help on the far side of the mountains. Five in the group perished during a blizzard near American Gap and were eaten by their companions. Back at the base camp by the lake cannibalism also appeared, leaving insanity and terrible family feuding in its wake. When finally help arrived from the California side of the Sierra thirty-six members of the original Donner party and immigrants who had joined them on the way overland were dead in the winter passes of the High Sierra. Fourteen were children. For many years thereafter wagon trains from the East avoided the route by way of Donner Lake, Donner Pass and Donner Summit. It had an unsavory name.

# The White-Tops Headed Endlessly out of Westport

Westport Landing at Kansas City was the accepted jumping-off place for immigrants who had come up the Missouri from St. Louis. Here in a dusty and profane midst of teamsters, blacksmiths, wheelwrights, horse traders and outfitters of all sorts from dealers in derringers to vendors of patent gold-separating machinery, the Westward pilgrim said good-by to the last traces of urban life. From there he mostly followed the course of the Platte River to its northern fork (*center*) and eventually came to Fort Laramie, not be confused with the site of today's Laramie town, shown in the sketch at the lower left. All rivers he forded until he got to California where, here and there at populous crossings, such as is shown in the old time photograph below, he might encounter a ferry.

# The Crossing Of The Great Plains Was An Epic Chapter In The Saga Of The Old West

When the immigrant trains reached Salt Lake the great majority of them went around the north end of the lake, past the sites of Corinne and Promontory to be, and then struck out in a southwesterly direction to follow the valley of the Humboldt to the Sierra. The trail boss (*above*), as drawn by Remington, headed the long procession of carts, white-tops and horsemen, this one evidently serene in his disdain for Indians. Often the wagon trains of the fifties, particularly those which planned to take the fork to Oregon, had schoolteachers among their numbers (*center*). Classic peril of the overland journey were the plains Indians, sketched below by Remington as they circle a wagon train in a maneuver which became familiar to most of those who headed Westward from armed outpost to armed outpost until the coming of the railroad in the last years of the sixties.

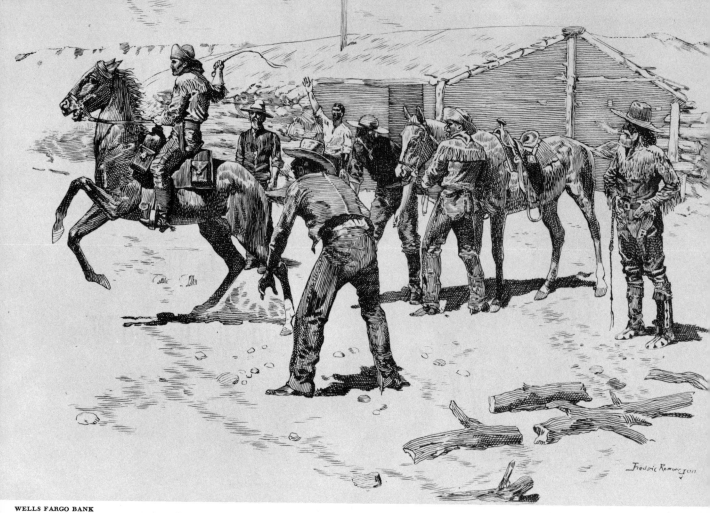

## THE NEWS OF THE GALLOPING PONY THRILLED THE LAND

For a few brief months while the eastern and western terminals of the Overland Telegraph approached each other, the legendary Pony Express raced letters from St. Joe to San Francisco in an unbelievable thirteen days. Above, Remington sketches a change of horse at a plains relay station. Below: In Sacramento hats were doffed, cannon fired, anvils smitten as the first rider from the East arrived in 1860.

## AFTER THE PONY, THE TELEGRAPH, THEN THE STEAMCARS

During the four years of the Civil War communications with the West were vital to the Union cause and largely exchanged by telegraph. With the cessation of hostilities, however, the minds of men turned once more to the dream, long since voiced, then temporarily shelved, of a transcontinental railroad. In 1867 the Kansas Pacific headed out of Kansas City with the eventual goal of Denver, but already the Central Pacific out of Sacramento and the Union Pacific out of Omaha were building toward each other and a rendezvous at Promontory. A. R. Waud, who drew so much of the West in its frontier years, sketched the end of track (*above*) of the Pacific Railroad somewhere west of Laramie and 100 miles south of the South Pass through which it was widely believed at first the rails would run. To keep the armies of tracklayers and graders in fresh meat, professional hunters (*right*), among whom was an as yet unheralded Buffalo Bill Cody, were retained to shoot buffalo and haul them to the "hell on wheels" which moved forward with the end of track. The railroad towns abounded in riotous living, Homeric drinking and sudden death, and Manifest Destiny was being accomplished in its final stage to an orchestration of gunfire and the singing of "Oh, My Darling Clementine."

# The Cars Recapitulated All That Had Gone Before

The continental destinies of the American people may be said to have been realized at many mileposts in the epic of a nation on the Westward march. Conceivably it was at misty California dawn when the Bear Flag raised on faltering halyards at Sonoma proclaimed that, in the Republic of California, America had reached the Pacific littoral at last. Perhaps it had an even earlier setting when William Clark in 1805 first sighted the Pacific and wrote in his journal, "Ocian in view! O! The joy!" It may have been at Promontory Point in Utah that wet and windy day in May of 1869 when a telegraphic circuit closed to tell the world that time and distance had, to all essential considerations, disappeared from the lexicon of continental United States. If the last of these choices is valid, surely its great, climactic consequence and moment was when the steamcars of the Central Pacific rolling all the way from Omaha, as shown on the page opposite, ground for the first time to a stop to allow the passengers to view the South Fork of the American River from Cape Horn. Here the cycle of continental destiny had been assured twenty-one years earlier with the first discovery of California gold. In the hand-braked progress of the Central Pacific's wood-burning locomotives down the grade to Colfax is recapitulated all the epic of the men who crossed the Great Plains in the perilous fifties, the dancing legend of the Pony Express, the handcarts of the Mormons, the lurching thorough-braced coaches built in far-off Concord. The memories of wagon trains of the vanished years, as drawn by Frenzeny above, rode the cars into California the Golden.

In the expressive vernacular of the time and place, "To See the Elephant" was to visit the Mother Lode in search of fortune, whether or not one found it. Charles Nahl's often reproduced painting, "Sunday in Camp," depicts a variety of miners seeing the elephant, each in his own fashion, in one of the liveliest of all pictures of early California. The phrase later came into less specific usage and meant to experience any exciting or instructive aspect of life in the Old West.

# IV

# *To See the Elephant*

## Gold on the American River Brought the Eyes of the World to California, Settled a Western Continent and Set the Seal of Authenticity on Manifest Destiny in an Impress of Precious Metal

**A** LATER GENERATION smitten with an overwhelming yet largely unrecognized poverty of everything desirable to life, character, laughter, adventure and somewhere to go, has invested its ancestors with a good many supposed virtues they never possessed and would have found a source of inextinguishable laughter if they had.

One of them is that America and later the United States came into being by reason of a vast spiritual yearning for a number of intangibles among which have always been mentioned a variety of liberties and a hanker to worship God. One of the earliest songs of a generation of school children not yet vanished told excited auditors that the Pilgrims sought "a Faith's pure shrine."

There is evidence to the contrary.

The United States we know and enjoy, whether its enjoyment is reasonable or not, came into being and without any equivocation at all out of a yearning for material possessions. These varied with the time and place from a clearing in the pine stands of Massachusetts or a south forty in Sangamon County, Illinois, to seventy-room mansions on Fifth Avenue and William Randolph Hearst's castle of San Simeon. The desire for tangibles may have now and then been complicated by sentimentalities occasionally expressed in the words "liberty" and "love," but liberty was seldom invoked except when it opened a way to material gain and diamonds have always been a girl's best friend.

The clear vision of the Jim Hills, the Fricks, Carnegies, Mellons, Morgans, Harrimans, Huntingtons and McCormicks who saw destiny with milled edges bearing the imprint of the United States Treasury, uncomplicated by any sentimentality at all, was the vision that built America and the West. This is not, of course, the philosophy fashionable in a generation of little men and unrealistic humanitarianism. It is merely fact.

The irrefutable evidence in the matter is found in a small but expressive lexicon of the Old West which includes Sutter's Mill, Captain John Marshall, the Mother Lode and gold. Until the discovery of gold at Coloma, as President James K. Polk discovered, it was all but impossible to get anybody save a demented fringe of fur traders who cared nothing for their own hair to venture on the far side of the Missouri. After the word of gold got around the populations of Vermont and New Hampshire melted like snow before a Chinook and it was impossible to keep anybody down on the farm in Illinois or Michigan. There was no talk of "a Faith's pure shrine" in California the Golden. The presentation Bibles that were sent along with the young men out of Boston on the sailing packets held no such fascination on the long voyage Westward as did the patent gold scales sold at wharfside in Panama to all well-advised pilgrims to the new Golconda.

When the gold was exhausted or began to run thin in the Mother Lode, there was silver in Nevada's Comstock or more gold in the Black Hills, and only after these ran out did the population of the West begin to think about less dramatic values, although often enough greater ones, in cattle, wheat, lumber, railroads, and base metals. Of all the Westering population of the United States in the nineteenth century only the Mormons had other than material motivation for following the sun across the continent, and, once they saw Deseret, it can never be said that the Mormons themselves had no use for property.

The fulminate that exploded the great continental rush of population to the American West was not the mercury fulminate of the miner's blasting machine but American River gold in the miner's rocker. If at the time there were any other values comparable to metallic gold in California they were commensurable in gold and devoted to its mining: foodstuffs, earth-moving tools, and whisky.

There never was a more frankly material civilization than that of California's Mother Lode nor one so unabashedly based on the procurement of the root of all evil. Let a hypocritical generation that mutters about spiritual values and human rights and counts its Cadillacs take off its hat to the Argonauts. They were honest.

87

# Gold Lured Men Westward in Every Weather

ROUGH GOING AT DUTCH FLAT

By the winter of 1850 not even the blizzards that made a nightmare of the High Sierra in the vicinity of Blue Canyon and Emigrant Gap had terror to stay the gold seekers headed for the Mother Lode. Ill-fated expeditions such as that of the Donner party foundered and perished in the deep drifts without apparent effect on those who came afterward, although more prudent prospectors (*below*) followed the same route under summer conditions with less misery and suffering.

## CALIFORNIA TIDINGS SOON GOT EAST

The wonders of California early found space in the periodicals of the
East. In 1852 *Gleason's Pictorial Drawing Room Companion* commis-
sioned a special artist to draw "The Great California Cedar Tree"
which was "first discovered by miners in the mountains of Calaveras,
California, in a forest called the Redwoods on Trinidad Bay" and had
an estimated height of 300 feet. Shortly afterward Charles Nahl, a
distinguished portrayer of the California of the pioneers, drew a fearful
grizzly bear (*ursus horribilis*) which, although he bore scant resem-
blance to the friendly bruin of the Bear Flag, might be expected by
all comers in the Mother Lode. Below, a prospecting miner in a popular periodical of the time dreams of the voyage home when he shall
have made his pile while sleeping beside his lunch basket, powder
horn and copy of Young's *Night Thoughts* or possibly a guidebook to
the New Eldorado.

# Avidly The East
# Read Of
# Golden Treasure

## GOLD WAS ON EVERY TONGUE

What the life of the cowboy was to the generation immediately following, the California gold seeker held of romance in the fifties. His attire and outfit were sketched in fullest detail by J. W. Audubon (*above*) and shop clerks in Philadelphia and under-graduates at New Haven resolved forthwith to go West where the properties of immediate and endless wealth were the miner's pick and shovel, his rocker and gold-washing pan. Frank Marryat found the subject for a drawing (*left*) in Mother Lode miners drawing straws to settle a fine point of law, while the great consummation of all, weighing their gold, was portrayed by *Gleason's* artist in the sketch below.

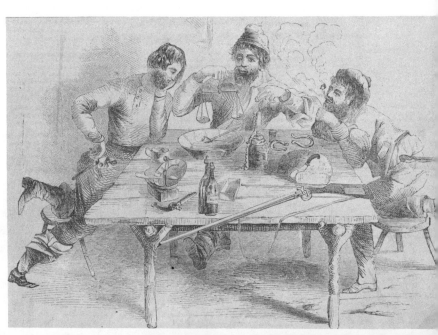

## CALIFORNIA—
## AND ROMANCE—
## HERE WE COME!

To men occupied with the work-aday life of cities in the East, California spelled the wild free ways of the Western continent, a release from drudgery, a refuge from enforced decorum, and escape from burdensome domesticity and convention. A dinner of beans and sourdough prepared by the open fire in a log cabin in some Dry Diggings (*top*) or Rich Bar was a vision of the good life that could come true with steamer fare by way of Panama. Rainy-day occupations of mending clothes and cobbling boots (*center*) were better than the sleet of winter in Boston's Atlantic Avenue, and even the surprise of finding Bruin in possession at the end of a day's toil at the rockers and long toms was implicit with romance and adventure. To some the bear looked friendlier than creditors, mothers-in-law and the hard-bitten employers they knew at home.

# Low Life and Industry, Each Had Its Reward

## THE PARABLE OF THE PRIMROSE PATH

Foremost of the California artists of the Mother Lode period was Charles Nahl, whose drawings of "The Idle and Industrious Miner" became classic of the time and place. In the above drawings a virtuous youth goes to his claim with the rising sun and shortly is seen depositing his profits with Adams & Co., Express, for forwarding to his home in the East. Below, however, the idle miner falls a prey to cardsharps and loses all and ends up, boozy and in no good shape, in a nearby gin mill, a horrible example of bad companions and lack of will power.

In far-off Paris, *L'Illustration* showed French readers the view (*above*) of life in a miner's cabin in California, while below, Frank Marryat in an often reproduced drawing depicts what happened at a funeral where gold was discovered in the miner's grave. "The preacher stopped and enquiringly asked: 'Boys, what's that?' took a view of the ground for himself and shouted 'Gold! Gold! And the richest kind of diggings! The congregation is dismissed!' The dead miner was buried elsewhere and the funeral party, the minister at their head, lost no time in prospecting and staking out new diggings!"

## HIGH JINKS ON SATURDAY NIGHT

In the remote towns of the Mother Lode, miners who organized a Saturday night dance, as shown above, tied a handkerchief around their partner's arm for lack of female companionship. Later, as suggested in the drawing at the left, female company became more readily available in the larger California towns and the miners who could raise enough pinches of dust indulged a hanker for champagne wine and tinned oysters while basking in feminine admiration as long as their funds held out. In the Green Devil Saloon, drawn by Alonzo Delano and shown below, anything went and, to a conservative eye, fun was unabashed and uninhibited. The French Four was for partners, lone performers favored with a Pigeon Wing.

IN LUXURY OR SIMPLE CIRCUMSTANCES, FARO WAS UNIVERSAL

The everlasting faro and poker games which, next to the bottle, were almost the sole relaxation of Mother Lode miners of a Saturday night attracted every artist who ever depicted life in the diggings. Above, W. L. Dodge draws "The Faro Players" for *Harper's,* while below is depicted a similar game in less opulent circumstances, a tent saloon serving in place of the more elegant premises of Dodge's drawing.

## EXCITEMENTS WERE RARE IN THE LIFE OF THE MINER

The first mining of the Mother Lode was by the placer method, shown in this contemporary sketch, the ore-bearing gravel from the river bottoms being washed first in pans by hand and then in riffles or long toms in which the heavy gold settled out of the sand in water brought, often from great distances, by wooden flumes. Below, W. L. Dodge drew "An Auction at Coloma" for *Harper's* at a time when entertainment was rare and a week end in town to bid on a pair of boots, a blanket or mining equipment was a festive occasion for the company-starved miners from Negro Bar, Hangtown or Secret Town.

# Sacramento Was the Entrepôt to All the Diggings

## SACRAMENTO LIVED BY THE RIVER

"Sacramento City," as the below lithograph of the levee at the California capital called it, was the center of banking and express between the diggings of the Mother Lode and San Francisco. In early days the arrival of a river boat with the mail (*above*) was a momentous event in the lives of the exiles to be celebrated with a rousing welcome. Later when river communications were established on a regular daily basis, the swift and graceful *Antelope*, queen of the river packets to San Francisco, was known as "The Gold Boat" because of the vast sums in treasure it transported every other night on its run downriver.

# The Robin Hood Legend Flowered Again in Murieta

That the Robin Hood legend of the chivalrous bandit who robbed the rich to give to the poor should be evoked in the Mother Lode fifties was natural to the frontier and its credulities. The ranking scholar in the field, Joseph Henry Jackson, believed there were several Murietas, or outlaws named Joaquin, which is the same thing, all of them Mexicans who troubled the peace of the California countryside in the years of gold. Every outrage against the Chinese, whom the Mexicans hated, every highway robbery, every murder untraceable elsewhere was laid at the door of the terrible, romantic, handsome Joaquin Murieta and his bloody lieutenant, Three-Fingered Jack. Joaquin levied taxes on rich ranchers (*above*) and ravished beautiful and not altogether reluctant women (*below*) at his pleasure. Since no known authentic likeness of the bandit exists, these romanticized pictures of his activities larcenous and amorous are purely imaginary. Californians of the fifties believed implicitly in his existence, and didn't they eventually see his head pickled in a bottle of whisky? What more could you ask?

## TERRIBLE JOAQUIN WAS EVERYWHERE AT ONCE

What Frank and Jesse James were to be to a later generation in the Border States, Joaquin and Three-Fingered Jack Garcia were to the miners and ranchers living from one end of the Mother Lode to the other. The circumstance that they were often reported in two places a hundred miles apart at the precise same time made no difference. Any crime not otherwise accountable was laid at Murieta's door, just as Jesse James was to be credited with every train robbery for which nobody else was hanged in Missouri and Kansas thirty years later. He waged pitched battles, as shown in the top drawing here, with miners staking their claims in Mariposa, Whisky Slide or Poverty Flat. Chinamen he murdered by the reputed score after tying their pigtails together for economy of effort in cutting their throats. The final extermination of Murieta's gang by Love's Vigilantes in the shadow of a gristmill in the wilds of Tulare Valley is depicted in the center of the page. Captain Love made a good thing of the story and collected the reward on Murieta's head, but there were narrow-minded folk who believed the whole thing was a put-up job.

When the various Murietas and their crimes against the peace and dignity of California finally aroused public sentiment, Governor John Bigler, early in 1853, asked the state legislature to authorize the organization of a special group of rangers under the command of Captain Harry Love to apprehend Murieta or at least the best Murieta he could capture and no questions asked. Soon thereafter Captain Love's bravos rode into camp with a bearded and gory head and a severed mutilated hand which they said had belonged to Joaquin and Three-Fingered Jack, respectively, and collected the governor's reward. Cynical newspaper editors, notably those of the *Alta California* in San Francisco, took a dim view of the triumph of law and order and charged that the whole matter was barefaced fraud and that the head was that of the first Mexican encountered by the rangers. No matter; the severed head and hand were exhibited as inducements to setting them up in saloons for many years, as suggested by the poster at the right. Alive or dead, Murieta was valuable to somebody.

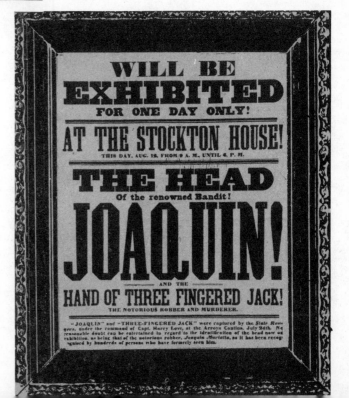

WILL BE EXHIBITED
FOR ONE DAY ONLY!
AT THE STOCKTON HOUSE!
THIS DAY, AUG. 12, FROM 9 A. M., UNTIL 6. P. M.
THE HEAD
Of the renowned Bandit!
JOAQUIN!
AND THE
HAND OF THREE FINGERED JACK!
THE NOTORIOUS ROBBER AND MURDERER.

"JOAQUIN" and "THREE-FINGERED JACK" were captured by the State Rangers, under the command of Capt. Harry Love, at the Arroyo Cantua, July 24th. No reasonable doubt can be entertained in regard to the identification of the head now on exhibition, as being that of the notorious robber, Joaquin Murietta, as it has been recognized by hundreds of persons who have formerly seen him.

## 'JUSTIFIABLE"

When, in the middle seventies, a lascivious invader of his home attacked the wife of Erastus Bradley, a Whisky Bar placer miner, Bradley shot him through the head and a jury termed it "justifiable homicide." The verdict was applauded by *The Illustrated Police News*, a notable believer in the sanctity of womanhood, when it ran this picture of the event a few weeks later. Such crimes would have been altogether unthinkable in the early days of the Mother Lode but became increasingly frequent with the influx of unsavory scoundrels in later years.

## BRET HARTE TOOK THE MOTHER LODE FOR HIS OWN

No better example of the body of folklore and legend that sprang up in the wake of California gold can be found than Bret Harte's celebrated short story, "The Luck of Roaring Camp," to illustrate which Henry Bacon painted the below scene, now in the collection of the National Academy of Design in New York. Background for Harte's stories of miners, gamblers, unfortunate women and all the sentimentalities of the Western generation were Knight's Ferry, Stent, Quartz, Tuttletown, better known as Mormon Gulch, and Jackass Hill. With such romantic overtones did he invest the Mother Lode that much of that part of the California countryside was advertised to a later generation as "the Bret Harte country."

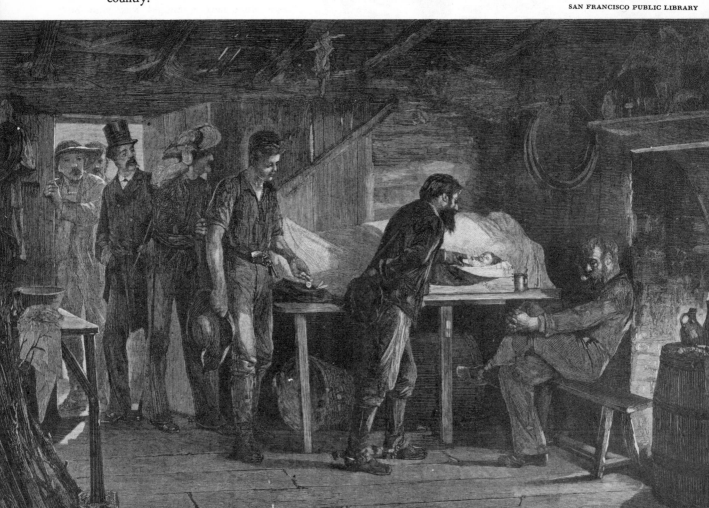

# Mediocrity Set In With
# The Decline In Mining

## LILIES AND LANGORS OF VIRTUE

Life in the hill towns of California more nearly approached that of any small community in the West as the production of gold dropped and greater bonanzas in Nevada, Montana or the Black Hills lured the adventurous element away from California. By 1876 election day in Dutch Flat as shown at the left might have been election day anywhere rather than in a once whooping diggings with sudden wealth on every hand. Morality and civic virtue, too, began raising their dreary heads and at Marysville the city fathers hired a dray team (*above*) to drag a house of pretty girls beyond the municipal limits. Most depressing evidence of the shift to mediocrity and uniformity was a rage to change the names of communities for the more respectable and inevitably less individualistic. Bedbug became Ione; Hangtown was changed to Placerville; Negro Bar emerged as Folsom; while across the hill in Nevada, Mormon Station became Genoa and Pizen Switch assumed the name of Yerington. Old times were changing, mostly for the worse.

THREE PICTURES: AUTHORS' COLLECTION

## GOOD TIMES LONG GONE

"I see by the *Delta* that the old Visalia House is being torn down," wrote an old-timer to the *Visalia Delta* in 1916. "If ever there were a hotel noted for its various incidents, it was this one. To say nothing of myself, there certainly were some roughs boarded there, such as Ketcham. Him and I were playing a game of horseback billiards when a stranger came in a little full and bothered us some. Ketcham out with his six-shooter and shot him three times. They carried him out and we finished the game and I left. Years after, Ketcham was shot and killed out in Utah." The scene depicted here may or may not have been the old-timer and Ketcham before the stranger arrived "a little full," but it depicts the spirit of horseback billiards, always popular on the frontier. Such robust doings in the hill towns were becoming less common with the advent of "progress."

# The Legend of Violence Lingered in the Hills

Although Murieta disappeared from the Mother Lode roads in the middle fifties and Black Bart dates from the late seventies, the name California suggested primitive violence and frontier customs long after the telephone was commonplace in country ranches and sheriff's posses were becoming the property of the new kinetoscope. *The National Police Gazette* was happy to startle its readers with the pictorial account (*left*) of Mrs. Clara Omo's defense to the death against a lecherous brute in the Feather River region as late as 1890, while only a few years earlier summer visitors to the Yosemite had been held up by masked miscreants (*below*) on the Sonora stage and forced to surrender their wallets and chatelaine watches.

TWO PICTURES: AUTHORS' COLLECTION

It should be noted that, elsewhere than in California, stages were still held up right down to the turn of the century. A lady bandit named Pearl Hart held up the last stagecoach running in Arizona Territory between Globe and Florence in 1899. She didn't get away with it but rated A for effort in the newspapers.

## DEAD-END KIDS IN THE DIGGINGS

After the passing of what Joseph Henry Jackson calls "The Age of Innocence," when the Mother Lode was a venture for Americans only, a lawless element began to show itself, as is suggested by Hubert Burgess's sketch called "Roughs in Town," which appeared in *Harper's*.

## MOST MINING TOWNS EARNED THEIR NAMES

Life in the mining towns of the Sierra foothills was filled with excursions and alarms throughout the years of gold. When future United States Senator from Nevada William Morris Stewart, a young man fresh from Yale, first came to the town of Rough and Ready in 1850, the diggings lived up to its name. A miner about to be lynched appealed to Stewart to save him from the mob which believed he had stolen a partner's savings. "Dare you stop it?" a stranger asked Stewart. "With you I dare," replied Stewart, drawing his revolvers. "Stop, you have got the wrong man," he shouted, and when the mob paused he soon produced evidence of the man's innocence. "Mobs usually act when the word of command is given," remarked Stewart of the episode, and all his life mobs listened to Senator William Morris Stewart, "Father of American Mining Law." Not all men accused of crime in the diggings got off so easily. A traveler through Bidwell's Bar in the early fifties reported that as he crossed the Feather River at breakfast-time three lifeless figures dangled from the bridge (*below*), mute evidence that Vigilantes had been riding the night before. The dry diggings that later was known as Hangtown, today's Placerville, was so associated in the public mind with informal executions that its name derived from them.

# Nevada City and Grass Valley Were Famed for Two Women

Nevada City and Grass Valley, neighboring diggings high in the wintry Sierra, were rich mining communities for a time, but each owes its perpetual fame to a woman of character and distinction: Nevada City to Eleanore Dumont, better known as Madame Moustache, and Grass Valley to the fiery Lola Montez, mistress of the King of Bavaria. Madame Moustache came from God-knows-where, settled in Nevada City and, despite all odds to the contrary, became a fixture of the place whose games of Rocky Mountain—since called Twenty-one—and keno were above reproach for honesty and decorum. Her ability to maintain her character as a gambler without reproach in a time when even men who followed the calling were of the half-world became her monument. The world forgot Nevada City after Madame Moustache departed for richer prospects at Bodie, but years later it was recalled to general awareness when a drawing in the *Police Gazette* (*left*) depicted "A Big Cornish Miner Saving the Life of a Friend from a Runaway Brute in Nevada City, Cal."

## SOME DIGGINGS HAD PASTORAL ASPECTS AS WELL AS GOLD

Although both Grass Valley and Nevada City were famous in their earliest days as mining communities—it was at Nevada City that Ott's Assay Office assayed the ore from Virginia City which caused the first rush to the Comstock in Nevada—both were fortunately situated in fertile valleys in the High Sierra which made agriculture possible after mining had declined. The water to activate this gristmill in Grass Valley came in open wooden flumes from far away in the mountains, perhaps from the Bear River.

## OVERTONES OF ROYALTY

Perhaps Grass Valley's strongest claim on the attention of the great world was as the chosen home of Lola Montez, favorite of the crowned heads of Europe, Bohemian of spacious proportions and, at the whim of King Ludwig of Bavaria, Countess of Landsfeldt with an annual income of $100,000. Lola's spider dance was the sensation of two continents and her relationships with such Old World notables as Czar Nicholas I and Alexander Dumas *fils* perfumed her name with delicious scandal. At long last, tiring of titles and tiaras, she settled down in this house in Grass Valley. Scandal pursued her, however, even into the Sierra and a provincial hypocrisy that could tolerate the Saturday night prostitutes of the Line raised eyebrows at the mistress of a reigning monarch. In a Grass Valley saloon Lola made dogmeat with a horsewhip of an editor who had attacked her in print, and fled to New York never to return. She was and is Grass Valley's greatest claim to immortality.

## NARROW GAGE TO VANISHED TIMES

Just as surely as the somewhat larger New York Central was the family railroad of the Vanderbilts, so the Nevada County Narrow Gage connecting Grass Valley and Nevada City with the Central Pacific transcontinental main line at Colfax was the family railroad of the Kidders. The destinies of the homely short line were those of Engineer John Kidder who built it and President John Kidder who later forsook his corduroys for broadcloth tails to manage it. Its wood-burning engine *Grass Valley*, shown here in two different views from old time wet plate photographs, was the pride of the countryside and even the Emperor Dom Pedro of Brazil, whose private car was briefly stopped for servicing at Colfax, wanted to see the celebrated wooden trestle built by Kidder across the Bear River. It was the boast of the management that no bad men had ever molested the narrow gage cars and old-timers recalled seeing sacks of minted double eagles en route to the banks in Nevada County lying unguarded in the baggage cars like so much cornmeal. The Nevada County Narrow Gage was a railroad man's railroad, having been the training school for the Southern Pacific's famed general manager, Joseph Dyer, in later years, and time dealt kindly with the little road. When finally it went to the Valhalla of all short lines, its steel trestle across U.S. Highway 40 near Colfax stood until the Second World War, a monument to vanished times and halcyon days.

From the great wooden trestle over the Bear River, passengers on the narrow gage sometimes caught glimpses of miners washing their clothes in the icy waters far below the precarious ribbon of steel on which the diminutive cars rolled.

## PRIMITIVE WAS THE LINE ACROSS THE HIGH SIERRA

It is difficult for an age which snarls through Colfax on its way east or west in dead of night aboard the *City of San Francisco* to imagine the pastoral beginnings of railroading in the High Sierra when the first light iron of the Central Pacific was laid on its way from Sacramento to Promontory. As in this atmospheric drawing by the distinguished Western artist E. S. Hammack, the wood-burning eight wheelers and wooden cars jolted to a stop at Colfax while Wells Fargo's men loaded the gold from transfer with the Nevada County Railroad on the way to San Francisco Mint. A few miles farther to the east the cars rolled through the snowsheds at Norden (*below*) where, in deep of winter, an entire community lived beneath the drifts with dispatcher's offices, commissary and a turntable under cover, seen at the right, where the helper engines for the grade from Truckee could be turned.

AUBURN AND FOREST HILL

HIS MOUNTAIN HOME.

SMASHING THE TREASURE CHEST.

THE LONE HIGHWAYMAN OF PLACER COUNTY.

# ARREST. STAGE ROBBER.

About one o'clock P. M. on the 3d of August, 1877, the down stage between Fort Ross and Russian River, was ...d by a man in disguise, who took from Wells, Fargo & Co.'s express box about $300 in coin and a check for ...32, on Granger's Bank, San Francisco, in favor of Fisk Bros. On one of the way-bills left with the box, the ... wrote as follows :

> I've labored long and hard for bread—
> For honor and for riches—
> But on my corns too long you've trod,
> You fine haired sons of bitches.
> BLACK BART, the Poet.

Driver, give my respects to our friend, the other driver; but I really had a notion to hang my old disguise hat ... weather eye.

*Respectfully*
*B. B.*

It is believed that he went into the Town of Guernieville ... daylight next morning.

About three o'clock P. M , July 25th, 1878, the down stage from Quincy, Plumas Co., to Oroville, Butte Co., was ...d by one masked man, and from Wells, Fargo & Co.'s box taken $379 coin, one diamond ring said to be worth ... and one silver watch valued at $25.   In the box, when found next day, was the following :     [Fac simile.]

*here I lay me down to sleep*
*to wait the coming morrow*
*perhaps success perhaps defeat*
*And everlasting sorrow*
*I've labored long and hard for bread*
*for honor and for riches*
*But on my corns too long youve trod*
*You fine haired sons of Bitches*
*let come what will I'll try it on*
*My condition cant be worse*
*And if theres money in that Box*
*Tis munny in my purse*
*Black Bart*
*the. Po 8*

About eight o'clock A. M. of July 30th, 1878, the down stage from La Porte to Oroville was robbed by one man, ...ok from express box a package of gold specimens valued at $50, silver watch No. 716,996, P. S. Bartlett, maker. It is certain the first two of these crimes were done by the same man, and there are good reasons to believe that the three.

There is a liberal reward offered by the State, and Wells, Fargo & Co . for the arrest and conviction of such ...rs.  For particulars, see Wells, Fargo & Co.'s "Standing Reward" Posters of July 1st, 1876.

It will be seen from the above that this fellow is a character that would be remembered as a scribbler and some- ...f a wit or wag. and would be likely to leave specimens of his handwriting on hotel registers and other public places. If arrested, telegraph the undersigned at Sacramento.  Any information thankfully received.

**J. B. HUME, Special Officer Wells, Fargo & Co.**

*Black Bart*

## BLACK BART'S SHOTGUN WASN'T EVEN LOADED

The eminently respectable-appearing old gentleman photographed above in a bowler hat and satin-faced Chesterfield is in fact none other than "Black Bart, the PO8," whose holdups of Mother Lode stages gave Wells Fargo's Chief of Detectives James B. Hume a bad time for years. Disguised with a flour sack over his hard hat and armed with a shotgun, Black Bart soon engaged the fascinated attention of newspaper readers by leaving at the scene of his various crimes the verses which appear on the poster reproduced above. In actual fact the mildest mannered of men, Bart soon was the central figure of a legend of ferocity and lawless enterprise. Eventually trapped in San Francisco by a laundry mark, Bart served a short sentence and thereafter disappeared from public life, although every stage holdup for years aroused speculation as to whether or not he had reverted to his bad ways. Eventually the *Police Gazette* gave Black Bart a national celebrity, as shown on the page opposite. Imaginative as the artist was, he was correct in one detail of the PO8's technique: he always operated alone.

CHARLES CLEGG PHOTO

COLUMBIA WAS WORLDLY, WEALTHY AND IN WINE

Most picturesque of all outposts of Wells Fargo's empire of banking and express was at Columbia, where their office, as shown here, stands to this day. Through its vaults in wooden treasure chests passed literally millions in gold dust and nuggets on their way to the gold scales (*below*) at the United States Mint in San Francisco. It was in Columbia that Darius Ogden Mills had an assay office which started him on the road to becoming the West Coast's most powerful banker and the frosty-faced dictator of the Bank of California. Columbia, because of its superior riches, lived high in a multiplicity of gorgeous saloons where champagne supplanted the conventional chaser of beer and to get "Columbia drunk" was very drunk indeed even by Forty-niner standards.

WELLS FARGO BANK

Prince of stage drivers for the princely firm of Wells Fargo & Co. was Hank Monk, whose admonition to Uncle Horace Greeley, "Keep your seat, Horace! I'll get you there in time," has become legendary. Monk (*above*) for many years drove across the Sierra Nevada between Carson City and Hangtown over precipitous mountain roads (*left*) where traffic was sometime impervious to less skilled drivers and where in summertime watering carts, as shown in this old picture, laid the dust twenty-four hours a day over hundreds of miles of highway. Stage drivers were the aristocracy of the West until the coming of the railroads, and an invitation to ride the box with them was a royal command and just as flattering.

PRINCE OF JEHUS, HANK MONK DROVE GRANDLY FOR WELLS FARGO

Stage drivers and old-timers who viewed the coming of the railroad with disapproval and claimed the iron horse wasn't here to stay were happy in wintertime long after the passing of the coaching routes to learn that the cars and engines of the Central Pacific were having rough going in Blue Canyon and Gold Run. Sometimes they were bogged down for days in the deep drifts and in the fearful winter of '89 no wheel turned across the mountains for weeks.

With The Palace for a backdrop, the corner of Market Street at Kearny in the nineties with the cable cars in their bright noontide and a fat policeman drinking at Lotta's Fountain is all a San Franciscan needs to weep for the glory and the grandeur that are gone.

V

# *Golden Gate*

## To the American Awareness San Francisco Has Always Been the City where Dreams Come True, the Old West and the New Merged on the Farthest Horizon of All

IN ONE OF HIS most beguiling and perceptive moments as the supreme essayist on the region, legend and folklore that is the American West, Bernard De Voto has remarked that, "aware that many signal though deserved favors of providence have set it apart from other towns, San Francisco nevertheless counts as foremost among them the fact that it is West. It is thinking accurately. For, stranger, San Francisco is West as all hell."

Not only is San Francisco aware that it is West. It started being that way almost the moment it was anything at all. The Argonauts had hardly gotten their first shave after landing from the voyage around the Horn aboard the first sailing of the S.S. *California,* and secured a change of linen to supplant undergarments and pleated shirts worn continuously from Panama City, than they got together and organized the Society of California Pioneers in 1850. They knew they were men set apart and dedicated and they spend the rest of their lives sneering cheerfully in alumni association meetings at anyone so downright misfortunate as to have arrived so much as a single steamer sailing later than they had. If promptness is proverbially an attribute of royalty, the pioneers were a case where it created royalty. Anybody who missed the first boat was a commoner for sure.

San Francisco also possessed a charming capacity for nostalgia and wistful reminiscence at a time when the things it became nostalgic about were still going on. By the early seventies the good old days were already well over the horizon. Nobody changed his money in *pesos* and *reales* anymore. The Spanish glazed sombrero was out of fashion and hardly anyone wore the serape of the first settlers.

By 1873 those gentle and most charming of all San Francisco chroniclers, Barry & Patten, the wistful saloonkeepers, were metaphorically crying in their beer because of the monolithic age of industrialism—cable cars, the magnetic telegraph and the cutaway frock coat—into which they had had the misfortune to live. The end of all good things had arrived when Montgomery Street had been graded and nobody at all had space for a rose garden east of Portsmouth Square, where once the San Francisco fog had dealt so kindly with posies.

Earlier perhaps than any of the world's gracious cities, San Francisco was able to shed a tear for *les temps jadis* and sigh for *les neiges d'antan.* The best of everything had been experienced, according to true believers, by the time of the invasion of the Pony Express, and their gaze was shudderingly averted from the time, still nearly a decade in the future, when Arcady should be no more for the coming of the Pacific Railroad. Well, anyway, they had known the best for a little.

This is a state of mind at once constant and progressive in the San Francisco story, and if the year Forty-nine was shot with stars and glory by the year Fifty— as indeed it was in fact—so the fifties assumed an epic grandeur in the sixties, until today the misty never-never land of the city's wonder years is the period known as "Before the Fire." "Before the Fire" takes care of everything: the Argonauts, the Committees of Vigilance, the Emperor Norton, Steamer Day, Sunday breakfast at the Seal Rocks, Lotta Crabtree, the cable cars, the Cobweb Palace, Belmont, Gertrude Atherton, Duncan Nicol and the Bank Exchange, Oysters Kirkpatrick, Lilly Coit, Addison Mizner and the Mid-Winter Fair. It is a repository of things stirring and gentle and wonderful that, though they will come not again, have never altogether departed.

If, by fortunate chance, archeologists five thousand years hence shall chance alone upon buried traces of San Francisco, having happily overpassed Detroit, Bridgeport, Scranton and Provo, we will all have a better name with posterity. For they will come upon things and artifacts and souvenirs expressive of a way of life in a proud and generous city of flags and fogs whose counterpart is not anywhere. It is a consummation to be wished for in Pisco Punch.

# Early California Amusements Were Various

### EVERYONE ENJOYED DOGFIGHTS, FISHING WAS SPECIAL

Every class and nationality was represented on Sansome Street in the early days when a dogfight started, from Chinabo to monocled gentleman and from shovel-wielding paddy to Yankee whittler. Another recreation which fetched the fanc of the pioneers was the organization of fishing parties off the Farallones, as shown below in *The California Mercanti Journal*. Not all the participants were good sailors and the artist captioned his drawing: "Not Sick, But Feels So Bad. Then as later, a split of the best champagne was felt to be a sovereign remedy for *mal de mer*.

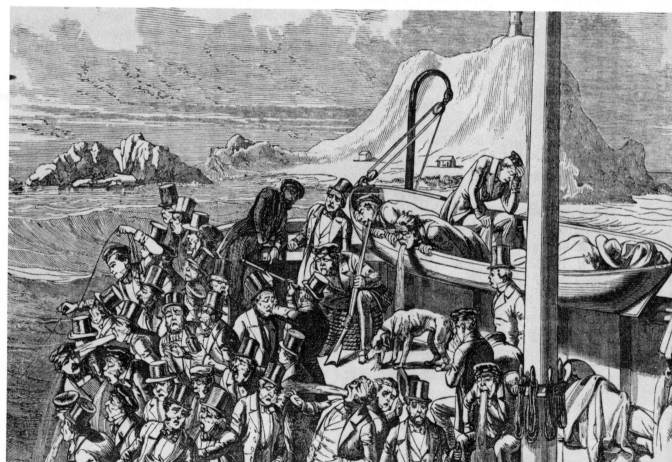

## HORSEBACK POOL, BILLIARDS AND LIVE ONES

Riding horseback into the nearest saloon was a gesture of abandon and good fellowship as much esteemed in San Francisco as in less urban reaches of the Old West. "We saw a drunken hombre yesterday riding into some of the saloons of the Plaza, *a la* Tom Hyer," said the *Alta California* reprovingly in 1851. "It is time these scenes of rowdyism ceased to be allowed among us." In the same issue the newspaper raises an editorial eyebrow at "careless shooting. A bullet grazes three gentlemen at the bar of the Hotel de Ville in Montgomery Street." At the lower left the glass of fashion of the time pauses for his portrait during a game of billiards while at the right is depicted that perennial sport, occupation and profession in all civilized lands, waiting for a live one.

# Steamer Day

Until the coming of the railroads, and m
especially in the fifties before the com
tion of the overland telegraph, "Stea
Day," when the side-wheelers of the Pa
Mail Steamship Company arrived from I
ama or departed thereto, was a red le
day in San Francisco. The steamship c
pany was organized in 1848 with ha
million dollars' capital by William As
wall, for whom the Atlantic seaport at I
ama was named, and continued in busi
until 1925. It ran six steamers on reg
schedule and in the fifties, according to
vin Harlow, "was overwhelmed with b
ness." Departure day saw all San Franc
in a dither, settling accounts, sending
the mail and seeing friends to the pier.

The arrival of an incoming steamer, signaled by the semaphore atop Telegraph Hill, was the occasion for a concerted rush to San Francisco's post office, depicted below by Andre Castaigne. So much of an institution were the lifted arms of the telegraph that in a playhouse, when an actor appeared on stage, his arms spread wide as accompaniment to the line: "What does this mean?" a voice from the gallery shouted "Side-wheel steamer!"

## PORTSMOUTH SQUARE WAS THE BEATING HEART OF TOWN

Steamer Day in the fifties brought all sorts of country types to San Francisco for the news and the mail, as shown in the above drawing by Gilbert Gaul. Miners in from the Mother Lode renewed city acquaintances, Spanish ranchers in colorful attire rode their horses to the hitch rack outside the Empire Saloon and old gentlemen bought knicknacks from Turkish street vendors. Portsmouth Square, shown below, was the Plaza. In the old photograph are visible the Bella Union, gaming and music hall of wide and evil fame, McLaughlin's Stage and Mail Office serving Oakland, Santa Cruz and Stockton, and the shop of John Piper, dealer in fruits and preserves. Piper shortly took off his storekeeper's apron and removed to booming Virginia City where he became proprietor, during his lifetime, of three opera houses and was known as one of the most celebrated theatrical impressarios of his day. Most of San Francisco's civic life of the period centered around the Plaza.

# The Best of Everything Was None Too Good in '53

THREE PICTURES: CALIFORNIA HISTORICAL SOCIETY

Two years after the discovery of gold at Captain Sutter's Mill San Francisco was beginning to assume aspects of urbanity with three-story stone buildings, such as those shown above in Montgomery Street at the foot of Washington, rising above a street life which still possessed overtones of the Spanish ranchers (*right*) whose picturesque attire and Castilian speech were still a commonplace on the streets. "Nearly all the residents in those days rode horseback," recorded the inimitable Barry & Patten, "used the Mexican saddle and all the jangling accoutrements, wore the vicuña hat, or broad-brimmed glazed sombrero and the comfortable, convenient, protecting serapa. . . . Hardly anybody said two bits in those days. It was '*dos reales!*' '*cuarto reales!*' '*un peso!*' Nearly all the newcomers had either crossed the Isthmus or come by the Horn, stopping at old Spanish cities *en route*, picking up sufficient *de la lengua* to ask for anything they wished." Two years after this account of life at the Golden Gate, San Francisco had its own Delmonico's, patterned on the great original in New York, where as shown below, everyone ate and drank the best of everything.

## BOMBAZINE, BON-BONS AND BOMBS

Gentle and wistful Barry and Patten would scarcely have recognized the Cosmopolis of the West represented by San Francisco a quarter of a century after the time of the scenes on the page opposite. At the Bohemian Club (*above*) matters of literary and artistic importance to the new world engaged the preoccupied attention of tail-coated members in a day before Low Jinx were born. At William Ralston's classic Old California Theater matinee-goers (*left*) patronized "the best managed and conducted theater in the Union" under the regime of Maguire and McCullough. Minstrelsy was yielding to vaudeville, but when *Pinafore* arrived for its second presentation in the United States—the first had been at Boston Museum—it advertised, "A Real Ship Manned With Real Sailors! Real Cannon! A Realistic Production!" Less approving of the muses was a crank who, a few years later, blew himself to pieces (*below*) while attempting to protest against the appearance of Mme. Nellie Melba at the San Francisco Opera. Quite literally hoist with his own petard, remarked the irrepressible *Chronicle*.

# '49 WAS A YEAR MARKED WITH A STAR

"SPICED, PLUMP AND *BUENO*"

The feeling of comradeship which existed among the California pioneers has no counterpart elsewhere in the American legend. The Argonauts who came around the Horn, the Forty-niners who braved the Isthmus, the men who shared the long *jornada* across the plains behind the plodding oxen, all were members of a fellowship deeper and more abiding in its emotions than any other confraternity. They had experienced things no man would ever again experience and, like Ulysses who had sailed the unknown seas before them, could say, "I am a part of all that I have met." And like Aeneas, remembering perils and hardships: "*Haec olim meminisse juvabit.*" Being Argonauts and Californians, the first-comers were immediately conscious that they were men set apart, in a way consecrated, and lost no time in capitalizing on their foresight in arriving days or weeks before those of less discernment. The Society of California Pioneers was organized in 1850 while scores of future members, to be admitted on a somewhat less exalted status, were still rounding the Horn or slapping mosquitoes at Chagres. Another primeval and articulate group associated itself from among the passengers who had arrived on the second run of the steamer *Panama* which had come in on August 18, 1849. Three years from that happy date to the minute, the *Panama* veterans, already legendary figures, sat down to an anniversary dinner, as shown here, at the Irving Restaurant in San Francisco. The menu included vintage champagne cooled with ice brought around the Horn from Saugus, Massachusetts, fresh butter from Goshen, New York, prime Havana cigars and oysters "three weeks from the shell, almost fresh, spiced, plump and *bueno*." The dinner was such a radiant success that it was repeated next year at the Lafayette, and the anniversaries continued as long as the last survivor could hold a glass of champagne to toast the great days that were gone.

Twenty years later 200 members of the Society of California Pioneers went from San Francisco to New York City to share recollections with other old-timers. On the way they stopped off at Potter Palmer's sumptuous hotel in Chicago (*above*). Later, when they checked in at the Astor House in New York (*lower right*), did they remember an earlier Astor House on the San Francisco waterfront in the winter of '49?

## THE RISING TIDE OF CRIME

By late in 1849 the criminal populace of San Francisco, largely recruited from the British penal colony at Tasmania, took on aspects of serious menace. Six times in two years the flimsy town was swept by devastating fires, four of them definitely known to have been set so that mobs of thieves could plunder the fugitives (*below*). It was a condition of affairs, according to Herbert Asbury, most nearly to approach criminal anarchy in American history. The Sydney Ducks, as the English toughs were known, and the "Hounds," rival gangsters, took pleasure in beating the Chilenos and abusing the prostitutes (*right*) in their quarter of town and contributed materially to the formation of the first Vigilance Committee in 1851.

# Building Gallows Became a Full-Time Occupation

Under the provocation of arson, murder and pillage so frequent as to be commonplace there came into being the San Francisco Committee of Vigilance, a group of armed citizens with military authority determined to take justice out of the impotent courts and put the fear of God in evildoers. Gallows building and other ominous gestures of retribution became visible around the city.

### UP, JENKINS!

The first victim of the Vigilantes was a Sydney-Town criminal of long record named John Jenkins. Seized by the Committee for stealing a safe, Jenkins was given a hasty hearing by members summoned by an alarm rung on the bell of Monumental Engine Company. Early the next morning a group of heavily armed men hanged Jenkins (*right*) from the ridgepole of an adobe in Portsmouth Square. The Sydney Ducks left town by the score, but not all of them.

## SAN FRANCISCO'S MOST SENSATIONAL SHOOTING

The reactivation of the Vigilance Committee for San Francisco's second cleansing in 1856 was occasioned by the city's most sensational murder, that of James King of William, editor of the *Bulletin*, by James Casey, a machine politician and local bad hat. The murder took place at the corner of Montgomery and Washington streets (*above*) and immediately a number of citizens who had been active in the Committee of 1851 held a secret meeting and reorganized. A thousand men were sworn in the first afternoon, the militia stacked arms and joined the extralegal forces of law and order and took over the entire conduct of the city's affairs. All business was suspended while James King lingered at death's door and when it became apparent that he would not recover the Vigilantes seized the jail where Casey was confined together with Charles Cora, a gambler who had recently killed General W. H. Richardson. Sheriff David Scannell, later head of the fire department and a notable San Francisco figure until his death many years afterward, surrendered his prisoners and they were brought to trial at the Committee's headquarters, known as Fort Gunnybags. The dramatic drawing of the murder was first published in *Leslie's* July 19, 1856, only a month after Casey had been hanged for it.

This old print shows the San Francisco Vigilance Committee assembling at the sound of the tocsin atop Fort Gunnybags, a warehouse near the waterfront which had been fortified with sandbags and mounted two cannon. Here Cora and Casey were held until the time of their execution.

Cora and Casey are shown in this drawing being escorted by a heavily armed delegation with a cannon from the city jail to be lodged for trial and ultimately execution at Fort Gunnybags.

A BAD END TO CASEY AND CORA

The hanging of Cora and Casey furnished San Francisco with its greatest sensation of the time. James King died six days after being shot by Casey and a cortege of 20,000 followed the editor to his grave at Lone Mountain. As the bells were still tolling Cora and Casey were hanged before an equally numerous throng (*below*) from the front of Fort Gunnybags on an improvised gallows which had seen service five years previous during the first law and order regime. It was easily the most celebrated hanging in the history of the West and had vast repercussions in the future political and social history of the community.

# The Town's Criminal Element Frequented Its Dives

San Francisco's organized crime at the time of the first Vigilantes had its focal point in the dives and among the denizens of Sydney-Town. In a generation which never used the word prostitute if an elaborate paraphrase could be devised, the "pretty waiter girls" of San Francisco's Barbary Coast deadfalls were world famous for their rapacity and total lack of moral inhibitions. In such fandango dives as the Bull Run, Occidental, Brooks' Melodeon and Billy Goat, which flourished in unbelievable squalor in Pacific Street, their duties were to separate sailors from their money by urging on them drinks into which aphrodisiacs had been insinuated and then sell them their personal favors in the fifteen minutes which usually separated the calling of each dance. At the zenith of its bad fame the Bull Run employed half a hundred "pretty waiter girls" who were "notorious as the most brazen, hopeless and abandoned women on the Barbary Coast." The strumpets gloried in such picturesque names as the Galloping Cow, the Roaring Gimlet, the Waddling Duck, Lady Jane Gray and the Little Lost Chicken. All were accomplished pickpockets and adept at rolling lushes, in which occupation they were in cahoots with the police. This woodcut of the "pretty waiter girls" plying their trade in the Opera Comique at Jackson and Kearny streets, better known as Murderer's Corner, is from the files of the *California Police Gazette* in the Bancroft Library and typifies the night life of the town's criminal element when the Vigilance Committee was called.

## THE PRESS WAS PRESENT

The work of the Second Vigilance Committee of 1856 concluded with the hanging of Joseph Hetherington and his accomplice Brace, who had been involved in several murders. The execution (*below*) took place before a large and enthusiastic audience on a gallows in the middle of Davis Street near Sacramento. Brace went insane before the noose was adjusted and a sack had to be tied over his head, so fearful were his blasphemies. Reporters and representatives of the press, including sketch artists (*left*), had a fine view of these macabre doings from a flight of steps leading to a ship chandler's loft in Davis Street and were able to give their readers a full account next day. Shortly thereafter the Vigilantes disbanded.

# In Life and Death Judge Terry Was Violent

## BLOODY JUDGE TERRY

Fieriest figure in San Francisco's early years was Supreme Court Judge David S. Terry, a secessionist agitator and duelist of note. During the disorders which occasioned the Second Vigilance cleansing of the city's criminal element, Terry stabbed a Vigilante policeman (*above*) during a street riot. The entire Vigilante force of the city was at once mobilized (*below*) and Terry locked up in Fort Gunnybags (*right*). The wounded man recovered and Terry escaped punishment—for a time.

## THE TERRY-BRODERICK DUEL WAS A GREAT SCANDAL

Three years after the stabbing episode, Terry was again in the news. This time it was as one of the participants in California's most celebrated of all duels, with David C. Broderick, a political opponent whom Terry blamed for his defeat in a local election. Terry killed Broderick (*above*) on the morning of September 13, 1859, at Lake Merced in San Mateo County. The ensuing scandal drove Terry from office while Broderick lay in state (*below*) in San Francisco.

## AN END TO JUDGE TERRY

It took thirty years for time to catch up with Judge Terry. In 1889, however, Terry was involved in another feud, this time with United States Supreme Court Justice Stephen J. Field, who had clapped him in jail for contempt of court. Terry swore to kill Field and the latter retained as bodyguard Dave Naegle, late of Panamint, Pioche, Bodie and Tombstone and a man who had made dogmeat of bad men by the score. Field and Terry chanced to meet in the railroad lunchroom at Lathrop; Terry reached as though for a gun and was instantly killed by Naegle. Everyone in California breathed easier with the professional fire-eater out of the way.

From the very beginnings of San Francisco journalism with the appearance of the first copy of the *California Star*, its editors and owners had a low emotional boiling point and were quick on the trigger. Duels between editors and other editors, editors and politicians, and outright assassinations of newspapermen became a commonplace and occupational hazard of the profession. The murder of James King of William, editor of the *Bulletin*, evoked the Second Committee of Vigilance and became California's most celebrated shooting. When General J. W. Denver, for whom the Colorado capital was to be named, killed Edward Gilbert, senior editor of the *Alta California*, in a particularly vicious duel with rifles (*below left*), it had national repercussions many years later. The Democrats were about to nominate Denver for the presidency when Republican papers recalled the unsavory encounter with Gilbert and his name was withdrawn. Grover Cleveland was named instead and won. C. A. Russell, editor of the *Evening Picayune*, exchanged shots with Captain Joseph Folsom, U.S.A., and when neither was harmed they resorted to bowie knives and both parties were seriously carved up. An editorial wag placed a sign over his office: "Subscriptions received from 9 to 4; challenges 11 to 12 only." Professional stand-ins for duelists were available for a fee and when, finally, two editors of a French language paper staged a duel with all Continental formality (*lower right*), personal encounters were pretty much laughed out of the picture.

# The Code Duello Was Often Invoked in the Early Days

## TUMULTS ATTENDED THE DE YOUNGS EVERYWHERE

The advent of seventeen-year-old Michael de Young and his brother Charles and what eventually became their *San Francisco Chronicle* marked an epoch in the history of San Francisco. On the strength of a borrowed $20 gold piece and limitless energy and audacity they soon had the most important newspaper property on the Coast. Because Mike de Young understood telegraphic code, they scooped the town on the death of Lincoln, but their high-handed operations made trouble in the end. When a crackpot professional friend-of-the-people murdered Mike de Young and was promptly acquitted, the San Francisco mob (*above*) drew his carriage in triumph through the streets. *Harper's,* in printing the drawing, remarked that it was an action "of dubious propriety."

### CAVIAR TO THE RESCUE

San Francisco was a hustling newspaper town second to none in the United States in the vital seventies and Paul Frenzeny was so fetched by delivery boys on horseback with umbrellas that he drew the well-known sketch at the right. The new day that came to San Francisco journalism with the rise of young William Randolph Hearst was typified by a resounding series of news beats, extravagant promotional campaigns and crusades. When a Southern Pacific train became stalled in snowdrifts in Northern California, the *Examiner* sent a relief expedition to its aid. Typical of the Corinthian tastes of the publisher was the menu for the stranded: caviar canapes, *foie gras* and roast chicken.

San Francisco in the sixties was a paradise of prostitution and boasted a red light district larger than those in other cities of the world many times its size. Love stores were cosmopolitan in recruiting their handmaidens but the Gallic reputation for adeptness in amour made French women in most requisition and in the fall of 1850, when the city was suffering a great dearth of Cyprians, the *News* caused a wave of enthusiasm when it announced that 900 women were being recruited in the bagnios of Paris for immediate export to California. The better grade of brothels centered around Portland Square and many of them were celebrated for their costly and ornate furnishings as well as for the professional skill of their inmates. The uptown resorts were usually honest in their dealings with customers, the picking of pockets and slugging of gentlemen in wine being frowned upon. Now and then, however, there was reported some lapse from perfect propriety and the *California Police Gazette* was able to instruct and edify its readers with an account of retribution such as that depicted on the page opposite. Here a madame is expropriating the shoes and stockings of two new recruits to her premises as assurance of continued residence.

# San Francisco's Love Stores Were Hilarious

The melodeons or variety halls of the Barbary Coast in the San Francisco sixties attracted as customers a class of roughs and nogooders who were customers for the favors of the chorus line after the performance.

## HIP AND THIGH WAS THE SMITING

Street fights (*above*), the shooting of his wife's paramour (*right*) by Henry Johnson, or Kate Smith begging for her life when discovered (*lower right*) in sin by her husband all delighted San Francisco when they appeared in the public prints. A few years later, as indicated by attire and hairdos ladies sometimes had a falling out over what started as a friendly game of poker. (*below*)

# San Francisco's Night Life Was Largely Donnybrook

Heady noises arose from the streets of San Francisco in the frenetic fifties. The razzmatazz of civilization on the prod saw strange sarabands in the vicinage of Portsmouth Square and its adjacent byways, as yet innocent of grading, drainage or, in many cases, police protection. In 1857 the *California Police Gazette*, ever anxious to point a moral and warn impressionable youth against the pitfalls of vice, printed the above woodcut with the ominous caption to the effect that Frank Lines, after having been feloniously rolled of his wallet during a casual evening in the hay, had returned "to clean out Madam Reiter's Bagnio in Sacramento Street." Below this stern pictorial admonition to professional ethics is shown a drunk being searched by the police after having been ejected from Our House Saloon for disreputable conduct. On the page opposite is a brief excerpt from a San Francisco police blotter of the time culled by the distinguished historian Alvin Harlow from the files of the *Daily Alta California* in 1852.

# From the Police Court Column

## of the Daily Alta California in 1852.

George Ditz was found insensibly drunk in front of the Custom House. He was taken up in a handcart and emptied in the police station. Fined $5.

Hyppolite Boveau, a Frenchman, fired a pistol in the street and did not know any better. Discharged.

Florence C. Stevenson got drunk and attempted to take a grocery on Dupont Street by storm. Fined $7.

John Gomez, a red-shirted, squalid looking greaser, was guilty of beating and maltreating his woman, quite an interesting specimen of the female sex. John accounted for her black eye by saying that the bedpost flew up and hit her. John was fined $25 and sent down for ten days.

Colonel Waters of the Curbstone Rangers was picked up helplessly drunk on Kearny Street and taken to the station house in a wheelbarrow. Fined $5.

Three Frenchmen with unpronounceable names were found very noisy on Pacific Wharf and fined $5 each.

A HARD OLD CASE.—J. Keyser was found miserably drunk on Pacific Street and taken in. When called up in the dock, he was hardly able to stand, being considerably affected with the trembles. He admitted having been on a bender for a whole week. Fined $5 and sent to the lock-up for five days.

Henry Foster, considerably noisy and furious, fined $25.

COLOR HARMONY.—Henry White and George Brown, being very blue, went into Green Street and blacked each other's eyes. Fined $25 each.

A greaserita named Carolina and an American named Hyde, with their heads wrapped up in several handkerchiefs, appeared in the dock to answer a charge of fighting desperately on Dupont Street. Fined $20 each and put in the jug for ten days.

John Briggs, found comfortably drunk on Long Wharf. Discharged on promise to reform.

E. Jones was found by Officer North on the corner of Long Wharf and Montgomery Street in a state of drunkenness and quite disorderly. He resisted the officer manfully, tearing his breeches and committing other small depradations. Fined $20 or ten days.

Mrs. Mark Quirk, proprietress of a rum mill on Stockton Street, was found punching the goard (sic) of a poor, ill-shaven, luckless wight that had drank until he had become weak in the knees. Fined $50 and the Recorder sent the man to jail for three days because he had become so drunk as to let a woman thrash him.

INDECENT EXHIBITION.—Antonio Rico has got a music box and a magic lantern. His pictures represent members of the human family in the Texas costume. Whilst the exhibition is going on, he grinds Yankee Doodle out of the box and charges two rials a sight. He was discharged and the indecent pictures ordered to be destroyed.

Susannah, the Indian woman, who has not been out of the station house for one week at a stretch in two years, was up again, with another attack of the prevailing epidemic. Sent down for 9 days.

Gaudalupe Parvenise, sleeping with a friend Sunday night, abstracted $10 from his pocket, for the purpose, he said, of preventing somebody else from taking it. Sent down for 3 months.

# Seeing the Elephant Could Entail Unforeseen Expenses

One of Pacific Street's most infamous resorts in Barbary Coast days was a combined brothel, music hall and tavern called Bull Run. Here the Bull Run's proprietor, Ned Allen, is shown assisting an employee in the discharge of her professional duties after a customer has been rendered senseless with drugged whisky.

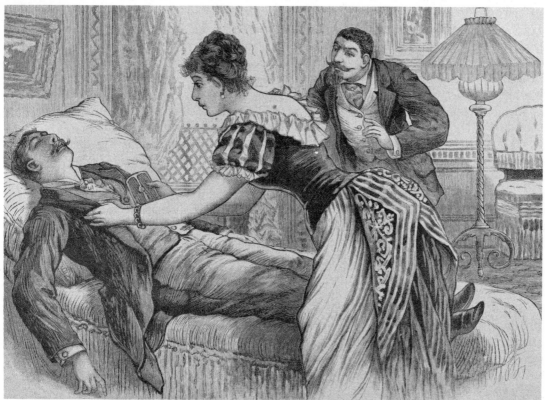

In later years the brothels of the Upper Tenderloin—Mason, Larkin, Eddie, O'Farrell and Turk Streets— were considered an improvement over the Barbary Coast in that patrons were never murdered and seldom damaged. It was entirely possible, however, for a customer to lose his wallet in a moment of inadvertent relaxation in even the best-upholstered setting.

AND THERE WAS THE ADDED HAZARD OF NOCTURNAL EARTHQUAKE

San Franciscans in the early years of the city found its profusion of bawdy houses a source not only of satisfaction and convenience but of perpetual hilarity. The intelligence that the collector of port or the mayor had been discovered in unbecoming surroundings when a brothel caught fire or that an alderman had mislaid his diamond evening studs in a house of mirth provided spicy items for the gossip columnists of the day, none of whom enjoyed wider circulation among the community's sporting element than reporters of the *California Police Gazette*, an impious *feuilleton* not to be confused with *The National Police Gazette* published at a later date in New York. In the spirited scene above recorded in woodcut the *Gazette* was able to depict for its readers the alarm and terror occasioned in one of the better Portland Square bordellos when a senator in "grotesque attire from a fancy dress ball" ran through the corridors. The *Gazette's* gossip paragrapher declared coyly that he knew the identity of the august solon but wouldn't divulge it unless he were asked. In the mid-sixties the entire town rocked with laughter after having first been rocked by an earthquake which drove the inmates and patrons of an Eddie Street resort (*left*) into the street in informal attire.

## TO LEARN ABOUT CONDITIONS AT FIRST HAND

In 1878 a legislative committee from Sacramento descended upon San Francisco to study its night life at first hand with an eye to enacting state-wide legislation against sin. Mostly they were interested in the nymphs of the Upper Tenderloin and consented to take a glass of wine in the interest of seeing everything. There is no record of their report or any laws based on it in the archives of California.

# By the Turn of the Century the Barbary Coast Was Tamer

Right up to the time of the Fire a man could have an evening's fun along Pacific Street (*below*) but he was less apt to be slugged or drugged or shanghaied. The well-heeled tourist out to see the elephant could, of course, patronize the elaborate bagnio conducted in the Upper Tenderloin by Miss Tessie Wall, a voluptuous blonde with a reputed capacity for drinking twenty-two bottles of champagne without moving from the table. Here amidst ornate upholstery (*right*) he might meet the leading San Francisco politicians of the time or socially correct seniors from Leland Stanford, occasionally with their fathers. Tessie enjoyed a reputation for strict propriety except, of course, in the line of business. Like Edie, she had class with a capital K.

SAN FRANCISCO CALL BULLETIN

# LILLY COIT 5

By fated chance, the ship bringing the little girl who was to become the most celebrated of fire buffs and one of San Francisco's most venerated characters sailed through the Golden Gate on the morning of May 4, 1851, just as the fifth of its great conflagrations (*above*) was reducing the town to the level of a collapsed opera hat. Lilly Hitchcock Coit, to whose memory the Coit Tower stands today as a San Francisco landmark, was fascinated and her first impression of the city in flames was to shape her entire life. At an early age she attached herself to Knickerbocker Hose No. 5, whose station was near her home, and answered all alarms to which its gooseneck hand pumper was toilsomely pulled on the run by members of the company. On her twentieth birthday she was made an honorary member of the Knickerbockers, an accolade which would have elevated her socially to the estate of the Crockers and Tevises had not her family already been there. At the left, Lilly is shown in a celebrated sketch which appeared in the *Police Gazette* and below, one of the fearful conflagrations to which San Francisco was subject and which she never missed attending.

## LILLY MISSED NO FIRES

Lilly's conduct as a young lady was the scandal and delight of San Francisco. Always headstrong and boyish, she sometimes went out in boy's attire (*above*) and had to be helped home after seeing the elephant. She went to cockfights in Marin County and smoked cigars at the Maison Dorée. In an age when ladies and liquor were never mentioned in the same breath, she unaccountably chose to have Silas Selleck, the "photographic artist," pose her (*right*) with a bottle in her hand. She was the toast of the Fireman's Balls and as long as she lived signed herself "Lilly Coit 5," much as royalty would sign "Regina" to show her membership in Knickerbocker 5. At the court of Napoleon III, where she dropped in one afternoon for a cup of tea and a chat with the Empress Eugenie, she was pointed out as *une pompière celebre*, and in time she achieved the status of a national figure. When, full of years and honors, Lilly answered her last alarm in 1929 San Francisco was bowed with grief for Lilly and for the old days that would not return. She had been one of the noblest Romans, one with White Hat McCarthy and the Emperor Norton, and when at her bequest the Coit Memorial Tower arose on Telegraph Hill where once the semaphore had signaled vessels inbound, sentimental San Franciscans thought it a pity the architect hadn't included a fire bell at its summit. Lilly Coit 5, they said, would have liked that.

# The Dawn of Banking in the Western Continent

WELLS FARGO BANK

## THIS WAS A DAY MARKED WITH A STAR, TOO

Early in the banking day of July 1, 1852, the staff of Wells Fargo & Co., newly arrived from the East, posed for their photograph before offices in Sam Brannan's new fireproof block in Montgomery Street between California and Sacramento. Porter, office manager, cashier and bookkeepers may even have appreciated that it was an epic moment in the story of the American West. Within a few years Wells Fargo Banking and Wells Fargo Express were to have absorbed all rivals in both businesses in California and become the dominant agencies of money and transportation, not only out of San Francisco, but wherever in the Western states and territories business was transacted, precious metals mined and freight transported. The name Wells Fargo itself was to become one of the legendary properties of the great days, synonymous with yellow and red Concord stages riding down the years with shotgun messengers, route agents and frock-coated cashiers in the supporting cast.

It may or may not have presaged impending calamity when returning travelers from the Comstock (*above*) reported that wild horses had invaded the Virginia City branch of the all-powerful Bank of California (*right*) and frightened the wits out of the customers.

But the Bank of California was indeed in trouble. The imperial manner and delusions of grandeur of William Ralston in financing every sort of business venture on the West Coast, mines, mills, railways, water companies, hotels, vineyards, manufactories and shipyards, had overextended its resources. Ralston, in the role of Lorenzo, had done more for the future of San Francisco than any living man of his generation, but he had all but wrecked the most powerful banking firm in the West to do it. As in other times of crisis, Wells Fargo was to stand aloof from the general ruin and assist to pick up the pieces.

Black Friday was August 27, 1875, when it became known throughout San Francisco that William Ralston was drowned in the bay while swimming, the victim of mischance or his own hand none has ever been able to say. Crowds besieged the banking offices he had so lately dominated and murmured threats against the Bonanza Firm of Flood, Fair, Mackay and O'Brien who had reportedly driven the bank to the wall. "They have killed San Francisco," said a newspaper of them. Happily neither it nor any of many other unsavory rumors was so. Simply, Ralston had dreamed too boldly to make his dream come true. No great national banking crisis followed, as some had feared. In a few weeks San Francisco's affairs were again on an even keel and William Sharon, Ralston's friend and business partner, had taken up where the great builder had left off. The tragedy, classic, austere and complete, was the tragedy of the greatest San Franciscan of them all.

## "COOLERS OF CHAMPAGNE WINE, STRATEGICALLY LOCATED"

Most radiantly sumptuous of all San Francisco's civic sarabands was mounted in 1879 to welcome former President Grant during his round-the-world tour. Public and private entertainments for the hero of the Civil War were on a scale to dim anything ever before seen in the shadow of the Golden Gate. Every yacht and charter steamer in the harbor escorted the liner *Tokio* into the bay and the guest of honor was transshipped to the side-wheeler *St. Paul,* which had been rented for the occasion by Louis Sloss and General John F. Miller, an old comrade-in-arms. There 400 guests, a number neatly fitting the qualifications laid down by Ward McAllister for New York's eligible aristocracy, partook of a caterer's luncheon of quail in aspic, *foie gras* and ices washed down by a Niagara of Mumm's best champagne. Grant made his debarkation "completely surrounded by. plug hats and ulsters" and a monster parade escorted him, inevitably, to The Palace. His entry into the Palm Court (*left*) was made in a chariot drawn by six white horses as thousands cheered.

Most spectacular private entertainment in the annals of the Golden Gate was the reception for President Grant given at Belmont by Senator William Sharon. Two thousand guests were conveyed by special trains to Belmont, where 100 carriages with 200 grooms and coachmen awaited them. Among the guests, reported the *Argonaut,* "were 101 ladies in white silks or satin, 83 in colored silks or satin, 61 wearing point lace, 143 wearing Duchesse, Valenciennes, Spanish blonde, Honiton, Smyrna, Chantilly and guipure; 313 ladies wore diamonds and 5 wore diamond necklaces. No lady was ungloved and only one gentleman." Special trains, thoughtfully scheduled to leave Belmont at one, three, four and six in the morning, returned the guests to San Francisco awash with water ice, champagne, claret cup, *foie gras* and lobster in aspic and firm in the conviction that since the court of the Sun King of France there had never been such sumptuous liberality of entertainment.

The Bay

Once Teemed

With

Walking

Beams

SOLONS IN WINE FRIGHTENED THE FAIR SEX

During the eighties complaints were sometime heard that the "Legislative Train" running between Sacramento and Oakland was the scene of unchivalrous conduct by statesmen in wine and ladies feared to ride it.

Like its cable cars, the ferries across San Francisco Bay to Oakland (*page opposite*) were for many decades beloved and familiar institutions. Driven by side wheels governed by massive walking beams, and later by propellers, until the construction of the Bay Bridge in the nineteen thirties scores of these humble and utilitarian but somehow romantic carriers plied between San Francisco's Ferry Building at the foot of Market Street and destinations at Oakland, Alemeda, Sausalito, and other hamlets across the Bay. Many of these vessels saw service for decades and their cabins with colored-glass transoms, their lunch counters and their personnels were known with affection by generations of Californians. Their almost indestructible engines passed from ship to ship, for years carrying passengers from the Southern Pacific's pier at Oakland where all transcontinental rail traffic terminated, and for many a world traveler his first view of America's most beautiful city was from the fog-wet deck of the *Sacramento, Piedmont* or *Sausalito*. When the Central Pacific's transcontinental trains had their terminal at Vallejo, passengers departing on the night train for the East had ample time for supper on the Vallejo ferry, while early morning arrivals took breakfast in the same manner. Here the artist has shown business and professional men in the early nineties ready to disembark at the Ferry Building for a business day in Montgomery Street or amidst the thickets of mansions on Nob Hill. Below, another view of the ferries and a sketch by E. A. Abbey showing the manually operated bells which guided ferries to their slip on foggy mornings before the coming of electricity.

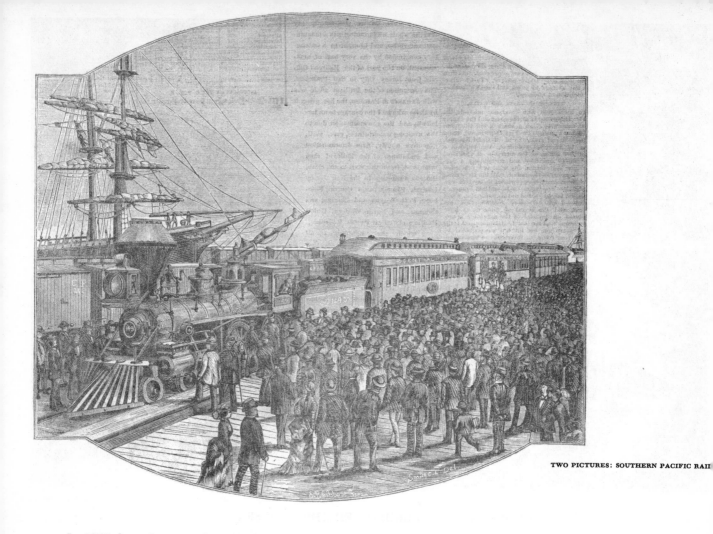

In 1876 the rail journey from New York to California conventionally occupied seven days. Tense was the drama, therefore, when Henry Jarrett, comanager of Booth's Theater in New York, announced that he planned to send a company of distinguished players across the continent in less than four days to keep a San Francisco engagement. Headed by Lawrence Barrett, the troupers entrained at Jersey City after their closing performance on Broadway and headed West in a snow storm of wonderful publicity. It was the major American excitement of the Centennial year and the *Lightning Express* captured the universal fancy in an age when railroading was implicit with romance. Bulletins followed the train's progress to Chicago, across Iowa to Omaha and then on the Great Plains of the authentic West. Money changed hands on split-second arrivals. The *Express* flew through Reno well ahead of time in a blaze of flares and red fire and arrived, as shown in this old print, at the Central Pacific's Oakland Pier in eighty-four hours, twelve less than advertised. Nobody was to top the record for years. It is notable that the Central's locomotive No. 149 hauled the train at top speed the entire distance between Ogden and Oakland, 782 miles, without change of engines, a practice only to become common in Diesel service three quarters of a century later.

For the better part of a century railroad travelers from the East have arrived in San Francisco with an opportunity to approach the world's most beautiful city by water. The piers shown in this drawing were built out into San Francisco Bay toward Goat Island in 1871 of timber and pilings brought from the summit of the Sierra Nevada. Excepting only the *Great Eastern* they could accommodate any ship afloat at the time. The Southern Pacific's passengers have always thought it a romantic way to arrive and depart and view with consternation the day when the ferries may disappear entirely and all traffic be by wheel across bridges.

# The Espee Was Always in the Public Eye

In 1871 when this old photograph was taken the Central Pacific, predecessor of the Southern Pacific, took its trains to wharfside at Oakland much as it was to do for the next eighty-odd years. The wooden cars, balloon stacks and sailing ship give a clue to the period while the twin stacks of the ferry *El Capitan* are visible at the left over the trainshed. It was a romantic era of travel but not the most luxurious.

he railroad's press agent, had such thing existed in 1878, would prob- bly have been at pains to keep the an Francisco newspapers from rinting the story of one youthful assenger who arrived aboard the ars from the East having had as raveling companion a man of The :loth who produced a long bowie nife with the explanation: "I can arry the Gospel with this, no need f a gun."

# The Wonderful Palace

A tangible manifestation of the city's affluence which no San Franciscan of any generation has been able to admire save with superlatives was The Palace, the first great luxury hotel of the West Coast, begun by the unhappy William Ralston of the Bank of California and continued to completion after his death by Senator William Sharon, the Bank's Virginia City manager. Located at the junction of New Montgomery and Market streets, The Palace rose in a façade spendthrift with bow windows for seven amazing stories. That it was vast beyond all possibility of profitable occupancy at the time of its completion bothered its owners not at all and San Francisco itself still less. It was a monument to the concrete virtues of the pioneers and eventually justified its construction as one of the most valuable hotel properties in the world. The northwest view of The Palace (*above left*) shows the cable cars of Market Street and, in the immediate foreground, Lotta's Fountain, to this day a monument to the memory of San Francisco's darling of the music halls, Lotta Crabtree. Below is shown the immense wonder and glory of the hotel's architecture, the Grand Court as it appeared in 1878. Here the beautiful carriages of such perfectionists in the details of living as Lloyd Tevis of Wells Fargo & Co. and James Flood of the Virginia City bonanza firm daily deposited their rich and fashionable passengers right in the very heart of the hotel itself. When President Grant put up at The Palace in 1879 a chariot drawn by six snow white horses with grooms and footmen in lavender liveries entered the Grand Court at a full gallop while thousands of admirers lined the tiers of galleries, cheering and waving what a contemporary newspaper account called "a sea of silk hats."

The first major social event at The Palace, the forerunner of innumerable dazzlements, was a banquet to General Philip Sheridan, as depicted above. Here the railroad rajahs of Central Pacific and silver kings of the Comstock admired each other's diamond shirt studs and broadcloth tail coats in a midst of almost paralyzing grandeur. The Palace was the first and forever the greatest public gratification of San Francisco's love of luxury and ostentation. Its opulent apartments occupied the site of "Happy Valley" which a decade previous had been a shantytown. No visitor of note to the American West thereafter but was feted at The Palace: Presidents Grant, Hayes, Harrison, McKinley, Roosevelt and Taft, the Grand Duke Boris of Russia, King Albert of the Belgians, Prince Louis of Savoy, the King of Hawaii, Lady Randolph Churchill and mere millionaires by the score, Rockefellers, two Morgans, Carnegie, Pullman, Huntington, Swift and shoals of Vanderbilts, Goulds and Fricks. At a dinner to Senator William Sharon in the seventies the menu (right) was engrossed on plates of solid silver which alone cost $40 each. "The banquet was of rare splendor," remarked a contemporary somewhat unnecessarily, "and was most emphatically a dinner to millionaires."

MENU

Huitres
Chablis
Consommé Royale
Sherry Isabella
Saumon glacé au four à la Chambord
Sauterne
Boudin blanc à la Richelieu
Château la Tour
Filet de Boeuf à la Providence
Champagne
Pâté de fois Gras
Château Yquem
Timbale de Volaille Américaine au Sénateur
Clos Vougeot
Côtelettes d'Agneau sauté au pointes d'Asperges
Sorbet
Bécassines au Cresson
Château Margeaux
Salade à la Française
DESSERT

THE HOUSE OF LORDS IN 1891

In the Grand Court of The Palace the carriages of the town's Crockers, McAllisters, Tobins and de Youngs daily presented a parade of wealth and fashion of a fabulous era (*right*) and their occupants dismounted in thickets of rare shrubs and potted palms from the hotel's own greenhouses. The first elevators in the West (*below*) were also a source of civic gratification to San Francisco as they took millionaires and kings up and down from their multiwindowed apartments. In its last day of doom after the earthquake of 1906, when it was reduced to "the damnedest finest ruins, nothing more and nothing less," the hotel burned (*lower right*) at the same time with the Grand Hotel across New Montgomery Street with which it had been connected by a bridge at the third story. At the right of the photograph is the profile of a mounted man; the United States Cavalry from the Presideo, participants in so many stirring moments in the saga of the Old West, stood guard at the telling of one more last chapter.

# Even the Last Moments of The Palace Were Splendid

## SUNDAY AFTERNOON AT THE OLD PUEBLO

The Spanish traditions lingered around the sleepy precincts of the Old Pueblo, which was coming to be known as Los Angeles, far later than they did around San Francisco Bay. In the late seventies Frenzeny and Tavernier drew this picture for *Harper's: "Correr El Gallo,"* showing a long-established sport which required the winning contestants to break the head from the body of a buried chicken at full gallop.

### NEVER HAPPENED BEFORE

From earliest times it was considered bad taste around Los Angeles to admit the possibility of rainfall or take any precautions against it, such as drainage or runoff ditches. In 1886 a flash flood destroyed twenty-five houses in downtown Los Angeles and carried away the new depot of the Los Angeles & San Gabriel Railroad. Los Angelenos were vexed when the event received pictorial treatment (*left*) in *Leslie's* and assured all who would listen that the thing was without precedent and would never happen again.

# Sex and Citrus Were Southland Commodities Always

From the very beginning San Franciscans were glad to associate sex crimes with Los Angeles and took inordinate pleasure when the *Police Gazette* for November 5, 1887, ran this picture on its outside cover with the caption: "She Tried to Cremate Him: After Shooting Dr. E. C. Harlan for Betraying Her, Hattie Woolsteen Sets Fire to His Body in a Barn Near Los Angeles, California." For their part, Los Angelenos rejoiced when it seemed likely that there was a modest but possibly steady demand for oranges and lemons from their part of the world. Early in the nineties the Santa Fe Railroad was shipping several hundred carloads a year from its Los Angeles terminal (*below*) and it seemed there might be a future in the trade. Fast schedules to the East had to be maintained even then because refrigerated fruit cars in 110-car trains were still in the future. Oranges were becoming synonymous in the public imagination with the sunny southland and have remained so ever since.

The arrest at Fort Scott in 1858 of border ruffians by Captain Sam Walker, a Federal officer, provided a scene of violence typical of the conflicts and emotions of the time and place.

# VI

# *The Border States*

## The Wars between Pro-Slavery Elements and Free-Soilers in the Kansas Fifties Were a Curtain Raiser to the Civil War Itself

To THE INFORMED American intelligence, Kansas was the border state and remained that way longer than any other, but in their time and way so were Missouri, Arkansas and Oklahoma as the frontier moved westward, largely behind the ever-advancing iron of the railroads.

Kansas, however, dominated the general imagination. Here the cold war between free-soilers and the South first flamed into the hot war that was to become a great civil conflict. Here the border ruffians and night riders set a pattern of lawlessness and bloodshed that was not to come to an end until the elimination of the Doolin gang of outlaws at Ingalls, Oklahoma, in 1893. Here, in the roaring cattle towns along the Kansas Pacific and the Santa Fe, Texans who rode north with the vast herds of the seventies acted more Texan than they ever did at home beyond the Red River. For a time, indeed, Kansas was little more than a Texas province, so greatly was it dominated by the trail riders headed for Abilene, Newton and Dodge City. And, long after the trail herds had disappeared and the waddies had gone back for keeps to Corpus Christi or Lampasas, Kansas occupied

156

national headlines for its perpetual skirmishes with the Demon Rum which were to foreshadow the national farce and calamity of prohibition four decades later.

Largely Americans would prefer to forget the chapters of border history coming under the classic heading of "Bleeding Kansas." So bloody and brutal were the annals of both sides, so atrocious the lawless and cowardly acts of both free-soilers and slave state men, that the triumph of righteousness and the nobility of a lost cause are not altogether clearly defined or visible through the smoke of burning homes and cities. History has discovered that John Brown, once venerated in song and folklore as the source and fountainhead of freedom, was no better than a murderous psychopath. Kansas history in the fifties was made by border ruffians and night riders and the names that emerge after the passage of the years are those of guerrillas, raiders and ruffians without peer in the American lexicon. And long after the War of the States ended at Appomattox, organized war against society was maintained by the James boys, the Daltons, Youngers and their associates, imitators and survivors, all of them conducting their operations throughout the states of the by then vanishing border.

It is to the legend and folklore of the cattle days in Kansas that the amateur of Americana turns with unabated enthusiasm, but because of its social, economic and personal overtones of Texas, despite its regional geography in Kansas, this is a saga which will be considered in this pictorial survey in the space allotted to Texans and their beef critters.

Lamentably, while the pictorial record of many stirring events in the record of Kansas and Missouri is available, some of the most characteristic episodes in the history of Arkansas went unrecorded by brush or pen. Where can one turn for the likeness of Sam Houston on his Gargantuan drunk at Little Rock in the course of which, after having consigned his every stitch of clothing to a campfire, he danced stark naked through the astonished streets? What picture file is repository for a drawing of the fabled General Albert Pike whose fame as a lawyer was matched only by his skill at self-publicization, on his way to court behind a hired brass band? What artist was present when Davy Crockett, at the now historic shooting match at Little Rock, won by surreptitiously poking a bullet into the bull's-eye on top of the bullet previously lodged there by his adversary?

Alas, A. R. Waud has given us a drawing of the legendary Arkansas traveler, but little more.

When one turns to Missouri, however, the prospect is far more cheerful, for Missouri rejoiced in the art of one of the most graphic of all painters of American folkways, whose scenes of country politics are unsurpassed for vividness and humor. George Caleb Bingham's county elections, backwoods electors, stump speakers and solons in Alpaca and silk hats constitute a rich treasury of American ways in a time of personal politics and elections floated on a sea of stone fence. So do his boating paintings of the Mississippi and its regional types.

In their way the border states were fortunate in their emergence at just the time they did. Some of their scenes and places, all of them of a static nature to be sure, were available to wet plate photography, but they had their season in the sun in the very heyday and flowering of the professional sketch artist of the illustrated periodical.

For this all students of the Western legend may be grateful.

## KANSAS BLED IN FACT AS WELL AS ORATORY

The scene above shows Missouri "Border Ruffians" on their way to vote against the Abolitionists in Kansas under the leadership of Senator David Atchison. Below is the Massacre at Lawrence by Quantrill's Guerrillas, one of the most notorious outrages of the years in which Kansas bled so profusely.

# Night Riders, Jayhawkers Gave Kansas a Bad Name

### THE PASTOR WAS A DEAD SHOT

The struggle for Kansas which raged over the question of whether the state should be slave or free-soil in the years immediately before the Civil War produced a wave of lawlessness unparalleled at any time or place elsewhere in the West. At Lecompton, territorial capital of Kansas, proslavery night riders threatened to tar and feather the Rev. Wallace Henry, an ardent advocate of the free-soil cause. The clergyman put the hoodlums to rout with a buffalo gun.

## BORDER STATES

### DEATH AMONG THE SWANS

When proslavery night riders in the Kansas wars murdered five free-soilers in cold blood at a gulch named Marais des Cygnes because swans had formerly nested there, the massacre incited both sides to accusations of bloodthirstiness and brutality only rivaled by those produced by the sack of Lawrence.

## BOOZE FLOWED LIKE BLOOD
## PART OF THE TIME IN KANSAS

Not all the controversy that characterized "Bleedi[ng] Kansas" in the abolitionist years was conducted [on] a high-minded level. One of the agencies seeking [to] colonize Kansas with Northern free-soilers was t[he] Massachusetts Emigrant Aid Society which raise[d] $5,000,000 for the cause. Eventually one of [its] agents, Charles Robinson, was tried at a "Territor[ial] Indignation Meeting," shown above, as a "False Be[l]shazzar" who had stolen lumber for his sawmill. [A] good deal of land speculation masqueraded in Ka[n]sas as humanitarian endeavor. In the center pictu[re] is shown a second trial of Robinson, free-soil pr[e]tender to the governorship of Kansas, which w[as] held in McCarthy's Hotel, Leavenworth, Kansas Te[r]ritory, in 1857. Newspapers reported that the tr[ial] was conducted by Chief Justice Lecompte with [a] minimum of Blackstone and a maximum of bourb[on] whisky and the affair came to nothing when Robi[n]son's friends spirited him out of town one nig[ht] when his guards were in a local groggery. In t[he] bottom picture Colonel Edwin Sumner is sho[wn] dispersing the Kansas Free State Government [at] Topeka, Fourth of July, 1856. No bloodshed a[t]tended the event although a number of people com[plained that patriotic ceremonies were spoiled an[d] it was impossible to hear the band hired for t[he] occasion by reason of the bad language of the di[s]franchised delegates with free-soil leanings.

## POLITICS WERE PERENNIAL

Court painter of border state politics in the stormy years before the Civil War was George Caleb Bingham of Missouri. A one-time politician himself who finally became disgusted with partisanship, Bingham devoted his mature years to painting charming canvases depicting political activities of his country contemporaries. His "Canvassing for a Vote" (*above*) is a classic of four-corners preoccupation with issues of the day. Thirty years later, when F. W. Freer drew this illustration for *Harper's*, politics were still the obsession of back-country Kansas and Missouri, but participants were less likely to produce derringers in a crisis and slavery was a dead issue. The argument underway in this village post office somewhere near Topeka concerns "Should James G. Blaine be honored with the Presidency when his mere nomination has so shamefully lowered the moral tone of the Republican party?"

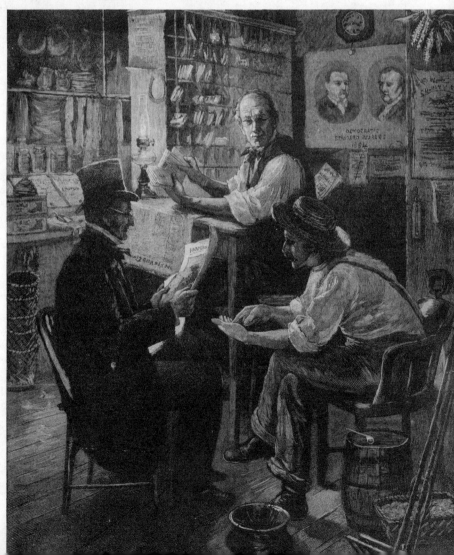

# The Arkansas Traveler Was Soon Part of the Language

Before the emergence of "On a Slow Train Through Arkansas" as part of the folk literature of the Southwest, the Arkansas Traveler was already an institution in the lexicon of the land. Somewhere in the canebrakes A. R. Waud sketched these rough-looking customers for *Harper's* and entitled the result "Arkansas Travelers." The camp scene below was drawn by the team of Frenzeny and Tavernier at about the same time and was called "Arkansas Pilgrims in Camp." They explained in the caption material that the women settlers whom they encountered in Arkansas border towns and camps made a good thing taking in washing while their men had hired themselves out to work on the railroads which by the middle seventies were becoming a national obsession, their lonely lines crisscrossing Arkansas no less than the other states and territories of the Union.

LIBRARY OF CONGRESS

## BORDER TOWN HAD TRIALS AND TRIBULATIONS

A heritage from the lawless days of night riders and border ruffians in Kansas and Missouri for years after the Civil War was a scourge of tramps and drifters who made themselves free of the countryside, invading undefended homes when the menfolk were away, and frightened women and children with their coarse ways and unseemly conduct. Usually their crimes were trespass and petty theft, not sufficient to stir up concerted action by the law on a widespread scale. Another menace of the period was fire, which raged through the shack towns and wooden-built cities of the borderland almost without organized forces for its prevention. Elsewhere fire companies and in large cities paid fire departments were almost universal, but in deepest Kansas or Arkansas the village pump and an informal bucket brigade, as shown below, was the best that could be hoped for for many years.

# Folklore Gathered Around Jesse James in His Lifetime

## THEY HAD A HANKER TO KILL

It is probable that intelligent estimate of their activities by later generations will never altogether remove the members of the Jesse James gang of hoodlums, murderers and highwaymen from the Robin Hood category assigned them by sentimental publicists in their own generation. There is no evidence outside the paper covers of nickel novels that they ever gave a thin dime to a widow, orphan or the deserving poor, although they themselves made widows and orphans by the score. They didn't even invent train robbery, which was practiced before them by the Renos in the Midwest and the Central Pacific bandits in Nevada. The above photograph, taken it is believed at Kansas City during one of their periodical sprees among the urban fleshpots, shows Cole and Bob Younger standing, Frank and Jesse James seated. Their armament of ten weapons between four men was typical of the times and their calling. At the right is Jesse as portrayed in his lifetime in the *Police Gazette*.

During the lifetime of Jesse James all train robberies west of the Mississippi and north of Texas were ascribed to his followers, while other and lesser bandits imitated his technique of stopping the cars, shooting the crews and blowing the Wells Fargo strong box. The holdup (*above*) of a Wabash train at Randolph, Missouri, and another near Moberly, never proven, still rated notches on the James boys' guns.

# The Saga of the Youngers, Too, Was One of Violence

Train robbery, as invented by the Reno brothers in Indiana in 1866, was not, at the time, a conspicuous success. The people of Indiana liked their railroads and were impatient with the law. As a result, nine members of the Reno gang were lynched (*left*) within a few weeks by Vigilantes operating under the motto: *Salus Populi Suprema Lex*, "Public Safety Is Higher Than The Law." The moral was, however, lost on the James boys.

## LIKE ROYALTY, OUTLAWS LIVED IN FEAR FOR THEIR LIVES

Like the royal houses of Europe, the bandits of nineteenth century America were united by ties of marriage. Many accounts of the career of Belle Starr, Missouri outlaw queen in her own right and at one time wife of Cole Younger of the James gang, attribute the beginnings of her lawless career to the death of her brother, Ed Shirley, a noted bushwhacker of Civil War times. Operating out of Carthage, Missouri, with a group of Jasper County border riders, Ed was assassinated (*below*) while eating dinner at an outlaw hideout near Sarcoxie. Romantic historians date Belle's dedication to a life of crime from this episode.

TWO PICTURES: AUTHORS' COLLECTION

## LEGEND IN THE MAKING

Reports of the death of Jesse James were weekly occurrences during his lifetime, representing a nationwide wish-fulfillment on the part of decent people. Only the week before he was in actual fact killed by Bob Ford at St. Joseph, the pages of the *Police Gazette* carried the eye-witness account of the extermination of the James gang "at Moberly, Mo." (*left*), accompanied by this stirring scene of their last moments. After James's death sentimentalists promptly arranged for him to have been hanging a "God Bless Our Home" motto on the wall when he was cut down by an assassin's bullet. Actually Bob Ford seized an opportunity when the outlaw wasn't looking and killed him under circumstances of convenience. It took time to evolve the legend that the ranking thug of the Old West had come to the end of the trail in circumstances of almost sanctified respectability. The more probable circumstance of the outlaw's assassination is depicted (*left, below*) beside the idealized version still cherished by the soft headed to this day. (*right, below*)

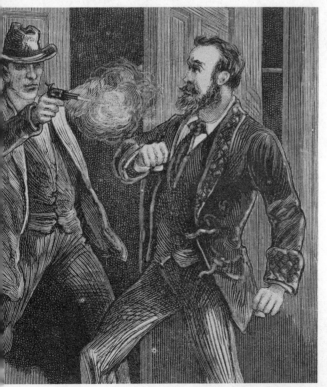

## DEATH OF AN OUTLAW

No funeral of a Chicago gangster in
prohibition times evoked more mawk-
ish sentimentality that the killing of
Jesse James by Bob Ford (*above*).
While the body of the outlaw (*below*)
remained on public view in a St.
Joseph undertaking parlor, his mother,
shown in a dramatic drawing in the
*Police Gazette* (*upper right*), waved
the stump of her arm blown off by "the
cowardly Pinkertons" and swore the
neighbors to a solemn oath against her
son's slayers. "Johnny, my boy," Mrs.
Samuels exhorted James's half-brother,
"look upon your sainted brother Jesse,
your murdered brother Jesse! Look
upon him and then upon your poor
brokenhearted mother! Oh, my heart is
broken; they have killed my sainted
son. He is in Heaven. He has gone to
Heaven. God will punish all who had
a hand in murdering him for money."
The next day (*right*), as the coffin containing James was being carried to
nearby Kearney, it was forced to ford a
stream so swollen that the remains
nearly floated away. A staff artist for
*Harper's* was on hand to record the
scene for posterity.

## END OF THE GLORY ROAD

Immediately upon the spreading of the news that the dead man whom Bob Ford had shot at the cottage above the tracks of the Hannibal & St. Joseph Railroad was the notorious Jesse James, townsfolk descended in swarms upon the premises, as shown in the above drawing which appeared a fortnight later in *Leslie's*. Shortly after the shooting of the West's most notorious killer, his goods and personal possessions were auctioned off to a morbid crowd of curiosity seekers who bid in his furniture, clothes and even his small pet dog, although the prices realized were not flattering. Years later *The Illustrated Police News* discovered Frank James, who had always had a weakness "for spoutin' Shakespeare" to his companions, now reformed and making a legitimate living (*bottom*) as a shoe salesman in St. Louis. It was a letdown from border banditry, but safer.

## KANSAS REVERTED TO BARBARISM EARLY IN THE GAME

Temperance movements first appeared in Kansas in the seventies, having their origins in, of all places, the wild towns of Abilene, Hays and Dodge City. The sodbusters who took over where their betters, the buffalo hunters and cattle trail riders, left off took a dim view of saloon life, hurdy-gurdy houses, shooting and uproar generally. They had all they wanted to drink on the farm and couldn't stand the idea of folk drinking under more urbane and civilized conditions. By 1880 bands of good women enlisted to do holy battle with the Demon were praying and sniffling around the doors of saloons in Topeka and Lawrence, interfering with business and annoying the thirsty. They took down names of patrons (*above left*) and marched through the streets (*above right*) singing about salvation through sobriety. They got themselves thrown out of numberless saloons (*below*), but on March 10, 1881, Kansas officially went dry among the hosannas of the women's clubs and the next day the state's first speakeasy opened for business in downtown Manhattan. Masculine mockers were once more assured of a refuge from respectability.

Although born in Kentucky, it was in Kansas that the name of Carrie Nation, archfoe of the Demon and the liveliest prohibitionist of them all, first achieved fame. Carrie's first husband, a rumpot of heroic proportions, died in delirium tremens, inspiring his widow, who soon remarried, to dedicate her life to warfare on strong drink. A motherly old party, she first ran amuck in Wichita, Kansas, in 1901, where she smashed up two saloons, doing such notable damage among the glassware and barroom nudes that she overnight became a national character. From Wichita she progressed to Topeka, Enterprise and other strongholds of sin, doing the Lord's work with a hatchet, defacing works of art behind the back bar and filling the wicked with terror.

# Carrie Nation
# Dearly Loved
# The Sound of
# Smashing Glass

Erratic, fanatic, anointed of the Lord and as busy as a biscuit, Carrie was the best news copy of her day and symbolized the forces of arid morality. Often jailed, she was seldom manhandled, and when she died in 1911, her obituaries recalled that "she had brought some praise and considerable scorn upon Kansas."

# Kansas, As Ever, Voted Dry and Drank Very Wet

## TWO BOTTLES OF OLD CROW WEREN'T GOING TO BE ENOUGH

As the fatal date of Kansas prohibition approached, provident citizens took thought for the future and began laying in supplies, some decorously, as above, and some in a spirit of abandon, as is suggested below. The well-to-do were able to make provision for weeks or even months, but the lower classes, who of course required whisky in the greatest quantity, soon found that a gallon or so wasn't going to be enough, and speakeasies began flourishing, green bay treelike, on every hand. The Kansas brand of temperance was to be a farce of cosmic dimensions for two full generations.

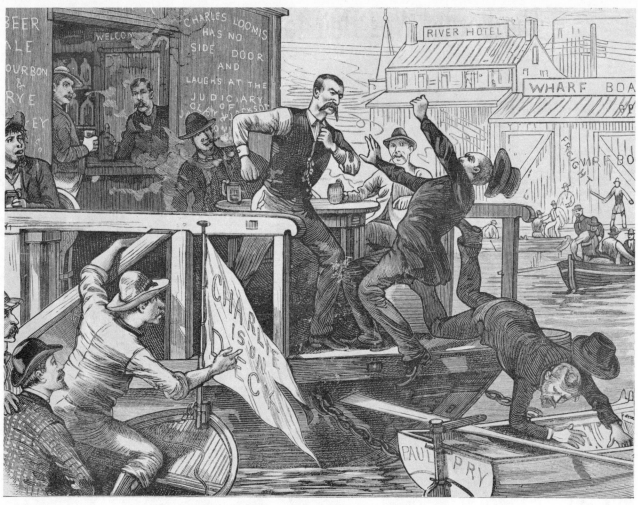

KANSAS DIDN'T SUBMIT TO OPPRESSION FOR LONG

In the best American tradition, Kansas, once prohibition had been made law, immediately seethed with rebellion against the oppressor. As on a later nationwide scale, speakeasies flowered on every hand and riotous intoxication and patriotism became synonymous overnight. At Kansas City, where its Missouri counterpart was handily adjacent and no such folly obtained, floating saloons such as this one moored themselves to the banks of the Kansas River and invited the thirsty aboard. Law officers from indignant Kansas sheriffs' offices were hilariously tossed in the river while thousands cheered. It all presaged an even greater revolt which convulsed the entire nation in 1919.

In the upper reaches of the river not available to navigation by deeper craft, bumboats and skiffs conveyed liquid refreshments to Kaw braves and honest cowhands with democratic impartiality. The wicked were as a troubled sea and rejoiced tumultuously. Sodbusters and temperance folk pretended it all didn't happen.

# The Border Was Heir to a Tradition of Gunfire

A POINT OF DISORDER IN THE LEGISLATURE

The tradition of lawlessness and bloodshed that had come into being in abolitionist times in Kansas was continued in its fullest vigor after the conclusion of the Civil War. Shown above is an episode in which Boston Corbett, the man who killed John Wilkes Booth after his assassination of President Lincoln, himself ran amuck while a special officer for the Kansas House of Representatives at Topeka. Corbett kept the lawmakers at bay at a pistol's point for several hours after looking overlong on the wine when it was red and was finally disarmed by an offer to buy him a drink.

Hand guns were also resorted to in County Court at Woodward, Oklahoma, when a lawyer, Ed Jennings, passed the lie to Senator Temple Houston, son of old Sam Houston of Lone Star fame, and the senator promptly ventilated him in the presence of judge and jury. So brilliant was Houston's reputation as a criminal lawyer and also as a gunman who had outshot Billy the Kid in a friendly match that it was felt no good would come of following the matter up and Jennings was buried next day and no more said.

"Running Things Their Own Way in a Cherokee Nation Store" was the caption on this illustration in the *Police News*, sub-headed, "The Trainor Gang of Outlaws Run Mr. Ruckworth's Ranche To Suit Themselves For Three Days." The word "ranche" is used here in its original sense as business premises, not as an establishment for the raising of livestock.

THE DEAD MAN HAD BEEN ARMED

When Captain Nat McKinney, chief of a band of notorious bank robbers, was slain in an attempted holdup of a hardware store in Forsythe, Missouri, so strong was the code of border chivalry even in the killing of an outlaw that his slayer Billy Miles called on bystanders to witness that the dead man had been armed before he claimed a reward.

## KANSANS HEADED FOR THE CELLARS AS CYCLONES APPROACHED

A classic manifestation of nature throughout the length and breadth of Kansas has always been the cyclone. Unlike fire, it could not be stayed by the hand of man and in country regions cyclone cellars were and are the only answer to an approaching twister. In the above illustration from *Leslie's* is shown a massive cyclone which left death and destruction in its wake as it tore through Rice County one evening in 1882, while below is the scene of devastation as a similar storm dismayed the natives of Emporia the same year.

## FIRE WAS OFTEN
## FOUGHT WITH FIRE

Although Oklahoma's Osage Indians were
not to take to silk hats and Lincoln motor-
cars for some years to come as a result of
oil discovered on their lands, oil seepage in
Oklahoma was a commonplace as far back
as the eighties. On one occasion a passenger
train of the Missouri-Kansas-Texas Railroad, a line already beset by bad men and
legal problems, was forced to run blindly
through a sea of blazing petroleum incidental to a forest fire near Broken Arrow.
Prairie fires, as shown below, were a hazard
of ranching and life on the plains everywhere. When possible, the inhabitants
fought them with backfire; when not, they
fled for their lives.

M.K.T. RAILROAD

# Fun and Games Were Robust in the Old Southwest

## ALL IN FUN

*Harper's Weekly* for July 25, 1874, ran this illustration called "A Saturday Afternoon in a Southwest Town," by Frenzeny & Tavernier. Many commentators believe the scene to have been Denison, Texas, toward which at that time the rails of the building Missouri-Kansas-Texas Railroad were headed.

## FUN WITH EGGS

Less ingenuous, although in other variations the sport was to continue down almost until the present, was the game of "Hit the Nigger" with an assortment of missiles ranging from coconuts to baseballs, and in this case ripe eggs. The African cranium was popularly supposed to be impervious to damage from assault and such a human target gallery was indispensable at county fairs and roving carnivals everywhere.

## SUMMER IDYLL

Water for the ever-lengthening rail lines of
the border states often had to be pumped.
Here in a drawing by Frenzeny & Tavernier a youth in west Kansas takes it easy
while a faithful mule does the work turning
a geared pump.

## WHEAT-FIELD OBITUARY

For many years after the extermination of
the buffalo a major industry on the once
populous plains of Kansas was the recovery
of animal skeletons to be reduced for fertilizer. Bone-picking outfits throughout
1874 and 1875 loaded between ten and
twenty tons of buffalo bones a day on the
cars of the Santa Fe Railroad alone, and
other roads transported commensurate tonnage. "In sorting bones for the market,
strange discoveries are sometimes made,"
wrote the Topeka correspondent for the
*New York Daily Tribune* in November
1874. "It is no uncommon thing, for instance, to find Indian skulls, legs and arms;
and in some cases the skulls and vertebrae
of women and children have been picked
up. The latter are usually tossed aside as
a sort of rude reverence for the helpless
and innocent; but no such respect is paid
to the bones of an Indian. The Indian skull

is said to be worth $1.25 for combs, and
the Indian thigh makes knife handles that
are beautiful to behold." This wheat farmer
on the Kansas plain obviously sees $1.25 in
combs in the discovery of his Ames plow-
share.

## FAR FROM SARATOGA OR LEXINGTON DOWNS

When the New York Academy of Design held a water color exhibit in 1876, J. D. Smillie's "A Scrub Race on the Plains" attracted widespread attention for its portrayal of a Sunday afternoon horse race in Kansas. Horse racing elsewhere in the United States involved only thoroughbred entries bred for speed and endurance over a stated course and the idea of wild mustangs and humble saddle ponies in competition engaged the fancy of the artist, as shown above.

Fishing through the ice for pickerel and ice fish, usually associated through the agency of Currier & Ives with New England and the Middle West, actually was a sport of national dimensions where climate was propitious. This scene, sketched by Charles Osborne, is believed to have been made near St. Louis and it appeared in *Harper's* in 1874.

# Sports and Hunting Were a Border State Heritage

CULVER SERVICE

Hunting wild boar, a pastime which had enjoyed a royal vogue in France and England for centuries, provided Arkansas huntsmen and their hounds with exciting and dangerous sport in densely wooded regions in the southern part of the state. Coursing jackrabbits formally was first inaugurated in the United States by the American Coursing Club at Great Bend, Kansas, in the eighties.

## SOONERS, SMALLPOX AND CLAIM JUMPERS

In 1888 the entire western half of the Creek Nation, embracing much of present-day Oklahoma, was sold by Chief Pleasant Porter to the United States government and next year these incredibly fertile acres were declared public land and available to homesteading. One of the greatest land rushes in history ensued. Various aspects of it are here depicted, counterclockwise: a smallpox scare in the streets of the new town of Guthrie; water vendors in Guthrie; the U.S. Army issuing instructions to immigrants on how to live in a new country; drilling in camp to insure military order and law enforcement; the arrival in camp of the Indian scout "Pawnee Bill" and his welcome by the tribes; and, below: "The Last Invasion—Sunday Services in Camp." New aspects of Western frontier life were the "Sooners" who came early and attempted to cross the line and stake claims before the bugle and left their impress on the regional vocabulary. There were also claim jumpers, land sharps, blacklegs, confidence men, all the accustomed retinue of new places, but it was almost their last stand.

# The Cherokee Strip Marked The End Of The Public Lands

## NOW THERE WAS NO BORDER ANY MORE

In 1893 when W. A. Rogers drew the picture above for *Harper's* showing the rush of settlers for homestead claims in Oklahoma's Cherokee Strip, the public lands of the United States open to homesteading were almost gone. A decade earlier when Frenzeny and Tavernier had sketched their famous "A Kansas Land Office" (*right*) for the same magazine, the handwriting had been on the wall. Now the last of the Indian lands had been expropriated and the border states were no longer on the border of anything, but part of the integrated economy of an ever-increasingly industrial nation. By the turn of the century, the homesteader, the "nester" of the contemptuous cattle barons only a few years before, was as obsolete as the night rider and jayhawker who had gone before him.

To the pioneers and to later day railroaders as well, the Rockies presented a terrifying façade of bottomless abysses and dizzying heights, as is suggested by Theodore Davis's drawing, made in 1868, of "The Overland Mail Coach Crossing the Rocky Mountains."

# VII

## *The Shining Mountains*

### The Colorado Rocky Mountains Have Meant Many Things to Many Men. Health, Hunting, Pelfrey, Treasure and Industrial Empire Were a Few

THE SHINING MOUNTAINS, the first white travelers called them as they came into view at sunrise over the Great Plains and as they can still be seen from afar off by breakfasters off Colorado trout in the diners of the Westbound overnight trains from Chicago.

Perhaps it was a better name than the one they came later to assume. It attracted three generations of men with hair on them who might never have been drawn, as by a fantastic lodestone, to the mere Rockies. The Shining Mountains were implicit with wonderment and adventure in a time when these things laid hold on the hearts of men and fired them to achievements hitherto denied to all but the gods of pagan mythology. In the tally of the place names of the Old West the Shining Mountains must take their place beside Wind River and the Sweetwater, South Pass and the Staked Plains and Pogo Agie. They were named by poets.

The first white men to see the Shining Mountains were Spaniards, probably a group of explorers under Father Escalante who penetrated as far north as Durango and Silverton in 1776 and named the dolorous canyon connecting these remote spots for the Rio de las Animas Perdidas, the Canyon of Lost Souls. The Spaniards saw nothing good in the prospect of Colorado; their fancy ran to mountains of solid silver and cities fashioned from blocks of 22 carat gold, all free to steal for the asking, or at least after a little murder of the Indians in the name of the Inquisition.

But with the French from Canada, who came to the Rockies before even Zebulon Pike in 1806, it was different. The French were *voyageurs*, trappers, and here they found an abundance of fur-bearing game past all imagining, enough beaver for all the tall hats which English gentlemen were even then beginning to wear as the hallmark of Western civilization. It was, in reality, the beaver top hat that brought the first enduring settlers to the Rockies. Enduring in the sense that they returned season after season until the middle thirties when the silk top hat was invented and the Colorado beaver was all but extinct anyway.

The trappers established the Rocky Mountains and incidentally Colorado. They set up a metropolis of sophistication in Taos, which they called Touse, and their forts and trading posts such as those of the Bent Brothers and Cerain St. Vrain on the Arkansas or Fort Laramie in eastern Wyoming were like small jewels of safety strung on a necklace of thinly worn overland trails. Bent's Fort was a bewilderment of luxury set down within wolf-call of the howling wilderness. There was ice in an ice house for chilling champagne, a billiard table, couriers to bring mint from the mountains for juleps and a vast kitchen in charge of a lady of color named Charlotte, who introduced pumpkin pies to the Cheyenne Indians. Riflemen manned the loopholes of the stockade night and day and at Laramie there were two bronze cannon at the postern gate. When the fur trade ran into one of its periodical declines the Bents signed on big-time names, Kit Carson and Lucien Maxwell, as professional meat hunters.

A consequence of the fur trade was, of course, the introduction of rivers of whisky into the Rocky Mountain regions and the final inheritors of Colorado, the searchers after precious metals in the fifties and sixties, discovered the noble red man so far gone in booze that his virtual extermination was no trick at all. The American Fur Company, the Hudson's Bay Company, the Rocky Mountain Fur Company and the independents strove mightily amongst themselves to see how much St. Louis whisky diluted beyond recognition to the white man's palate they could unload in the fur trade on the Indians who gratefully drank themselves to death forthwith. When the Federal government, in one of its infrequent bursts of activity in the West of the time, began searching the steamers going up the Missouri for contraband liquor for the Indians, the American Fur Company set up a distillery of its own at Fort Union and imported corn and other grains by the boatload and with the blessings of the inspectors, who were told, quite truly too, that the Indians were to be its ultimate consumers.

The discovery of gold in California with its consequent tidal flow of Forty-niners across the Great Plains resulted in the first intimations that there might be gold in the Shining Mountains. Immigrants who first encountered the Rockies at the base of Pike's Peak and followed the escarpment of the mountains northward toward Fort Laramie panned the streams as they went. The colors in their pans were poor, but such encouragement as they did receive was at the junction of the South Platte with a small creek abounding in choke cherries, the Cherry Creek and, finally, Denver City of a few years later.

"These mountains are supposed to contain minerals, precious stones, and gold and silver ore," read a contemporary account of the region. "It is but of late they have taken the name of Rocky Mountains; by all old travelers they are called the Shining Mountains from the infinite number of crystal stones with which they are covered and which, when the sun shines on them, sparkle so as to be seen at a great distance. These same early travelers gave it as their opinion that in the future these mountains would be found to contain more riches than those of Indostan and Malabar, or the Gold Coast of Guinea, or Peru."

The future Denver City came into being largely as a real estate speculation of General William H. Larimer of Leavenworth. On the eve of the first Christmas at Cherry Creek there arrived in town a wagonload of merchandise driven by Richens Lacy Wootton, known to subsequent history as Uncle Dick. Most of the merchandise was in barrels, which turned out to contain a truly gratifying quantity of Taos Lightning, a regional spirits distilled according to an ancient Mexican formula which laid the recipients of Uncle Dick's hospitality in windrows.

Suddenly, mysteriously, all of the United States began to whisper rumors of gold in the Pike's Peak region. Nobody seemed able to trace the vague reports although subsequent investigation was to disclose that most of them originated in the border towns of Kansas and jumping-off places for the West where the California trade had begun to ebb. St. Louis wagon dealers displayed three-ounce gold nuggets allegedly taken from Cherry Creek right in the heart of Larimer's real estate. Newspapers in Kansas City shamelessly told of fortunes recovered from nearby Clear Creek by the veriest amateurs in the business of prospecting. Pike's Peak, to hear tell, was itself partly if not wholly composed of free gold and probably was the ancient site of the cities of Cibola sought by the Spaniards.

Blacksmiths in New Haven let the fire die on their smithies. Iowa farmers failed to plant their corn. Railroad brakemen in Georgia hit for Missouri without turning in their switch keys. "Now there is *shenanigan* going on," a Denver City resident protested. "This thing is being done by speculators here and on the Border and should be denied by all the papers." His was a voice trailing down the wind and all America echoed to a new slogan destined to join the great repository of such matters along with "Remember the *Maine*" and "Fifty-four forty or fight." It was "Pike's Peak or bust."

The first of the great Pike's Peak rushes ended like its slogan: bust. Thousands of prospectors milled about the base of the mountains, a few following the streams to their sources, none of them instructed in the sort of mining required by the region and few equipped for the brutal winters that swept in over the crest of the mountains from the wastes of Utah and Wyoming.

And then, wonderfully enough, came Golconda.

Up Clear Creek, approximately fifty miles west of Denver, a prospector named John H. Gregory staked a claim that began to yield more than mere colors. Then substantial returns, better than $4.00 a shovel, were uncovered. Like San Francisco in forty-nine, Denver became deserted overnight. Merchants hastened up Clear Creek with their stock in wagons. Gamblers, saloonkeepers, lawyers, all the professional riffraff of the frontier set up for business in the communities that soon lined the slender flow of by now discolored water: Black Hawk, Gregory Point, Central City, Nevadaville. This was the real thing, the true fissure, known farther to the West in the language of the Comstock as bonanza.

To put a final panache on good fortune there arrived shortly thereafter Uncle Horace Greeley with two other reporters of national fame, Henry Villard of the *Cincinnati Commercial Enquirer*, and A. D. Richardson of the *Boston Journal*. The three signed their famous report authenticating the news of gold in Colorado which was printed next day in a special edition of the newly established *Rocky Mountain News* and, later, in the *Tribune* in New York and other reputable papers throughout the United States. Colorado had found gold at last and, what's more, had proved it.

Prudently Greeley added that while gold was indisputable there were already more people on hand than the country could provide for and that the wealth itself might not be endless. Nobody paid him any mind. Colorado became the mecca of countless thousands who overflowed into the Rockies to discover other bonanzas undreamed of by the proprietors of the riches in Gregory Gulch: Leadville, Creede, Telluride, Silverton, Ouray and Red Mountain. In the crowd were names that were to make news for generations to come: Uncle Dick Wootton, Horace Tabor, William N. Byers, Senators-to-be Edward Wolcott and Henry Teller, Soapy Smith, Charlie Boettcher, George Mortimer Pullman, Eugene Field, Roman Nose and William McGaa. Colorado, with a golden gleam in its eye, was headed for a rendezvous with destiny.

## O PIONEERS!

After the first few disappointed Pike's Peakers of the fifties had turned back from Colorado (*above*) because the rivers didn't run with gold, the surge to Colorado became intensified, so that 1859 and 1860 saw a full tide of cheerful men and stout wagons such as those drawn by Frenzeny and Tavernier at the left pressing into the high passes of the Rockies. Still others were crossing the Great Plains from Kansas and Nebraska afoot (*below*), carrying all they possessed on their backs in the firm belief that in a little time they would be rich beyond all necessity for hardship, labor or suffering.

## A DANIEL COME TO JUDGMENT AMONG THE POTS

Often enough the first justice administered in Colorado mining camps followed the pattern of Cherry Creek where vigilante law took over until formal courts could be organized. Elsewhere, however, court might convene in a frontier saloon, as shown here in Alfred Mitchell's "A Trial Scene in a Colorado Mining Town," with all the stock characters of the diggings, the miner, merchant, teamster and Chinese laundryman participating, while the saloonkeeper, always a first citizen, presides as magistrate.

## FIRST GIRL IN TOWN

The first woman in any mining camp, no matter what her status— and she might be madame, prostitute or respectable housewife—was invariably welcomed with glad civic acclaim. All firsts in the Old West, the first piano, the first baby, the first arrival of the steamcars, were an occasion and celebrated with suitable rites, almost invariably including gunfire and the consumption of bottled goods.

Colorado's first newspaper, *The Rocky Mountain News*, came to Denver from Omaha by ox team goaded on its way by William N. Byers as part of the Pike's Peak rush of 1859. Byers was already a public person, having surveyed much of Nebraska for the Federal government and laid out the city of Omaha. The *News* was first established in the loft of Uncle Dick Wootton's store in Auraria on the south side of Cherry Creek. As in all newspapers of the frontier, compositors and editors worked with firearms handy against Indians, the opposition or border ruffians who resented the coming of law and order as represented by the press. The *News* beat its competition, the *Cherry Creek Pioneer*, to the street with Vol. I, No. 1 by a matter of minutes and promptly absorbed its good-natured rival. Very shortly the Byers paper was to achieve celebrity in the best tradition of gunfighting editors and frontier journalism. Below is shown the Washington "acorn model" press on which it first was printed and next it the "News Block" in Larimer Street to which it shortly moved with the Overland Daily Mail and United States Express Company as cotenants.

# THE STORY OF THE ROCKY MOUNTAIN NEWS

*The Rocky Mountain News* began a campaign to abate lawlessness in the Cherry Creek Diggings, which soon resulted in vigilante law taking care of some of the community's hard cases, as is shown at the right. A group of thugs under the leadership of George Steele shortly thereafter kidnaped editor Byers with the avowed intention of "stopping his attacks by stopping his breath," an eventuality which Byers escaped when one of the ruffians proved to be an old friend. The outlaws then charged The *News* building in mounted formation, as shown below, while editors and printers reached for handguns and rifles and returned their fire from the windows. In the ensuing melee Steele was shot and killed by a law-and-order partisan named Noisy Tom Pollock and the leaders of the night riders landed in jail. The affair ended with the Vigilantes in full control.

CLIMBING LA VETA PASS

ANTONITA.

CLOSE QUARTERS

PETERSON'S D

TOLTEC GORGE

OACHING FROM CHAMA

CHAMA. NEW ME

A MOUNTAINEER.

PAGOSA SPRINGS

LEHMAN'S.

TRES PIEDRAS

DURANGO

PASS IT AROUND

THE LOOK OF THE DESOLATE SAN JUAN

## DURANGO IN THE EIGHTIES WAS WILD AND FREE-WHEELING

In the southwestern corner of Colorado in the triangle formed by the New Mexican and Utahan boundaries, the San Juan basin first attracted settlers for its cattle grazing and the prospects of silver. In 1881 the narrow gage rails of the Denver & Rio Grande came into its most populous city, Durango, by way of Alamosa and the Toltec Gorge, as shown in the montage on the page opposite. Later the rails radiated from Durango to Silverton on the north and Farmington, New Mexico, on the south while Otto Mears's sensational Rio Grande Southern to the west made Durango the narrow gage capital of the railroad world. Although vigilante law made hanging at Durango's "Hanging Tree" a common occurrence during the eighties, the only legal hanging there, shown above, created a vast sensation when Bill Woods rudely murdered another customer in Charlie Dustin's Saloon and was executed with all formality against a background of the Rio Grande freight depot. Below, Durango's first baby, always an event in a frontier community comparable with the arrival of the first piano, attracts gifts from the sentimental miners, including a handy-size derringer for future use.

## SPACIOUS TIMES IN GREGORY'S GORGEOUS DIGGINGS

Fifty miles west of Denver in an improbable mountain fastness of the Rockies, a new diggings at Gregory's Gulch came in with a whoop and a holler in 1859. Nearly $200,000,000 in gold was eventually to be taken out of "the richest square mile on earth" and Central City soon acquired for itself a multiplicity of gorgeous saloons, a splendid luxury hotel, an opera, railroad, red light district and all the properties and attributes of a bonanza camp. Wiped out by the inevitable "Great Fire" in 1875, it arose in even greater splendor, much of which remains to this day. In the drawing below by Edward Jump of a Central gambling hall frequented by miners in the early days of the town, the wheel of fortune spins in the background, a faro dealer keeps cases at the left and a keno man tips the keno goose at the right, all to the cheerful music of an orchestra consisting of flute, fiddle and harp. Central, from earliest times, had its fun in style.

## GOLDEN NIGHTS IN EUREKA STREET

In the golden noontide of Central City's fortunes, the Colorado nabobs such as Haw Tabor, shown being helped into his coat, John Evans and Dave Moffatt, who built the tunnel, played for high stakes in the upstairs parlors of the Teller House where the original furnishings today make it a museum of frontier memories. Evening dress, liveried servants and limitless champagne were taken for granted and Central achieved a reputation for fast ways comparable to Denver City itself. Central folk in search of culture attended "Faust" and "Carmen" at the incomparable Central Opera in Eureka Street (*left*), and still do, while the narrow gage trains of the Colorado & Southern (*below*) snaked the ore out to the smelters.

## COW HANDS IN COLORADO

Of the illustration by Rufus Zogbaum on the page opposite, "Painting the Town Red," Dr. Robert Taft, the ranking authority on the art and illustrations of the Old West, is of the opinion it is the first important picture showing the American cowboy at play. If such is indeed the case, it set the pattern for a tremendous volume of cowboy art yet to come and perhaps a pattern for cowboys themselves in relaxed moments, for the men of the Old West very soon learned what was expected of them by Eastern editors and readers and were ever ready to oblige. Zogbaum's picture appeared in *Harper's* in 1885. At the top of this page, cowboys having innocent fun with the townies were depicted in the *Police News* under the caption, "Lift Those Mudhooks"; this purported to show a group of Colorado waddies on a bender in a frontier shop. Still another un-named artist for *Harper's* drew the two sketches of Colorado plains life shown at the right and entitled respectively, "Returning from a Miner's Meeting" and "I've Been Looking for You." Firearms, whisky and tumult occasionally complicated by assassination were properties which the rest of the world came to associate with cow hands through the agency of the public prints.

## THE HOGGER HAS
## WHISTLED FOR BRAKES

From Durango to Silverton the
narrow gage rails of the Rio
Grande followed the precipitous ravine of Animas Canyon—
the River of Lost Souls—deep
into the San Juan Mountains.
The spectacular wood engraving on the page opposite occupied two full pages in *Harper's*
and was made from a wet plate
photograph posed for William
Henry Jackson, dean of photographers of the Colorado frontier. The drawing at the right
by O. V. Schubert gives some
idea of a brakeman's life on the
car tops before the coming of
air brakes as the wooden freight
cars rolled perilously through
the night in the high passes to
Leadville, to South Park, to
Cripple Creek.

# ONCE THE NARROW GAGE RAN EVERYWHERE

aving lost its battle with
e Santa Fe for the Raton
d the Southwest, the Rio
ande turned westward
ward Silverton, Ouray,
eede and Durango. The
e over Veta Pass, shown
re, was one of the most
cturesque in Colorado.

FRENZENY & TAVERNIER

## VARIOUS WERE THE GOALS OF THE PILGRIMS OF THE PLAINS

Not all the pilgrims of the plains dreamed dreams of bonanza and saw visions of boundless wealth. A large majority of them, to be sure, were headed for Cherry Creek or the Gregory Diggings at Central City, but a substantial number set their courses for the rich agricultural regions, such as Greeley (*above*) on the margin of the Great Plains where irrigation (*page opposite*) was making the dream of the *New York Tribune's* matchless Uncle Horace come true of a West living by the soil and not the mine, by grain rather than the reducing mill. Many Colorado ranchers lived high on the hog, as is suggested below by Mary Hallock Foote's "Going to the Dance," and evolved a frontier society with amenities of politeness. "The only woman who can claim company among men in the field of Western picture" is Dr. Robert Taft's estimate of Mrs. Foote, who was for many years a resident of Leadville and lived to be over ninety at Grass Valley, California.

# BY ELEPHANT TRAIN TO SNOWY LEADVILLE

Often the diminutive trains of the railroads of the wood-burning era which laid their light iron above timberline—the Rio Grande, the South Park, the Colorado & Southern and the Colorado Midland— found themselves snowbound when tempests raged in the high passes and passengers had to be rescued from the drifts in sleighs. A legend of the folklore of the Columbine State is that of the circus train which, due to an unexpectedly fearful blizzard, lost its head of steam on the way to Leadville. True to the best tradition that the show must go on, their attending mahouts got the elephants out of their cars and the circus arrived in time for performance by elephant power.

## THE ROCKIES DREW ARTISTS AND PHOTOGRAPHERS ALIKE

By 1891 when Charles Graham drew "Over the Rockies in an Observation Car" for *Harper's*, Colorado's scenic wonderments were an economic asset undiminished to this day. Further to publicize the state's attractions the Rio Grande Railroad provided the great photographer William Henry Jackson with a private train (*below*) from which to secure shots of mountain scenery otherwise unobtainable.

## DIAMOND DUST MIRRORS

In a few years Denver's unpaved streets, such as Fifteenth from below Blake Street, with their spans of oxen and blasphemous bullwhackers, were to be replaced by such gorgeous hostelries as the world-famed Windsor Hotel (*below*), which English capital built in the rococo style so much admired in the opulent eighties. At the left is what the management, English to a scruple, chose to designate "The Ladies' Ordinary."

Here amidst diamond dust crystal mirrors and lobbies "where a vital company had partaken of Life in roistering years of gold and silver," in the words of Gene Fowler, the great of a generation passed: Grant, Buffalo Bill Cody, Lawrence Barrett, Lotta Crabtree, Richard Mansfield and Haw Tabor. A mixologist in the Windsor men's bar named Harry Heye Tammen was destined to write Colorado history in .45-caliber letters when he and Fred Bonfils acquired the *Denver Post*.

## THE TABOR GRAND
## WAS DENVER'S GLORY

The magnificence that obsessed the age of sudden riches found its fullest expression in the Tabor Grand Opera House at Denver, shown in this rare photograph from the Western Collection of the Denver Public Library, as it neared completion. Neither Tabor nor his associates from the Leadville diggings were fond of "Faust" or "Carmen" but they admired to wear evening dress complemented by large diamond studs and washed their favorite whisky down with vintage champagne to show they knew about Life. When the Tabor Grand opened with deafening civic fanfare the ceremonies included recitation from the stage of an original poem so bad that Eugene Field, sitting in Box F, had to be restrained by friends from hurling a heavy mahogany chair at its composer behind the footlights. *The Rocky Mountain News* did not, however, share Field's opinion of the doings, and simply headed its account of the opening of the Moorish gem with the single word: "Perfection."

TWO PICTURES: WESTERN COLLECTION

Less socially exalted circles than those frequented by Tabor, although he was at home in them too, had their rendezvous in a generous multiplicity of Denver saloons, plainer than the Windsor, but where the liquor was just as satisfying and the bartenders equally mustached.

# The Primrose Path of Dalliance Was Market Street

Throughout the seventies and eighties no metropolis in the West was wider open as a gambler's paradise than Cherry Creek Diggings, which had recently assumed the more elegant name of Denver City. Its dealers, monte throwers and proprietors of its brace games as well were largely recruited from the Mississippi River steamers where play was beginning to run thin, from Natchez-under-the-Hill and Vicksburg Landing. In Denver City they congregated in Larimer Street, drank deep with Colorado's silver senators in the bar of the Windsor Hotel with its diamond dust mirrors and grew rich on the money of miners who poured into town from Georgetown, Leadville, Central City and other suburban diggings to see the elephant. Favorite games in Ed West's gaming rooms in Larimer Street (*see picture*), where erudite and personable young ladies dealt faro, were faro bank, roulette, Spanish monte imported from Colorado's San Luis Valley where Spanish influence was strong, and keno in that order. West, according to Forbes Parkhill, ranking authority on Denver's spacious days, was the Queen City's highest toned gambler and as such attracted the patronage of Colorado's most august and patrician senior senator, Edward O. Wolcott, whose huge drooping mustaches and enormous bets were famous all the way from the Brown Palace to Canfield's in Saratoga. When, in 1888, Wolcott was candidate for United States senator, enemies charged that he had lost $22,000 in an evening playing poker at Ed West's. The bold old man scorned to deny the charge. "It's nobody's business but my own," he roared in the columns of *The Rocky Mountain News*, "and besides, I had won the money at the races the day previous."

## NEVER A DULL MOMENT
## AFTER DARK IN DENVER

Upon one lamentable occasion the management of the sedate and opulent Windsor Hotel in Larimer Street was obliged to curtail the merriment of a party of titled English gentlemen who violated the house rules by asking ladies to their room to have target practice by shooting out the window at insulators on the telegraph poles in the street.

THREE PICTURES: AUTHORS COLLECTION

Almost any taste for frivolity could be indulged in Market Street after dark and ladies of the evening and a game of cards with a professional gambler in a bedroom upstairs at Mattie Silks's place could make for a cosy and also costly night's entertainment.

Diners in the Navarre in the days when that now respected restaurant provided games of chance as well as food and drink were once startled when Mme. Ada La Monte, a popular madame, called attention to an underdone mountain trout by slapping the waiter's behind with the defective entree and sending it back to the chef.

# Leadville Gloried in Its Carbonate Kings

## RICHES CAME OVERNIGHT TO LEADVILLE

Leadville's first great strike in precious metals, the Little Pittsburgh Mine, made postmaster H. A. W. Tabor (*right*) the first of many fortunes. After the initial find bonanza piled upon bonanza as prospectors brought rich samples to town to be assayed, as depicted above in a sketch by A. C. Redwood. Big-time operators from Denver and the East (*below*) arrived in camp, each followed by numbers of men of property with interesting things to sell. Iron, Fryer and Carbonate Hills became the source of such sudden wealth that Leadville was swept by an orgy of speculation in mining properties. Tabor became Lieutenant Governor of Colorado. Railroads arrived in town and Leadville, sooty, crime-ridden, squalid and tumultuous beyond most, took its place in the gold-and-dross legend of the mining West.

An English visitor getting off the train at Leadville one late evening in the eighties was startled when he was accosted by a hotel runner who loudly announced to those on the platform that "he would put a bullet through any man who said the Clarendon wasn't a first-class house." The Englishman stayed at the Clarendon. The episode was typical of rough and ready Leadville, most of whose original city had been brought, as shown at the left, over corduroy roads and passes 13,000 feet above sea level. Even when it had achieved metropolitan greatness with gaudy hotels, militia companies and the Tabor Opera, whose stage is pictured at the foot of the page, Leadville remained a shooting town, so that the *Police Gazette* captioned the lively scene depicted below: "Guns for Four. An Early Morning Picnic on a Leadville, Colorado, Thoroughfare in Which a Coroner Participated." Supreme symbol of Leadville's loyalties was a huge silver dollar which towered above the roof of the Tabor Bank and gave the town's eccentric first citizen the title of "Silver Dollar Tabor." When the community's first public school was built, critics complained that it was "inferior in every way to Madame Purdy's Hurdy-Gurdy House and a disgrace to the city." Nobody ever questioned the de luxe nature of Leadville's bagnios.

## CRIPPLE CREEK HAD ITS NIGHT TO HOWL

Last of the great Colorado bonanza camps, Cripple Creek, on the far side of Pike's Peak from Colorado Springs, was discovered in 1890 by Cowboy Bob Womack and in its long activity, according to its official historian, Marshall Sprague, produced $433,000,000, nine tenths of it in gold, in its 475 mines. The excitements marked the transition period from the old time conduct of discoveries in the Black Hills and the Comstock to the final industrialized bonanzas of Nevada's Southern Mines after the turn of the century. In the above drawing the Cripple Creek Mining Exchange learns of a newly uncovered lead in Portland Mine, the camp's greatest producer. Below, Slim Jim Prescott, night bartender in the Palace Hotel, exacts pay from a group of free-loaders who seek to walk out on their bill.

## GLITTERING PROPERTIES OF GOLDEN YEARS

Greatest single source of wealth in Cripple Creek's tumultuous history was the discovery of the celebrated "vug" or geode in the Cresson Mine, where $1,200,000 in pure gold crystals were taken out of a single small opening in a four weeks' period. Coming when the affairs of the camp were declining, the spectacular bonanza notably augmented the already spacious fortunes of Bert Carlton, King of Cripple Creek, and extended the life of the Cresson itself for another twenty years, during which time the property produced $45,000,000. In this drawing Dick Roelofs, "the miracle miner of Cripple Creek," is depicted showing his great underground discovery to Carlton. At the right is Spencer Penrose, in his way almost as spectacular a property of Cripple Creek's golden years as the Cresson vug. Suspected at first of being a mere Eastern playboy, and brother of Pennsylvania's remarkable Senator Boise Penrose, he made a number of satisfactory fortunes in Colorado and proved one of the most durable pioneers in the record. His capacity for poker, whisky and all-night hurrah is still legendary and his monument is the Broadmoor Hotel which he built at Colorado Springs when the neighboring Antlers reproved him for riding saddle horses into the bar and shooting drinks out of the hands of more conventional customers.

BROADMOOR HOTEL

# Disaster Lurked in the Lower Depths of the Mines

Not all the deep mines in Colorado were for the recovery of precious metals. The state is rich in coal deposits ranging from the comparatively valueless lignite in the San Juan to rich mines in the vicinity of Crested Butte. At Crested Butte in 1884 there was enacted one of the mining tragedies of the West when a subterranean explosion of undetermined origin fired the lower levels of the mine and resulted in twenty deaths from suffocation and burning. Above is *The National Police Gazette's* version of the disaster while below *Harper's* depicts the grief of the dead miners' families with the caption "Victims and Mourners."

## MANY MINING TOWNS NOW
## SLEEP THE LONG SLEEP

The life span of Colorado mining towns was often pitifully brief and as early as 1875 Frenzeny and Tavernier were drawing ghost-town pictures for *Harper's,* such as that at the bottom of the page, identified simply as "A Played Out Gulch." More durable were some heroic souvenirs of the great years such as French Louis du Puy's Hotel de Paris at Georgetown, shown at the top of the page. French Louis, an eccentric hotelier and restaurateur, built the premises of Vermont granite to last the ages, laid down the finest cellars in the entire Rocky Mountain region and played host to the nabobs in the grand manner of Vatel and Brillat-Savarin. Himself a notable individualist, French Louis was temperamental and, it was said, hated his customers. Certainly if one of them neglected to savor the full bouquet of a rare Chateau Margaux or failed to comment favorably on his *caneton Lamberty,* he was asked never to return. In the center of the page is Eureka, once, for a brief span, a booming hamlet amidst the encircling peaks and now but a place mark in old maps of the region. The narrow gage Silverton Northern Railroad of the Pathfinder, Otto Mears, once reached to Eureka out of Silverton, but in 1938, when the great Sunnyside Mine was closed, Eureka fell asleep, probably forever.

The white-topped wagons heading out of Kansas into the sunset had many destinations: California the Golden, the Southwest through Santa Fe, the homesteads of Wyoming and Utah or even farthest Oregon on the rim of the world.

# VIII

## *The Great Plains*

### From the Missouri River to Great Salt Lake, Broken Only by the Rocky Mountains, Stretched the Unknown Sweep of the Prairies and the Plains, a Land of Buffalo Grass and Limitless Promise

L IKE THE WATERWAYS of the Mississippi and the Missouri, the Great Plains of the Western United States, lying roughly from Omaha to Great Salt Lake, played an incalculably important part in the development of what Bernard De Voto has called "the continental mind," the awareness before it was altogether accomplished of a continental destiny for the American people.

214

Across the Great Plains, until he encountered the Rocky Mountains or, beyond them in Colorado and Utah, the Great American Desert, the Forty-niner followed one of the several routes to California the Golden. Across them in the same generation the Mormons propelled their "divine handcarts" toward a somewhat less substantial consummation that was eventually to prove more enduring than the gold of the American and Yuba: Deseret. Before either of these mass exoduses in the direction of the Western horizon, the fur trade had brought the factors and *bourgeois* of the American Fur Company, the Hudson's Bay Company and the Rocky Mountain Fur Company. There were even a few independent operators in the business struggling for a foothold in the mountain fur trade and there were noble roamers, titled huntsmen from beyond the Atlantic, cartographers, naturalists and Westward-lookers of indefinable category past all counting. Zebulon Pike's account of his exploration of the Shining Mountains had been published in 1810 and from that time forward the infiltration of white men across the Great Plains was incessant almost to the turn of the century when the last tremendous waves of European immigration receded and the West was, to all intents, settled land.

The distances across the Great Plains constantly, of course, diminished with time. It was nowhere near as far from Council Bluffs to Ogden aboard the Pullman Palace cars of the Pacific Railroad in 1870 as it had been for the Latter-day Saints fleeing Nauvoo in February of 1846.

The proper geography of the Great Plains, as Mr. De Voto points out, was evolved slowly and painfully, not so much by cartographers as by interested parties to the settlement of the West who listened closely to returned voyagers into the prairie unknown. That the region was available to agriculture was seriously doubted from the first: it was a fine place for "buffaloes, wild goats and other wild game," but corn or wheat or timothy or melons, no! The Santa Fe Railroad, today the mightiest carrier of grainstuff in the world, never anticipated when it started out from Atchison in 1866 that the greatest volume of its revenue freight would be boxcars sealed for the carriage of the wheat of Kansas and Nebraska and Oklahoma. It was going to tap the Shining Mountains in the vicinity of Pike's Peak and it was going to carry gold and silver ore to the smelters! It just happened that its deadly rival, the Denver & Rio Grande, got the ore trade while it lasted.

The folklore of the Great Plains, however, revolves neither around the fur trade which first made them its stamping ground nor the sodbusters who came into their inheritance through the later agency of the McCormick reaper and binder. It was the running battle between hostile redskins mounted on swift ponies and the bearded guards and drivers armed with Sharps and later Henry rifles on the stagecoaches of the Great Overland & Pike's Peak Staging Company that will forever be associated in the popular imagination with the far-reaching prairie. The wagon train with its hollow circle of white-tops enclosing hard-bitten sharpshooters who fired through the wheels while the womenfolk loaded is the apotheosis of the plains, not the rendezvous at Green River of the long hunters and Indians mutually awash with whisky, bad feeling and a determination to cut each other's throats financially or, failing that, literally. The true epic of the Great Plains in the years of their continental dimension was one of motion and passage, all of it inevitably Westward.

## THE GREAT PLAINS WERE A SEA OF BLOOD

Attack upon the immigrant wagon train on the plains is as much a part of American folklore as Valley Forge or Ben Franklin's kite. No stage line had a name more associated with running fights with the hostiles than bearded old John Butterfield's Overland Stages for the Far West, shown above at departure time from the offices in Atchison, Kansas. Foreshadowing things to come and the end of staging itself were the premises next door of the Atchison & Pike's Peak Railroad, whose first length of rail laid at Atchison in 1866 was the primal link of today's far-flung Santa Fe Railroad. Occasionally, as shown below, Indians attacked lone travelers, but most men did not travel alone in the time and place. When hostiles appeared running parallel to a wagon train on their swift ponies, as shown opposite, the wagon master ordered a conventional maneuver which brought the teams into hollow square for defense. From then on there might be three classic denouements: annihilation by the Indians, a standoff with the redskins in retirement or, most dramatic of all, the arrival at the last moment of the United States Cavalry and the ensuing slaughter of the enemy to the last warrior. As shown in the lower drawing, plains settlers were never immune from ambush.

INDIAN AMBUSH OF WAGON TRAIN AND HOMESTEAD WAS A FRONTIER CLASSIC

## THE GALLOPING PONY
## ACHIEVED IMMORTALITY

The Pony Express that was to achieve immortality in the legend of the Old West came into being in 1860 and lasted only until the completion of the Overland Telegraph in the fall of 1861, but in that brief time it fired the American imagination and drew attention to the ever-crescent importance of the West as no other agency was able to do. It was organized by the great express and staging firm of Russell, Majors & Waddell to transmit letter post from St. Joseph, Missouri, which was the end of track of the Hannibal & St. Joe Railroad, to San Francisco over the route of the Overland Mail via the Oregon Trail up the Platte River, Fort Laramie, South Pass, Fort Bridger, Salt Lake and across Nevada by way of Deep Creek, Fort Churchill, Carson City and Genoa. It crossed the High Sierra south of Lake Tahoe, where U.S. 50 runs today, by Meyers, Strawberry, Sportsman's Hall and Hangtown. Seventy-five relays of ponies mounted by skilled riders traversed the 1,966 miles of desert and mountain from the Missouri to California in ten days. On the page opposite are three drawings showing respectively a group of agents for Russell, Majors & Waddell planning the route across the Great Plains, a Pony Express rider sketched by Carl Bolmar leaving Fort Kearney and another rider somewhere west of Salt Lake passing the then-building Overland Telegraph. In other parts of the West experiments were made carrying the mail in wind wagons on the plains and via rail, as shown above and at the right, and in a particularly bandit-infested region of Wyoming the United States Army once acted as mailman, as depicted at the bottom of the page.

# Destiny Rode the Thoroughbraced Concord Coach

ROMANCE AND GOLDEN DESTINIES RODE THE STAGES

"In the far West the stagecoach may be called the advance guard of civilization," wrote *Harper's Weekly*'s artist-reporter team of Jules Tavernier and Paul Frenzeny during a tour of the Far West in 1874. "Lines beginning at each railroad terminus lead to Arizona, New Mexico, Texas, Wyoming, Montana and other remote regions although it cannot be many years before the stagecoach will be superseded, and the traveler will no longer be compelled to jog for days and nights over the rough trails that serve as apologies for roads in those far regions. It is not altogether an enjoyable way of making a journey; but on the whole its pleasures and excitements more than counterbalance its inconveniences and discomforts." On the page opposite the artists depict a lonely post office where, in the absence of other business, mail sacks are exchanged on the fly; a pause for breakfast where the stage stops at a "home station"; the driver calling for the readying of a fresh relay of mules at a station perhaps a mile down the road and, finally, a station on the plains where the tired travelers put up for the night. Occasionally, too, in Utah and Colorado Frenzeny and Tavernier encountered a populous and well-guarded wagon train heading into the mountains in search of mining prospects in those wild and inaccessible regions. "The old excitement of danger from Indians has given way to almost complete security," they comment, "but enough remains to give spice to the trip." The greatest risk of staging then was being caught in a blizzard on the plains, such as is depicted on this page by the Western artist and contemporary of Frenzeny and Tavernier, A. R. Waud.

PICTURES: WESTERN COLLECTION

STAGING THROUGH THE EYES OF THE ARTIST, WAUD

## "THE TALL FAR-TRAFFICKING SHAPES"

To the men and women of the West the railroad was an article of faith. Those who went out before it said: "Things will be better when the steamcars come." To those who came after the rail was laid the smoking engines inching across the prairie or twisting into the high passes with their trains of yellow wooden coaches and brakes running hot on the downgrade were never a commonplace. All good things, the stream of life itself, flowed east and west over the ribboned steel, behind the main rods of the locomotives obedient in their guides. Its names were as familiar as those of the Old Testament: Santa Fe, Northern Pacific, Kansas City Southern, the Rio Grande, Hannibal & St. Joe, Arizona Central, Union Pacific, Kansas Pacific, Texas & Pacific. Mostly their names ended in the word Pacific because that was where the hearts of men lay in the ineffable dawn of the continental morning.

In the East, at Schenectady, Taunton, Boston and Manchester, master engine builders, William Mason, Holmes Hinckley, Matthias Baldwin, Rogers, Brooks, Cooke, Amoskeag, were designing railroad locomotives of a beauty and usefulness such as no man had seen before and advertising them to western railroads in elaborate lithographs resplendent with classical mythology and figures of allegory. For a brief span in the American consciousness beauty of design was synthesized with utilitarian engineering as it was never to be again. Such ornately elegant wood-burners as the Tiger, outshopped by Matthias Baldwin, hauled eight or ten of the coaches of the time across the prairie with ease, and more powerful engines with smaller wheels would head thirty boxcars into the foothills without urging. Whether they could afford them or not, presidents and master mechanics of railroads in Kansas and Nebraska and Dakota Territory gazed in enchantment on the lithographs and ordered what they saw there for their roads.

When engulfing blizzards roared down from Canada, filling the cuts and passes of the Sierra and the Cascades and obliterating landmarks on the Great Plains, the exhaust of the laboring engines was muffled and sometimes stilled altogether. But ranchers and townsfolk alike knew that all night long men were beating their equipment against the drifts and soon would come through. In the early days they marveled at the thrust of wooden wedge plows and flangers powered by from two to ten engines laboring under a canopy of smoke. Later came the rotaries and the rails were almost never closed after that.

## COURSE OF EMPIRE: WEST

All the main line railroads which commenced to penetrate the West after the Civil War, the Illinois Central, Santa Fe, Union Pacific, Burlington, Chicago & North Western, Central Pacific and finally the Northern Pacific and the Great Northern, were avid in colonizing the region traversed by their rights of way. Agents spread the word of fabulous agricultural resources in Europe and posters advertised the desirability of removing to the new land in overpopulated cities in the East. Often the carriers had been built with generous land grants from the Federal government and these were offered for sale on easy terms over a period of years. The poster at the right advertised the trains of the Union Pacific in the year 1867, by which time its rails extended all the way to North Platte "300 miles west of the Missouri River, and over 200 miles nearer Denver and Salt Lake than any other railroad line." The U. P. trail was still a long spell from its rendezvous with history at Promontory but it was on its way. As the iron penetrated ever farther toward the Pacific, passengers who got down from the cars at Julesburg, Cheyenne and Laramie discovered vast numbers of Indians lounging on the platforms and begging alms from the new inheritors of everything in sight. Frenzeny and Tavernier found these squaws exhibiting their papooses for two bits a look as the Palace Cars ground to a halt somewhere in Wyoming.

FRENZENY and TAVERNIER

Almost every artist who attempted to depict the West in the early days of its settlement was fascinated by the railroad stations and the types he encountered there. Here was a study of all the men and women who were making a new country almost before the very eyes of sketch artist and painter. Here were motion, life and activity concentrated as nowhere else in the whole United States. Before the coming of George Mortimer Pullman and his wonderful dining car, trains stopped three times a day for twenty minutes at stations designated as having restaurants. The deplorable quality of the food, it was generally felt, was only equalled by the manners of the customers.

Sometimes passengers who got off the cars to see the sights were themselves objects of interest to the natives, as when depot loungers at Corinne, Utah, got their first intimations of *haute couture* when the first bustle got out to take the air. Travel tended to broaden everyone concerned.

## THE SHORT LINES ALSO SERVED

Railroad building during the formative years of the West was not all of it dictated by prudence. Financing railroads and laying rails, often from noplace to nowhere, became a national mania bordering on clinical insanity. The vast fortunes acquired by titans of transport such as the Vanderbilt dynasty in the East and Stanford and Huntington in the West were powerful incentives to reckless financing of hundreds of railroads with slim excuse or none for their very existence. Locomotive builders, rail salesmen and tool manufacturers added to the dementia with high-pressure salesmanship for their products. Scores of short lines were built as feeders to the transcontinental carriers, following the old stage routes north and south from the main lines of Union and Central Pacific, Santa Fe and Burlington, often to be absorbed by the larger road as branches. The pastoral scene above shows the daily passenger train on the San Luis Valley Southern in deepest Colorado where it connects with the Rio Grande's Alamosa branch. Great things were once planned for the S.L.V.S. but its last tie was finally spiked at Jaroso (*below*), only thirty-one miles from its beginning at Blanca.

## RIDING THE CARS WAS NEVER DULL

Life on the cars aboard which a nation was riding to golden destinies in the Western land was always exciting. The exhilaration of
riding across whole states and territories at twenty-two miles an
hour, which was the Union Pacific's average in the early seventies,
was something to tell about back home. Occasionally there were
wrecks along the line, but mostly they were freights, as above,
and nobody was hurt or killed save the inevitable Indians stealing
a ride on the rods. Disasters to passenger trains in the Far West
were few and far between due partly to the lack of dense traffic
and partly to the long vistas available to the engineers' view.
Sometimes (*right*) that enviable man was able to shoot wild game
from his cab. Occasionally tragedy struck, as when (*below*) a
Central Pacific conductor discovered a suicide in the lower berth.

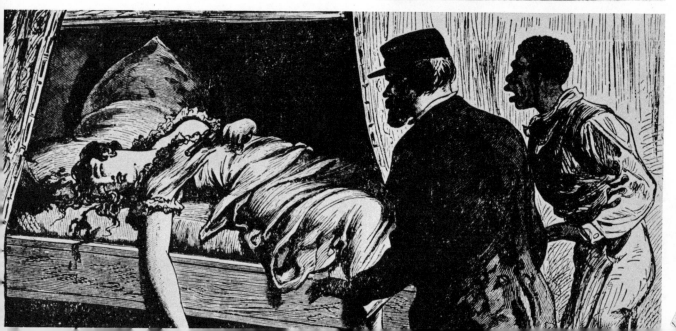

## THE PLAINS WERE A GREAT SEA, THE TRAINS WERE SHIPS

Rufus Zogbaum portrayed the progress of the Westbound immigrant aboard the steamcars in admirable detail in his "The Modern Ship of the Plains" which appeared in *Harper's* in 1886. A stove and fuel were provided by the railroad, simple necessities of life were sold by train butchers. Progress was slow, since immigrant trains were least important of all traffic and were sidetracked for everything else, but sooner or later they reached their destination at the end of track in Nebraska, Wyoming or Kansas, and a few days later saw the new settlers (*below*) breaking ground behind oxen financed by the railroad that had brought them out.

...is immigrant from Sweden was brought ...m New York by agents of the Burlington ...ilroad and settled on a homesite on the ...braska prairies. That he had done well ... himself by the time this photograph was ...ken is witnessed by a robust family, two ...nnected sod houses and even a perambu-...or.

...tertainment and social life were scarce on ...e great plains in a time innocent of mov-...g pictures, radio and television, and re-...val meetings conducted by itinerant ...angelists were looked forward to as an ...otional release and social gathering. ...eir excesses were many and the immoral-... induced by their hysterical atmosphere ...entually brought them into disrepute in ...spectable communities.

...s railroad monopolies increased in power ...nd discrimination in the plains states, ...rmers in revolt against the carriers be-...ame organized in societies known as the ...rangers. Often they were dominated by ...ackpots, boss haters and radicals, al-...hough the meeting here pictured in *Har-...er's* would appear innocuous enough. Most ... all the Grangers hated and feared some-...ing known as "Wall Street," and its ...icked ways were the subject of their most ...passioned oratory.

## IMMIGRATION WAS AT FLOOD TIDE

From the moment he arrived at Castle Garden in New York (*above*), the immigrant from the Old World was an object of solicitous attention from the booming railroads of the West. His person was solicited through the agency of glowing prospectuses (*left center*) and he was packed into coaches (*lower left*) which though far from commodious were a vast improvement over the ship's steerage he had just left. Arrived at the end of track (*below*), the railroad's land agents showed him his future home while the former tenants sat morosely by.

## MISCHANCE LURKED EVERYWHERE

Not every story of hardship and toil by immigrants seeking the Western Land had a happy ending. One family of hopeful land seekers met with "an appalling catastrophe" when their team attempted to run down the tracks at Lincoln, Nebraska. Others lost their homesteads through mischance or chicane and went to work for the very railroads that had brought them west, as sketched by Theodore Davis at the right. Still others were caught in blizzards on the Great Plains and perished miserably. Their fate was drawn by Paul Frenzeny in his "After the Thaw," reproduced at the bottom of the page.

## MISCHANCE RODE THE PRAIRIE WIND

If the hopeful settler on the Great Plains escaped the arrows of the Indians, grasshoppers, droughts and the speculations of land sharps, there were always other hazards of nature to combat and overcome. A favorite theme of Western artists, the prairie fire, is depicted above by the ubiquitous team of artists, Paul Frenzeny and Jules Tavernier, for *Harper's*. At the right is a version of a cyclone in western Kansas which appeared in *Leslie's* for July 4, 1885, showing the dugout which, then as now, was a refuge from hurricanes in many regions of the Southwest. At the bottom of the page is Rufus Zogbaum's celebrated "After the Blizzard," portraying the fate of a frontier family who failed to make it back to their ranch after a shopping trip to the nearest town for supplies.

## FRUITS OF FRONTIER TOIL WERE SWEET

But if the perils of homesteading on the Great Plains were many, so were the homely compensations, as is suggested in this drawing of pioneer satisfactions by A. R. Waud, to whom the West was a never-ending inspiration for drawings of place and character. Society on the frontier had few organized diversions, but when there was a barbecue at the county seat (*below*) the ranchers came from miles around to join in the festivity, talk politics, crops and gossip. The scene shows the roasting of oxen preparatory to a Fourth of July jubilation at Lincoln, Nebraska, in 1876, the Centennial Year.

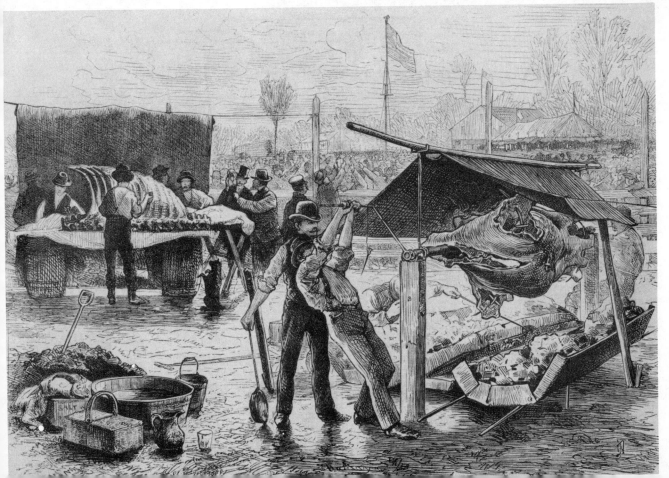

## WHISKY FINISHED OFF THE TRIBES

A dramatic property of the old days on the plains was the attack and chase by hostiles of a lone white man with the odds against him a hundred to one (*below*). With the passing of time, however, repeating firearms and the white man's whisky between them contrived the ruin of the red man. When General Sherman was asked for military guards for the Union Pacific, then building out of Cheyenne, he observed that the only protection the tracklayers needed was sufficient whisky in circulation among the Sioux. It killed them like flies, the medium of its circulation being "The Whisky Peddler of the Plains," shown at the left.

The wild free ways of the plains were represented to the entire world by Buffalo Bill Cody's American Wild West show, which played to packed grandstands in Europe, England and the United States for nearly thirty years. Star performer of the show, next to Cody himself, was Annie Oakley, "Little Sure Shot," the champion marksman of all time, shown here being presented at London to Edward the Prince of Wales, later King of England, and Princess Alexandra. Born in Darke County, Ohio, Annie had never seen the prairie until the Wild West visited Omaha.

## LO, THE POOR INDIAN GOT DAILY POORER

"It needs little familiarity with the actual, palpable aborigines to convince anyone that the poetic Indian of Cooper and Longfellow is only visible to the poet's eye," wrote Horace Greeley during his trip across the continent in 1859. "The Indians are children. Their arts, wars, treaties, habitations, alliances, crafts, properties, commerce, comforts, all belong to the very lowest and rudest ages of human existence. . . . Any band of schoolboys, from ten to fifteen years of age, are quite as capable of ruling their appetites, devising and upholding a public policy, constituting a state or community, as the average Indian tribe. And unless they shall be treated as a truly Christian community would treat a band of orphan children providentially thrown on its hands, the aborigines of this country will be practically extinct within the next fifty years." How well this prophecy was justified by history in less than Greeley's estimated time is evidenced by W. M. Cary's "An Old Squaw Begging for Food at a Frontier Station."

## THE SPIRIT AND THE SPACE OF THE GREAT PLAINS

Perhaps the most celebrated of all drawings portraying the spirit, properties and characters of the continental pilgrimage Westward is A. R. Waud's "Pilgrims of the Plains," reproduced on the page opposite. Almost equally known and admired is Charles Graham's "A Train Stopped by Antelopes," which first appeared in *Harper's Weekly* in 1884. The scene was identified by the artist in the accompanying letterpress as Green River, Utah, and the train as of the "Central Pacific Railroad." Graham was mistaken in his identification since, if he actually meant Utah, the railroad there at this time was the narrow gage Denver & Rio Grande. If he meant Green River, Wyoming, which seems more probable, it is and was located on the main line of the Union Pacific where the rails begin their ascent of the Wasatch Mountains before descending Weber Canyon to Ogden.

TERENCE DUREN

## THE EVERLEIGH SISTERS WERE A LEGEND IN OMAHA, TOO

Minna and Ada Everleigh, who were to become legendary figures in the annals of commercialized love in the American West, were heirs to the great tradition and spacious ways of Julia Bulette, Tessie Wall and Mattie Silks. Even their beginnings in Omaha in the nineties gave promise of the splendors that were to be later associated with their Chicago bagnio when they were recognized as the foremost madames of the continent and the carriage trade from the city's Gold Coast drove up to their midnight doors. With the community of feeling and action which was to characterize their entire lives, Minna and Ada had made unhappy marriages back in Virginia, and in the mid-nineties set up their first plush brothel in Omaha, then a cow town of carnival proportions. The *ton* of their bagnio enchanted the waddies from Fremont and Grande Island who carried home the details of the Tiffany stained-glass ceiling in the foyer and the $15,000 gold-plated piano played by a professor in evening dress. The piano was still in Minna's Riverside Drive apartment in New York when she died in 1949. Terence Duren, a Nebraska artist and student of the Everleigh legend, has shown Minna Everleigh as here depicted in her ornate brass bed in the days before she was exclusively a madame. Below is a medallion of Miss Ada by the same artist. "A girl has to start somewhere," said Minna of Omaha, but soon they were off to greater glories in Chicago, where one of Chicago's howling social swells lent notoriety to their establishment by being found shot to death in one of its bedrooms under deplorable circumstances. The Everleigh Sisters always had class.

WORKING THE BAR

TERENCE DUREN

## THE EVERLEIGHS' CUSTOMERS NEVER KNEW A DULL MOMENT

In addition to the elegances and conveniences described on the page opposite, Minna and Ada maintained a full-time bar at their Omaha establishment where the customers could be sluiced and gentled, or beguiled as the case might be, with strong waters of the most approved brands. Omaha before the turn of the century was a town of liberal inclinations and the cow pokes and businessmen who formed the sisters' clientele wanted the best of everything. Minna was the brains of the partnership, Ada the glamor. By the time they had removed from dusty Omaha to Chicago's Gold Coast they had established commercial amour on a strictly champagne basis, requiring good manners and evening dress on the part of their customers. Love, they felt, achieved a higher plane through the agency of a swallowtail coat and opera hat, a convention scrupulously observed by a distinguished clientele recruited from the best families of North Astor Street. The Everleigh girls deplored anything as shabby as a business suit on their premises.

## WYOMING HAD ITS SHARE OF BRAVE DOINGS IN THE SEVENTIES

The story of Cattle Kate Watson is depicted in a different pictorial version elsewhere in this book in the chapter devoted to pistol-packing madames. The equally graphic account of her bad end together with her lover Jim Averill in the Sweetwater Valley of Wyoming shown on the page opposite is from *The National Police Gazette* of the time, which was 1889. Most folk felt that Kate and Jim had it coming to them, if not for cattle stealing, then for maintaining a bawdy house frequented by thieves. In Sheridan, Wyoming, loose morals were frowned upon, too, as is suggested by the above drawing of a hotel clerk refusing two Cyprians with the phrase: "My chambers are full, all six of them." At the left below a cow poke takes exception to the house rules of the Rawlins House, Rawlins, Wyoming, while at the right two embattled frontiersmen at Green River, having but one revolver between them, take turns firing at each other, to the obvious detriment of trade in the Gold Nugget Saloon.

In 1877 when this photograph was taken from the slope of Mt. Davidson, Virginia City was the cosmopolis of the West, sharing honors for spacious urbanity and worldly ways only with San Francisco.

# IX

## *The Comstock*

### The Greatest Concentration of Readily Recoverable Riches in History Once Made Virginia City, Nevada, the Cosmopolis of the Western World

THE CONTINENTAL CONSEQUENCES of the Comstock Lode were not as far-reaching as those of the discovery of gold in California, but the resources of wealth produced in the mines of Virginia City had a tremendous impact on American economy and no bonanzas in the history of the world laid so compulsive a hold upon the human imagining as those discovered in the Territory of Western Utah in the shadow of Mt. Davidson.

Until the year 1859 Nevada's role in the American record had been neither dramatic nor influential. Its green valleys along the base of the High Sierra had been the westernmost marches of the Mormon Kingdom of Deseret, a realm extending as far to the south as San Bernardino, but the recall of all Mormons from their far-flung outposts by the fiat of President Young in 1856 had almost depopulated it of permanent residents save for a few farmers and cattle ranchers who moved into the deserted Mormon holdings at Las Vegas, and for the proprietors of staging and teaming businesses along the routes to California.

The largest of these staging stations, comprising a blockhouse, stables and a few scattered dwellings, was Mormon Station, which later changed its name to Genoa and remains to this day one of the most beautiful small towns in the West, an oasis of green meadows and stately trees between the grim Nevada desert and the towering ever-snowy peaks of the Sierra. Mormon Station's bright noontide of stages and freighting lasted throughout the fifties and in the sixties it was briefly a swing station on the route of the immortal Pony Express, but the discovery of the Comstock was to change the entire complexion of Nevada's economy and with its booming bonanzas Mormon Station was to recede ever further into the shadows.

Throughout the fifties the stages of George Chorpenning and Absolom Woodward followed the old Immigrant Trail along the banks of Carson Water to change horses at Mormon Station for the assault of the Sierra. So did thousands of California-bound pilgrims, an almost microscopic number of whom turned up Gold Canyon, a ravine in the side of Mt. Davidson, to prospect for minute quantities of gold reported from the region. For a time the present four-corners township of Dayton was known as Pause-and-Ponder because it was here the voyagers must make up their mind whether to take a chance on the lean Gold Canyon diggings or continue to the proven camps of the Mother Lode beyond the mountains.

For a full decade a mere handful of impoverished prospectors earned their Saturday night whisky in Gold Canyon. They took a full decade to work their way up the five miles of sage-grown gulch to the future site of Gold Hill, but when finally they did achieve it they made a discovery which was to change the entire history of the West, was to finance the Union cause in a great impending war and was to make the name of the Comstock of consequence on every bourse and mining exchange and in every chancellery in the world.

The discovery was not gold but silver, and silver was to become almost overnight synonymous with the destinies of Nevada, the Silver State, the Hard Money State, the One Sound State.

In the fall of 1859 a prospector in the Washoe Diggings, as the future Comstock was first known, sent a friend a sample of heavy, dark blue ore taken from his claim on the side of Mt. Davidson. The friend, Judge James Walsh of Grass Valley over in California, took the sample to Ott's Assay Office in neighboring Nevada City and the assay proved it to be silver ore of almost unbelievable richness.

That night Judge Walsh saddled his horse, loaded a mule with provisions and set off for western Utah over the pass at Donner Summit. He had told no one of his intentions, but when, at dawn, he looked back over the route he had come, most of Grass Valley and Nevada City were following his tracks. The rush to Washoe was on.

No gold rush in history rivaled in concentration and intensity the fantastic

243

reverse trek across the Sierra. Once prosperous diggings in the Mother Lode became depopulated overnight even as San Francisco had been depopulated with the discovery of gold in the Sierra foothills. Virginia City, as the new camp on the side of Mt. Davidson was shortly to be known, became in a space of weeks a bursting community of five, ten and finally fifteen thousand people which was to reach an all-time zenith in 1875 with 25,000 permanent residents. Stores, hotels, saloons, fire stations, brothels and private residences rose in florid profusion. The best road companies in the theater in the days of the road's effulgent glory played in Piper's, the Alhambra and the other theaters of Virginia. At one time six Shakespearean companies were playing the Comstock at the same time and there were minstrel shows, tent shows, raree shows and dog and pony shows past counting.

In 1875 Virginia City was razed almost in its entirety by one of the sudden and almost unobstructed conflagrations common to Western mining camps, but so much in the ascendency were the Comstock's fortunes at the time that within a few months an entire new community, this time of brick and stone to replace the earlier shacks and boardinghouses, rose tier on tier on the mountainside. Fine new theaters and places of public assembly were constructed. The International Hotel, boasting the first elevator west of the Palmer House in Chicago, rose six splendid stories to the amazement and pride of Nevada. The thirst of the Comstock, notable even in a time and region of universal thirst, was sluiced in more than 100 gaudy saloons, some of which, like the Sazarac, the Smokery, Delta and Bloody Bucket, became legendary throughout the West. There were four wards, each with its own public schools, fire department and precinct police station. Millionaire's Row in B Street saw the silk hats and fine carriages of the mine superintendents and stock speculators and their wives' gowns came from Worth in Paris by special handling. The second telephone exchange west of the Mississippi (the first was in San Francisco) served Virginia City's multiplicity of business houses and stately residences.

Through Pullmans came to the depot of the Virginia & Truckee Railroad and the private palace cars of celebrities were so commonplace as to arouse little attention. President Grant, General Sherman, Baron Rothschild, Helena Modjeska, Adelina Patti, Booth, Barrett, McCullough and Artemus Ward arrived, to be dined into insensibility at public banquets or play to evening-dressed audiences in Piper's Opera where David Belasco was stage manager.

Throughout the closing decades of the nineteenth century, Virginia City was the Cosmopolis of the Western World.

Names of national significance first assumed overtones of importance on the Comstock. Senators William M. Stewart and John Percival Jones were the first of a long line of "silver senators" to lend picturesque flamboyance to the legislative and social scene in Washington. The first two women to live on the Comstock were Julia Bulette, a courtesan whose murder was a celebrated case throughout the West, and Eilley Orrum, a washwoman who became the first Nevada millionaire through her casual mineholdings. The huge fortunes of John Mackay, James Flood, James Fair and William O'Brien, wealth which was to dominate San Francisco for generations and make itself felt in the capitals of the Old World, derived in their entirety from the mines of the Comstock. Marcus Daly, later the copper king of Montana, and George Hearst of the newspaper dynasty made their first strikes on the Comstock and improved their already effulgent fortunes elsewhere.

Senator William Sharon, whose princely ways staggered even San Franciscans accustomed to opulent display, had his beginnings in Virginia City as resident manager for Darius Ogden Mills's Bank of California. Adolph Sutro, a cigar maker who was to become the most popular of all San Francisco's mayors, first achieved fame with his tunnel, built against fantastic opposition, to drain the lower mines of the Comstock.

The most colorful and celebrated of all frontier newspapers, *The Territorial Enterprise,* which came to Virginia City from Mormon Station by way of Carson City with the first pioneers, was for years the strong voice of authority in the mining world. On its staff while a humble district man, Samuel Langhorne Clemens first adopted the pen name of Mark Twain. Other editors and *Enterprise* staff men of note included Fred Hart, Joe Goodman, Wells Drury, Rollin Daggett and William Wright, who wrote under the pen name of Dan De Quille and whose *The Big Bonanza* was to become the recognized and authoritative history of Nevada in its time.

The wealth in silver and gold produced by the deep mines of the Comstock had a profound effect on the economy of the nation and monetary policies of the world. In the course of the Civil War the admission to the Union of one more state with proper sympathies was essential for President Lincoln's plan of an Emancipation Proclamation, and Nevada's annual production, even at that early date, of nearly $25,000,000 in bullion, would greatly aid the Union Armies. Despite the fact that it possessed less than a sixth the population required for statehood, it became the thirty-sixth state in 1864.

A very substantial portion of the wealth of the Comstock enriched the city of San Francisco in the period before the fire of 1906 and traces of the lavish financing made possible by the ore of Con-Virginia, Gould & Curry, Hale & Norcross and other celebrated mines in Virginia City remained in the city that was rebuilt after 1906: the magnificent Palace Hotel, the Flood and Sharon buildings, the Fairmont Hotel, the Pacific Union Club and the *San Francisco Examiner.*

The staggering personal fortune of John Mackay, richest and most farsighted of all the silver kings, made itself felt throughout the entire world when Mackay acquired a monopoly of the world's cable services while his wife spent fabulous sums entertaining in London and Paris. Mackay's generosity after his death was to finance many good and useful institutions.

By the turn of the century it was apparent to informed operators that no more great bonanzas were forthcoming on the Comstock. While vast resources remained deep in the side of Mt. Davidson, their recovery was becoming increasingly costly and dangerous, and finally reached the point where deep mining was no longer economically justified. It is not true that the mines of the Comstock "gave out." Simply they became unworkable.

Gradually the shadows settled over the once throbbing metropolis of the Nevada desert. The new discoveries of Tonopah and Goldfield lured hard-rock miners to new bonanzas. Old-timers, "hot water plugs" as they were called, moved to California to escape the severe Nevada winters. Businesses closed, the railroad was torn up, houses were dismantled to be re-erected as far away as Los Angeles. So far as its once tumultuous mining industry was concerned, Virginia City had become a ghost town of shuttered dwellings living in splendid memories of the past. The Comstock knew a long twilight before new bonanzas in tourist dollars were to bring it back from the margin of total oblivion.

### CONFEDERATE SYMPATHIES WERE COMSTOCK CURRENCY

In the nourishing crisis of Secession the Comstock's suddenly revealed resources in treasure lent Nevada an importance to the Union cause quite unwarranted by its scanty population as a Territory. "Nevada, coin thy golden crags, with Freedom's image and name," wrote Emerson in his "Boston Hymn," while President Lincoln, less elegantly but with equal urgency, said: "It is easier to admit Nevada than raise another million soldiers," and thus Nevada, with one sixth the then required population to justify a single Congressman, became "the Battle-Born State." Throughout the early days of the War, Virginia City was a hotbed of Secessionist sympathizers who met in the bar room of Jacob Wimmer's Virginia Hotel, as shown here, and actually organized military companies who were to rise to the support of Jeff Davis and overwhelm Lincoln's friends in Nevada when the time was ripe. There were many tense moments on the Comstock when a sudden turn of Confederate fortunes might actually have precipitated open bloodshed, but the firm loyalist editorial policy of Joe Goodman's *Territorial Enterprise* and President Lincoln's clear evaluation of Nevada's assets stemmed the tide of Southern advantage and after the elevation of Nevada to statehood treason was too dangerous to flourish. The gatherings at Wimmer's assumed fewer military overtones and gray uniforms and Secessionist sentiments disappeared overnight.

# Pioneer Nevada Dearly Loved A Fine Hanging

As in all frontier societies of the American West the social cream of the community in Virginia City was its fire companies. Part military, part social, they were arbiters of good times and powerful political factions as well. This rare photograph taken on Fourth of July morning in 1862 shows Young America Hose No. 2 posed, appropriately enough, in front of Young America Saloon in South C Street, while the main thoroughfare of the growing cosmopolis of the West reaches away in a vista of false fronts to the north. The fire companies of the Comstock were largely influential in keeping Secessionist symapthies in Nevada in abeyance and eventually securing its loyalty to the Union cause in the Civil War. They were also notoriously prone to marching in civic funerals such as the one depicted below showing the hanging of John Millain, convicted of complicity in the murder of Julia Bulette, Virginia City's first, most notable and now legendary courtesan.

llain's execution, the most gala to date in vada, put a term to one of the celebrated rder cases of pioneer times. The Bulette, orite courtesan of the miners and notable her good works among the sick and edy in the Comstock's first terrible win- s, was found murdered for her jewels, d the apprehension of Millain as an ac- mplice caused a sensation throughout the est. His eventual hanging, as here de- ted from the files of the *California Po- Gazette*, was attended by all Virginia y *en gala*. Father (later Bishop) Patrick nogue attended the condemned. Mem- s of the staff of *The Territorial Enter- se* inspected the gallows. Women waved dkerchiefs and men munched sand- hes and passed fraternal bottles as the p was sprung. Then everyone went back town, the intelligentsia to attend a lec- e scheduled for that evening by a local y who had made good, Mark Twain, on adventures in the Holy Land.

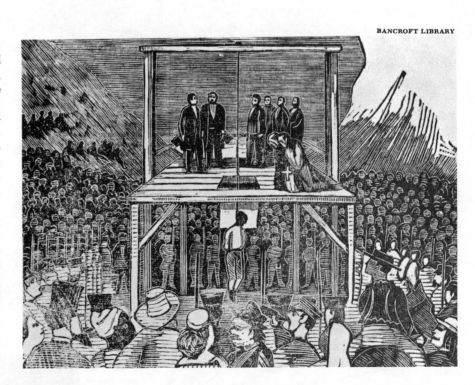

## THE COMSTOCK'S BEGINNINGS WERE STIRRING INDEED

The discovery of the Comstock Lode was painted in later years by James Harrington in a canvas visible today at San Francisco's De Young Memorial Museum. It was first simply known as the Washoe Diggings, but one night a windy no-gooder named Old Virginny Finney smashed a bottle of whisky by accident and, unwilling to let the episode go to waste, shouted, "I christen this place Virginia." The name stuck.

"STRUCK IT RICH."

## BONANZA!

All over Sun Mountain prospectors were staking claims and "striking it rich," as suggested above, making the claim stick with a Colt's Navy revolver if necessary. Everybody (*left center*) in the rough shack town was telling everybody else what a big future lay in store for the diggings and that they were all going to be rich. Characters along the town's main drag, as yet innocent of the name destined for immortality of "C Street," included bearded old George Hearst, founder of the newspaper dynasty, John Mackay, soon to be the richest man in America not even excepting W. K. Vanderbilt, William Morris Stewart, Yale man and "father of American mining law," Adolph Sutro, future mayor of San Francisco, and gamblers, gunmen, drifters, saloonkeepers and roughnecks past counting. The Church of Rome was represented by Father, later Bishop, Patrick Manogue, and the frail sisterhood by Julia Bulette. Eilley Orrum, a washwoman from down Silver City way, moved her boardinghouse and star boarders, Joe Plato and Sandy Bowers, up the mountain, married Sandy, and become the first Comstock millionairess. Mines with magic names began as holes in the hillside: Ophir, Con-Chollar, Chollar-Potossi, Burning Moscow, Best & Belcher. Saloons outnumbered all other business establishments ten to one and Wells Fargo came to town. Browne visited the local assay office (*bottom*) and found two heavily bearded fellows telling what they were going to do when they, too, struck it rich. Their names were James Fair and Marcus Daly

THE RUSH ACROSS THE SIERRA TO THE NEVADA DIGGINGS DWARFED ALL OTHERS

The rush to Washoe which followed just ten years upon the transcontinental rush to the California gold fields was the most dramatic
anabasis in search of precious metals in history. The Forty-niners of
California traversed a hemisphere by a variety of routes and modes
of travel: around the Horn, across the Isthmus, via Mexico and over
the Great Plains. They came by ship, by steamcars in Panama, afoot,
by wagon train, on muleback. The period of immigration lasted a
full decade. The rush to Washoe was concentrated. It was almost
all from California by way of three or four available passes in the
High Sierra and it came pell-mell, almost overnight. So dense was
the concentration of gold seekers bound for Virginia City that for
days at a time the road via Echo Summit to the south of Lake Tahoe
was impervious to westbound traffic and even the Pony Express cooled
its heels at Mormon Station awaiting a chance to breast the human
tide. A few fortunate and well-heeled prospectors and gamblers came
aboard the classic Concord coach, as shown above, although fares
were high and progress uncomfortable. A far vaster number came
afoot carrying their possessions and equipment on their backs or leading mules. Occasionally they encountered a discouraged wayfarer
homeward bound to California (*below*) who said Washoe was another hoax or that the diggings had petered out. The pilgrims paid
him no mind. They knew the Comstock was the true El Dorado.
They were right.

## ALL THE WORLD HEARD THE CALL

The best contemporary reporter of the Washoe gold rush, who combined the talent of a first-rate sketch artist, was J. Ross Browne, staff writer for *Harper's New Monthly Magazine*. He visited Nevada first during the great hurrah of 1859 when the diggings were newly discovered and again four years later when Virginia City was a proven camp on its way to becoming a metropolis. The sketches on this page were inspired by his earlier impressions of the crossing of the Sierra, the one above being entitled, "Go It, Washoe!" while that below bore the caption, "Carambo!—Caraja!—Sacramento!—Santa Maria!—Diavolo!" At the top right is Browne himself on the stage driven by "Old Charlie," a notoriously profane and alcoholic jehu of the time who proved after death to be a woman. In the middle is the less luxurious mode of travel by ore wagon whose jolting was eased by the universal bottle. At the bottom "Hurrah for Washoe!" shows pilgrims fresh out of Sacramento and filled with optimism as they assay the Sierra foothills, confident in the future, each a millionaire-man in his mind's eye. Many indeed were just that.

## BREASTING THE HIGH SIERRA

The ascent of the Sierra really began at Hangtown which, by the time the rush was on to Washoe, had yielded to respectability and was calling itself Placerville. From here the freight wagons and plodding footmen climbed steeply to Sportsman's Hall, the Pacific House, Swift's Station, Strawberry and eventually the margin of Lake Tahoe. Swift's Station, shown in the old photograph at the left top, has disappeared from the maps. Kyburz in the lower picture is still a roadhouse stop on U.S. 50. Particularly interesting in this photograph is the watering cart at the bottom painted with the name "Lake Bigler," as Lake Tahoe was then known. Throughout the sixties the entire length of staging road from Placerville to Carson City was watered constantly in summer to lay the dust. Incoming optimists sometimes met outgoing defeatists (*above*) on the road and everybody stopped at Strawberry for dinner, as shown below. The place was named for a particularly mean innkeeper named Berry who fed horses in his stable straw instead of hay. Browne reported that the quality of the food was only matched by the abominable manners of the guests.

## VIRGINIA ACHIEVES BONANZA AND BROWNE DISCOVERS VIRGINIA

Browne found Carson Valley, as the pilgrims descended the King's Canyon and Kingsbury Grades from Tahoe, littered with the bones of dead animals which had perished the winter previous (*above left*), as well as many curious characters (*upper right*) who told strange tales of the new diggings on Sun Mountain. When he achieved Virginia City itself he discovered a shack town leaping in throes of wildest optimism. The below sketch of three confident sourdoughs on their claim he entitled "Indications, sure!" while the scene in the local assay office represented the dream of every prospector in the West as the assayer reports, "Silver, certain, sir!" Virginia City was on the way to being the wildest, richest and noisiest mining town of the American continent.

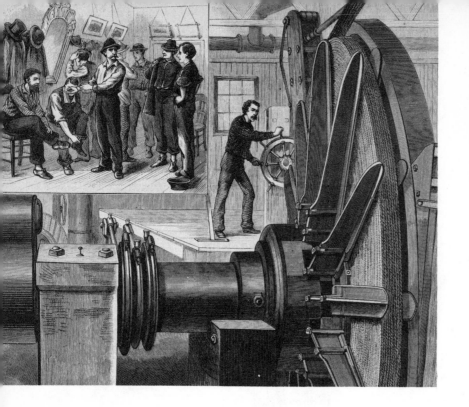

## AS *LESLIE'S* PORTRAYED THE COMSTOCK IN '78

The deep mines of the Comstock poured out riches with only minor interruptions for three full decades and were the wonder of the mining world. Most of the miners themselves were of established American stock, with a sprinkling of experts imported from Cornwall and known as "Cousin Jacks." The equipment, which included up to the minute explosives, pneumatic drills, air conditioners, ice water at every hand, telegraphic communications between each level and the surface, underground rest rooms and hoisting machinery that was a marvel of precision and speed, was viewed with awe by thousands of visitors every year. So great was the public preoccupation with the Nevada bonanzas that New York and San Francisco newspapers carried thousands of words of telegraphic news from Virginia City every week for thirty years. When the Frank Leslie Western Expedition came west from New York on a year's tour of the vanishing frontier, it devoted scores of pages of beautifully executed drawings and well-written typeset to its stay on the Comstock. All the drawings on these two pages are from *Leslie's* in 1878 and were the work of Harry Ogden and Walter Yaeger, staff artists on the expedition.

More than 300 miles of shafts tunneled under the windy slopes of Sun Mountain and were populated in continuous eight-hour shifts by nearly a third of the 25,000 population of Virginia City perched atop the mine hoists. There were literally hundreds of miles of narrow gage railroad, its cars hauled by a breed of mule which never saw daylight and was known as a "Washoe Canary." Like their superintendents and laborers in the depths, owners of the mines were familiar with every inch of their underground workings. At the top left Jim Fair, one of the three or four wealthiest of all the silver kings, is depicted in miner's garb carrying a lantern on the 2,000-foot level of Con-Virginia.

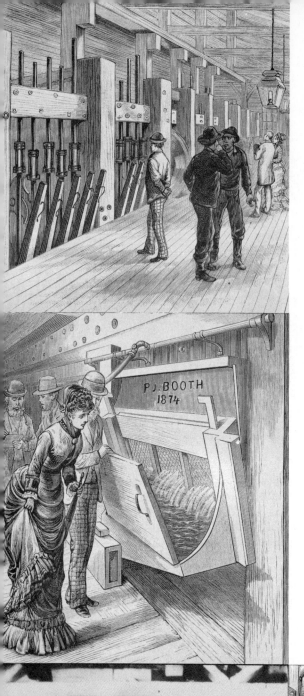

## THE INCREDIBLE UNDERGROUND WORKINGS OF THE COMSTOCK MINES HAD THEIR COUNTERPARTS ON THE SURFACE IN VIRGINIA CITY

No less fabulous to visitors were the vast surface counterparts of Virginia City's underground workings, its tremendous operations for the recovery of gold and silver from the quartz in which it was found. The lower reaches of Virginia City were lined with miles of great reducing works; so were the hillsides of Gold Hill and Silver City and so was the margin of Carson River all the way from Empire to Dayton, a distance of seven miles. Shown on this page at the top is a stamp mill where ponderous iron stamps mounted on eccentric shafts reduced the tough Comstock ore to powder. The center picture shows the flow of crushed ore and water on the way to the settling tanks while at the right bottom are the settling tanks themselves where the silver is amalgamated with quicksilver. The pump at the Union mine (*below left*) was installed at a cost of $547,000, had a flywheel 36 feet in diameter and a cylinder 100 inches in diameter. From this complex of machinery three quarters of a billion in pure gold and silver were eventually recovered.

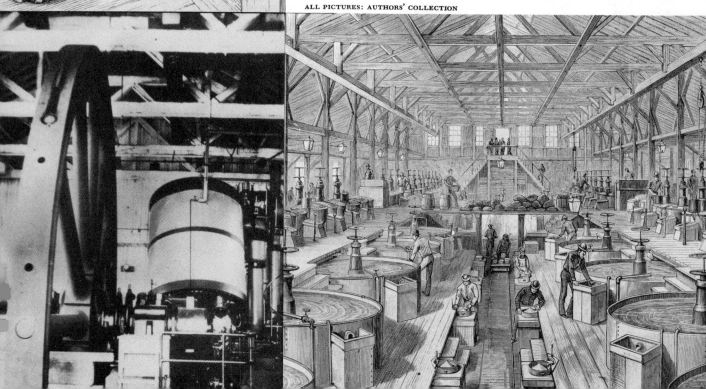

Foreign visitors accustomed to the crude reduction processes used elsewhere in the world of precious metals marveled at the perfection of the Comstock's cyaniding works, assay offices and bullion handling, where the one and only consideration was the recovery of every last ounce of silver and gold from every ton of ore brought to the surface. In the *Leslie's* drawing above workmen are manipulating the silver amalgam and distilling the quicksilver in the retort house of one of the mines. Below pure silver is being poured into molds for shipment to Carson Mint or the vaults of San Francisco.

## SAN FRANCISCO WAS SENSITIVE TO VIRGINIA

Throughout the sixties, seventies and eighties the fortunes of Virginia City were reflected directly and dramatically in the fortunes of San Francisco. As the mines under Sun Mountain emerged into bonanza or sank into borrasca, so millions were made or lost by San Francisco speculators in Comstock mining shares. The frequent panics and unstable banking conditions of California in this era were directly attributable to the mania to get rich quick in Best & Belcher, Consolidated Virginia, Burning Moscow, Ophir, Hale & Norcross or any of the other magic names on the certificates representing ownership in Nevada mines. The scene in Montgomery Street in 1878 during a temporary panic in the market was sketched for *Leslie's* by Walter Yaeger, a distinguished staff artist, and its caption proclaimed that "for days the uttermost consternation and confusion prevailed." But if San Francisco speculators lost immense fortunes playing the Comstock market, the city also arose in wealth and splendor on the basis of the tangible recoveries of nearly $700,000,000 from Virginia City's mines, almost all of which passed through the countinghouses and treasure vaults of Montgomery Street. For three full decades Virginia City regarded San Francisco as a combined bank for its resources and its most desirable residential suburb.

## EXCITEMENTS WERE VARIOUS AND CONSTANT

Inside information about what was toward in the deep shafts under Virginia City was priceless to unscrupulous speculators in San Francisco. Confidential reports from mine superintendents in Nevada to their principals in Montgomery Street were made daily, sometimes hourly, on the telegraph circuits looping across the High Sierra. Always they were in code, but the operators depicted here retained a female wire tapper to intercept the precious messages and a coding expert to decipher it for them. The result might be huge fortunes made on the basis of advance and presumably secret information. In the scene below a San Francisco mob menaces a Montgomery Street dealer in Comstock shares, blaming him for the decline in the market, while he dares them to shoot him.

The composing room of *The Territorial Enterprise* with its Washington hand press and whiskered printers was typical of such institutions in its time and place. The Sharp's rifle against the type cases and Colt's Navy revolver on the imposing stone were as much properties of the frontier newspaper shop as the type stick and printer's devil. Type stick in hand at the left is Steve Gillis, lifelong friend of Mark Twain and a celebrity in his own right throughout California and Nevada.

# Territorial Enterprise.

VOL. 1.　　CARSON CITY, NEVADA TERRITORY, SATURDAY, DECEMBER 17, 1859.　　NO. 45

A fabled property of the Old West, *The Territorial Enterprise* was at once the first newspaper to be published in Nevada Territory and the archetype and pattern of frontier newspapers everywhere. It first saw the light of day in Mormon Station (now Genoa) in 1858, moved briefly to Carson City, as indicated in the above logotype, and finally moved to Virginia City with the news of the great bonanzas being there uncovered. Primal architects of the *Enterprise's* fortunes were Joseph Goodman and Dennis McCarthy, whose whisky-drinking, gun-toting staff soon set the approved pattern of frontier journalism everywhere from Alder Gulch to Tombstone. One of its earliest reporters was Sam Clemens, who was soon signing his stories with a by-line destined for immortality: Mark Twain. In its golden noontide of the sixties and seventies *The Enterprise's* owners were reputed to take home the week's profits on Saturday night in fire buckets filled with gold double eagles. Many of its staff became celebrated in Western letters and included not only Clemens and Goodman, but William Wright, who as "Dan De Quille" was the most famous mining editor of his generation, Fred Hart, celebrated for his "Sazarac Lying Club," Wells Drury and Rollin Daggett. Judge C. C. Goodwin, for many years its editor, was one of the really great and scholarly figures of Western newspaperdom. This spirited drawing by E. S. Hammack shows *The Territorial Enterprise* as it looked in South C Street the year Mark Twain joined the staff.

Dull moments in the course of the affairs of *The Territorial Enterprise* in its golden years were infrequent. The first thing a new reporter or editorial writer was asked by the management when he reported for work was, "How well do you shoot?" Staff members were expected to defend their opinions and news stories personally and went armed as a matter of course. Indignant readers intent on horsewhipping the editors were shot up with such regularity that the urge was largely discouraged. On his first day on duty as a Comstock editor, Wells Drury, a diminutive youth, was attacked by a whip-wielding ruffian, put him to inglorious rout with a handy Colt's while bystanders cheered.

Less available to gunfire was the tempestuous, Irish-born actress, Matilda Heron, when she called at *The Enterprise* to protest an unfavorable review of her performance at Maguire's Opera as Camille. "An exponent of the elemental passions," as Miss Heron was described, she frightened the managing editor on duty cruelly so that he was forced to beat a retreat to the Old Magnolia Saloon where no woman might follow. It was a close shave.

One of the celebrated shooting feuds of frontier journalism was that between Joe Goodman, one of the early founders of *The Enterprise's* stormy destinies, and Tom Fitch, proprietor of the rival and equally outspoken *Virginia Daily Union*. When Fitch remarked in print that the editorial policies of *The Enterprise* "resembled the love of God," Goodman was able to complete the tag to the effect that they surpassed all human understanding and called Fitch out under the terms of the code duello. At the first exchange in a formal encounter, as here depicted and reprinted by permission of Harold's Club, Reno, Goodman hit Fitch in the kneecap, crippling him for life. It all added to the reputation of the terrible-tempered *Territorial Enterprise*.

# COMMOTIONAL WAS *The Territorial Enterprise*

It was on the staff of *The Territorial Enterprise* that a young reporter named Sam Clemens first, in 1863, started using the by-line Mark Twain. In later years Clemens, shown above at the time of his Virginia City adventures, confessed to having appropriated the nom de plume from Captain Isaiah Sellers of the Mississippi River Steamer *J. M. White*, who wrote ship's news for the *New Orleans Picayune* on the side. Sellers' gravestone at Bellefontaine Cemetery, St. Louis, also appears above.

## Pioneer Newspapering

In 1863 *The Enterprise* moved from the premises whose primal print shop is shown on a previous page to fine new quarters in South C Street, standing to this day. Here Mark Twain wrote his celebrated hoaxes amidst the excitements of the composing room rather than in more austere editorial quarters upstairs.

## THE TERRITORIAL CAPITAL, TOO, HAD ITS OWN EXCITEMENTS

No less than the neighboring Comstock Lode, Carson City, Nevada's capital, shared the robust overtones of frontier journalism. A legal prize ring where mine owners, railroad lobbyists for the all-powerful Central Pacific, pioneer lawyers and a notably corrupt judiciary lived a fantastic jungle night life, Carson's early newspapermen fought for keeps with no holds barred. The town's rugged individualism was personified by Sam Davis, editor of the *Carson Appeal* and brother of Bob Davis of the *New York Sun* of fragrant memory. On one occasion, as the result of political differences, Davis knocked down C. N. Harris, editor of the *Index*, in a corridor of the state capitol, as shown above. Fined $75 for assault, Davis paid under protest, complaining that he had also smashed a valuable Malacca stick beyond all repair. After that, Editor Harris, as seen in the drawing below, took to looking around doorways before entering the Old Magnolia.

## THE COMSTOCK PARTICIPATED
## IN ALL THE EXCITEMENTS

Although its own Virginia & Truckee Railroad was notoriously free from brigandage throughout its long and useful life, Virginia City participated, at least vicariously, in the very first of all the many train robberies in the shooting years of the West. The occasion was the looting at Verdi, a few miles west of Reno, of the Central Pacific's through sleeping train for the East, No. 1, on the night of November 4, 1870, a curtain raiser for scores of similar robberies to come, and it was engineered by E. B. Parsons, a well-known Comstock gambler, and Jack Davis, a hitherto presumably blameless man of Virginia City business affairs. The robbery set a pattern for years to come and the Wells Fargo box in the express car yielded $40,000 in hard gold currency. Wells Fargo's detectives were on the scene next morning, rewards almost as large as the loss itself were posted, and armed posses rode off through the Washoe Hills into which the miscreants had disappeared. All were apprehended in a matter of days and stiff jail terms imposed. The C.P.'s No. 1 suffered further indignity when, the very next day, it was once more held up and robbed by another enterprising gang at Independence, Nevada, 400 miles to the east.

WELLS FARGO BANK

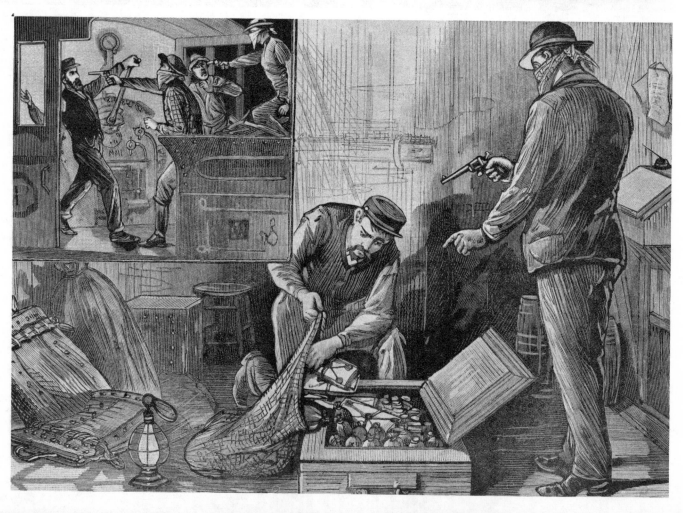

## THE COMSTOCK WASN'T LONG ON DECORUM

Like any other vital occasion in Virginia City, funerals were invariably an excuse for excess among the bottles, as is depicted above. Elections too (*below left*) were floated on a sea of spirits with the polling place located handy to the right saloon, while it was notorious, as is suggested below right in a drawing by J. Ross Browne, that every hotel in Washoe provided a chambermaid with every room. A scandalized Boston clergyman in the sixties remarked, "In Nevada they observe the Sabbath the way we celebrate Fourth of July!"

SAZARAC SALOON

## TEMPLE OF FRONTIER THESPIS

Ranking theatrical impresario of the West in 1864 was Tom Maguire, whose D Street opera in Virginia City, shown to the rear in this photograph, was one of the notable playhouses in the frontier tradition. Maguire telegraphed Artemus Ward, a leading monologist of the day, asking what he would take for twenty nights, and the Comstock was convulsed when Ward wired back, "Brandy and soda!" To Maguire's came Adah Isaacs Menken to thrill the miners in "Mazeppa" so that they made her an honorary fireman, and in an aisle seat at Maguire's sat Mark Twain on opening nights as drama reviewer for *The Territorial Enterprise.* In the middle sixties Maguire sold out to John Piper and removed to greater horizons in San Francisco, where he promptly embarked on the losing end of one of the greatest newspaper-theatrical feuds of history with the youthful but even then dangerous De Young brothers.

## LOLA MONTEZ AND LOTTA CRABTREE WERE FAVORITES

John Piper, Maguire's successor, had started business on the West Coast in Forty-niner times with a saloon next door to San Francisco's Bella Union music hall in Portsmouth Square. Following the rush to the Comstock, he bought out Maguire and, before his death, was to be owner and proprietor of three operas bearing his name and an even greater number of saloons. The melancholy tale depicted here was a classic of the American theater in the great days of the road: the optimistic arrival of a Shakespearean company on the morning steamcars, the seizure of their trunks by a hardhearted landlord when bad reviews in the *Enterprise* and *Union* closed the show, and their eventual departure from town in sorry case down the winding right of way of the equally hardhearted Virginia & Truckee Railroad which has refused them free passage away from their latest Waterloo. Barrett, Booth, Joe Jefferson, Adelina Patti and Caruso fared more happily at Piper's, where Maude Adams was to make her first stage appearance and David Belasco was once stage manager.

## HIGH JINX, LOW JINX, THE COMSTOCK HAD THEM ALL

In the fall of 1865, the *California Police Gazette,* which kept close watch on Virginia City as one of its prime sources of news of high life, was able to make its readers happy with the above sketch of a moment of relaxation in the National Brewery Saloon just as the police arrived. Against such contingencies, Virginia at the height of its fortunes maintained ten precinct stations in as many wards.

The melancholy event shown here in *The National Police Gazette* (no connection of the earlier weekly of similar name in California) shows Charles Fosgard, an engineer at the Con-Virginia shaft, just as he blew out his brains after an unfortunate encounter with luck at the farobank table in the Sawdust Corner Saloon. A reporter for *The Territorial Enterprise,* shown here in a bowler hat, who was present at the sensational moment afterward, wrote for his early edition: "Mr. Fosgard seemed to have been suffering for a long time from that fearful depression which sometimes seizes people in this section. It is particularly severe in persons of a certain temperament and is very apt to increase with time." The suicides of prostitutes in Virginia City were so commonplace that the newspapers hardly bothered reporting them.

When J. Ross Browne reported on life on the Comstock for *Harper's New Monthly Magazine* in the early sixties, he sketched this drawing showing the "hurdy-gurdy" girls in one of the town's night spots. Elsewhere such establishments were known as fandango houses, but the name never seems to have been common in Virginia City. Whatever the name, the occupation of the inmates was the world's oldest.

Nothing gave the frontier so big a laugh as a misplaced horse. The legend of the horse in the barroom itself occupies an entire chapter of Western folklore. Here an artist in *Leslie's* finds it hilarious when "A Horse Attends an Auction Sale in the Store of M. M. Frederick, at Virginia City, Nevada."

Eastern readers, too, were delighted when Jim Fair, one of the bonanza kings, sent down a basket lunch complete with champagne and *foie gras* to the 2,000-foot level in Con-Virginia mine in anticipation of entertaining a group of distinguished guests whom he was showing the property. A shift of Cornish miners, new to the country, thought it the solicitous gesture of an indulgent employer and were engaged in the cheerful demolition of the refreshments when Fair and his guests, visible in the background, arrived on the scene.

## "RIDERS SHAKING THE HEART——"

Throughout the riding years of the Old West no single firm, not even the Bank of California, ranked the princely banking and express firm of Wells Fargo & Co. in prestige and favorable celebrity. With the decline of the Mother Lode and subsequent rise of the Nevada bonanzas, Virginia City became the most important of all Wells Fargo's far-flung branches and outposts, and its great South C Street offices, shown here, was a vice-regal palace of inland empire. Hence, until the coming of the Virginia & Truckee Railroad in 1870, the Comstock's millions went down the grade and across the lofty Sierra to San Francisco in the thorough-braced Concord coaches of Wells Fargo. They were not often molested, for the company maintained a shotgun messenger service of legendary deadliness backed up by a detective agency almost as fatal. The Boot Hills of the West bristled with headstones engrossed at the company's expense with the legend, "Wells Fargo Never Forgets."

Wells Fargo's aristocratic stage drivers like Hank Monk and Baldy Green would never have tolerated such disgraceful scenes as this, representing as it did the decline in public manners and morals incidental to the advent of the steamcars. Madame Bentz's company of female minstrels, having concluded their run at Piper's Opera, paused briefly for refreshment before boarding the Virginia & Truckee's night sleeping train for Oakland. Pilgrim feet became tangled on the depot platform and this provocative scene was enacted before the train captain was able to highball out of town.

Rising six fantastic stories above C Street with its upper windows commanding a view of more than 200 miles of Nevada desert, the International Hotel established Virginia City as the Cosmopolis of the West, not even excepting San Francisco. The International, third of the name, was built following the Great Fire of 1875, possessed the first elevator, or "rising room" as it was at first known, west of Chicago's Palmer House and delighted the nabobs with its profusion of Turkey carpets, potted palms, mahogany furniture and a cellar of almost unimaginable resources. Special friends of the house like John Mackay and Adolph Sutro were encouraged to visit this wealthy crypt and draw their own from the wood. Like Denver's Windsor, the International at last fell on lean years and was destroyed by fire in 1914. At Austin, Nevada, 175 miles to the east, the flames were visible from Virginia City's first International Hotel which had been loaded on an oxcart and re-established there during one of the Comstock's temporary descents into borrasca in the sixties.

## STAKES WERE THE HIGHEST OF ALL AT THE INTERNATIONAL

When this spirited scene was reproduced in 1882 in the *Police News* in Boston the caption read as follows: "'Give me a stack of thousand dollar chips!' Ranchman Joe Timberlake's great play in bucking the tiger and losing $42,000 in Virginia City, Nev." Aside from this single source, no record survives either of Joe Timberlake or his great play and the episode might be regarded by severe scholars as apocryphal, but it shows the hold Virginia City still maintained on the public imagination and its established reputation for spendthrift ways.

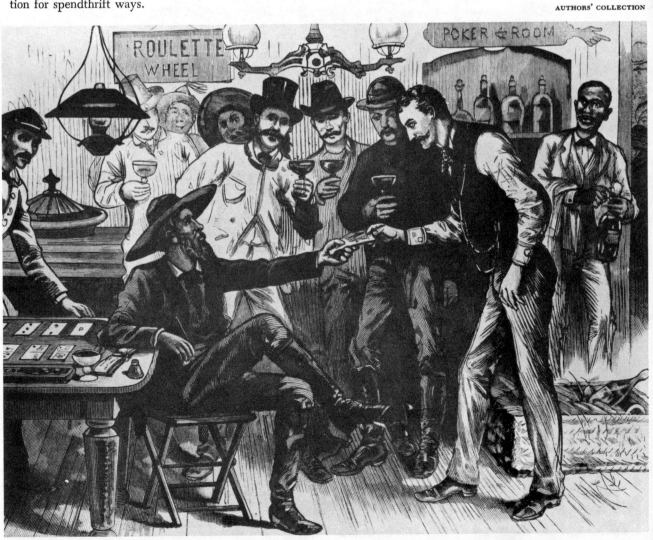

"THERE ARE ALWAYS LOSERS AND FINDERS.
THERE IS NO ABIDING PLACE . . ."

"John Brown's Body"

Like Virginia City, the capital city of Carson in Eagle
Valley, twelve miles removed from the Comstock, quiv-
ered with the impact of bonanza millions. Here was the
United States Mint, here the seat of Federal justice, here
the home office and shops of the wealthy Virginia &
Truckee Railroad. Carson was the staging and railroad
entrepôt to the Comstock and its affairs fluctuated with
those of the mines under Sun Mountain. The white man's
gambling habits were easily imitated by the Washoe Indians of the region and the artist who drew this scene
for the *Police News* in the seventies captioned it: "He
Played All His Clothes in Except His Breechclout—A
Washoe Indian Gambler Sacrifices His Wardrobe in a
Card Game at Carson, Nev." A few miles to the north in
Washoe Valley arose (*below*) the mansion of Sandy
Bowers and Eilley Orrum, first of the eventual bumper
crop of Comstock millionaires. Eilley claimed the gift of
second sight and was known as the Washoe Seeress;
Sandy couldn't read or write, but they were indisputably
rich and even went to London "to see the Queen." When
Eilley died, a poverty-stricken old lady many years later,
their story became one of the pathetic sagas of pioneer
times.

## JOHN L. IN WASHOE

Nevada's liberal attitude in all matters of personal freedom caused its selection as the setting for numerous championship boxfights over the years, none more exciting to the world of sport than that between Jim Corbett and Bob Fitzsimmons in Carson City in 1897. For the occasion scores of special trains, many carrying the glittering private cars of the nabobs, rolled in on the V. & T. The one that attracted most attention bore in person John L. Sullivan, former heavyweight champion of the world and now on duty as official fight correspondent for Joseph Pulitzer's *New York World*. On the platform waited a delegation of "local sports in well groomed tiles" and the Silver Cornet Band to escort John L. to the Arlington Hotel. Sullivan had sustained a slight arm injury when his train had made an emergency stop back in Wyoming and carried his arm in a sling, as shown in this drawing by a staff artist for the *Police Gazette*, which was also giving the event full coverage. At the Arlington Sullivan held court in a thronelike red plush armchair in the bar. Surprisingly, he made an excellent and conscientious reporter.

## NOT LIKE THIS IN TOMBSTONE!

On another occasion the *Police Gazette* found Carson City a dateline for pictorial news when it was visited, briefly be it said, by millionaire Ed Schieffelin, owner of the Toughnut Mine and founder of the fabled fortunes of Tombstone, Arizona. Schieffelin, en route to visit old time prospector friends in Virginia City, stepped off the cars of the V. & T. for lunch at the Ormsby House where, much to his amazement, the management made him wear a coat in the dining room. Where did they think they were, Ed demanded in tones of outrage, Delmonico's?

Throughout the sixties, seventies and eighties, scores of stamp mills such as this commenced their eccentric rigadoon in the far places of the West, in Treasure Hill, Hamilton, Jumbo, Como, Austin, Eureka, Bodie, Pioche and Panamint City. In each the cry resounded, "Greater than the Comstock." None were.

# X

## *Greater Than the Comstock*

### The Magnetic Lure of the Cry, "Greater Than the Comstock," Drew Many Men to the Far Places of the West

FROM THE VERY BEGINNINGS of its fortunes the Comstock was the standard of richness to which all other bonanzas were compared. Covertly whispered among a favored few who were to be let in on a good thing or openly proclaimed to the world, the phrase "greater than the Comstock" was possessed of a magic which overnight emptied whole established communities of their inhabitants and sent them hasting on dusty *jornadas* across mountain and desert. Circulated in mining and speculative circles in San Francisco, "greater than the Comstock" was a rumor to send obscure shares soaring and to depress the market in com-

274

paratively sound and productive operations in Virginia City, and the device was never too shopworn to carry with its merest utterance a sort of assurance of miracles at hand for the fortunate few who got in on the ground floor.

"Greater than the Comstock" was first used to describe new discoveries at Bodie and on the Reese River early in the sixties, which shows the estate in public imagining to which the Comstock had attained almost from the beginning. As the fortunes of Virginia City soared uncertainly but in an over-all upward graph for the next two decades, the implications of the comparison became ever greater and it was last used to rally the faithful, the true believers in new bonanzas, to Tonopah and Goldfield, Rawhide, Bullfrog and Rhyolite long after the Comstock itself had sunk into irretrievable borrasca.

"Greater than the Comstock" was the password of a confraternity of believers whose membership ranged from nabobs in top hats and striped cashmere trousers in the great mansions of Nob Hill to the weariest sourdough begging a grubstake for himself and his aging burro with which at last to discover the true Eldorado toward which his steps had led over a lifetime. It was the open sesame to the vaults of the all-powerful Bank of California with which Senator William Sharon charmed the ever-skeptical moneybags of the coast, Darius Ogden Mills. It was the incantation with which shady stock promoters unloaded such salted diggings as the Little Emma—to the tune of millions—on English investors and brought Anglo-American relations to an all-time low. It was the rallying cry of desert rats like Shorty Harris and Death Valley Scotty, the *in hoc signo vinces* of an entire generation of great men and small men on whom the lure of precious metals was an almost religious compulsion.

Its oriflamme was a prospector's pan and no Henry before Harfleur could have incited his troops with greater eloquence to valiant deeds than did a hundred grizzled sourdoughs bursting into saloons and billiard parlors of the frontier with the cry, "Greater than the Comstock."

Throughout four decades in which its name was used as an advertisement of other and always lesser bonanzas, Virginia City maintained a contemptuous aloofness, only now and then raising its voice to snarl at a rival, as did the columns of *The Territorial Enterprise* when it denounced Panamint as "merely another opening in the base metals range."

Other bonanzas turned to borrasca, the lights flared briefly and were dimmed all over the West, but the Comstock remained unassailable in performance. Time after time new riches were uncovered in the depths of Mt. Davidson to silence the faint of heart who proclaimed its wealth was at last exhausted. Each revival and fresh evidence of its vitality gave new meaning and new effectiveness to "greater than the Comstock," until, of course, the final decline of Virginia City's own fortunes toward the end of the century.

Curiously enough, the phrase was never used to promote the one and only bonanza which outproduced, outlived and outguessed the Comstock: the incredible Homestake in South Dakota, whose largest single shareholder, George Hearst, had had his own beginnings in Virginia City. The Homestake never needed promoting. It simply produced. Endlessly.

One of the earliest and, as it proved, longest lived of all camps to bask in the reflected glory of the Comstock comparative was Bodie in California's Mono

County, near Mono Lake, but so close to the Nevada border that its sister community, Aurora, actually is in Nevada.

Bodie's gold production antedated the discoveries in Gold Canyon by seven years but it was not until 1862 when the Comstock was already a proven camp that Waterman Body, "the Dutchman from Poughkeepsie," found substantial deposits there and the rush was on. "Greater than the Comstock" was used for the first time to promote dissolute and booming Bodie and traffic over the Sonora Pass wagon road brought into town all the conventional properties of a well-provided camp: whisky, girls, firearms, mining supplies, roulette tables and knockdown dwellings. Bodie wasn't greater than the Comstock, but new discoveries kept it in operation until comparatively recent times and "the bad man from Bodie" made its wickedness part of the legend of the West.

Contemporary with Bodie's emergence were the diggings on the Reese River in central Nevada for which Austin was the entrepôt of such surrounding camps as Tuscarora, Treasure Hill, Hamilton and, at slightly greater remove, Eureka in the White Pine region.

Austin's gaudy flowering began in 1862 and the cry "greater than the Comstock" was at concert pitch three years later when the Virginia City mines suffered their first brief descent into borrasca. This was the first of the Comstock's many short-lived recessions and men of little faith in considerable numbers deserted Sun Mountain for the widely touted diggings of the Reese.

Virginia City's first International Hotel—it was to have three of them—was loaded bodily on a wagon and set up in Austin where it is in serviceable operation to this day.

Of all the great local excitements of the Old West, the slogan "greater than the Comstock" was most cunningly used to exploit the fortunes of Panamint City, high in the Panamint Mountains on the rim of Death Valley.

Panamint had only the slimmest background of mining resources, but it came into being in the middle seventies when the impact of the Big Bonanza in Virginia City had aroused the entire West to a hysteria of mining enthusiasm and was shortly boomed with a great booming by experts, Nevada's peerless and fearfully bearded Senators William Morris Stewart and John Percival Jones. Associated with them was Trenor Park, a San Francisco aristocrat, and under their skilled manipulation Panamint shares soared mightily on the mining exchanges of the world. In the case of Panamint, "greater than the Comstock" was simply a sort of singing commercial, cynically associated with a purely speculative venture in stock promotion.

Panamint was the apotheosis of the phrase and when Panamint folded up it was relegated to the category of outmoded superlatives, there to gather dust until it was recovered and once more furnished forth with all its implications of glory at Tonopah and Goldfield after the turn of the century.

Amusingly enough the phrase "greater than the Comstock" was to reappear as conversational currency in Nevada long years after the world had come to believe the last bonanzas in precious metals had been uncovered and the destinies of the West as a source of gold and silver had come to an end. Hailing the fantastic emergence of Las Vegas as the twentieth century gambling center of the known universe, a Reno banker was quoted in the *Las Vegas Sun* to the effect that Vegas' "spectacular growth and prosperity exceeds that of Virginia City's Comstock Lode during the 1870s."

"Could be, could be," muttered the still animate and still dangerous *Territorial Enterprise* from its perch on Sun Mountain. "Yet this 'greater than the Comstock' cry has about it a prophetic and not altogether reassuring ring. We could, for Las Vegas' sake, wish for some less fatal precedent. Throughout the latter nineteenth century a long succession of boom and bust bonanzas were hailed by interested parties as 'greater than the Comstock.' The Reese River diggings were to be greater than Virginia City; so was Bodie, so indeed were brief-lived Panamint, fraudulent Rawhide and dubious Treasure Hill, Bullfrog, Rhyolite, Greenwater and Silver Peak. Any diggings that came along was greater than the Comstock for a week at least, sometimes two. Wishing Las Vegas well, as do all Nevadans, we could wish also a more cheerful comparative. 'Greater than the Comstock' be words of doom."

Thus, nearly a century after the first promoter of some forgotten diggings gave birth to the phrase of its diminishment, Virginia City was still able, aloof and cynical, to smile on all its detractors. It had been in business longest of them all.

One of the expectations that went with being "greater than the Comstock" was the future community's very own railroad. Austin and Eureka did indeed achieve notable short lines in the best bonanza tradition. So did Tonopah, Goldfield, Bullfrog, Bodie, and Rhyolite, but the sound of the iron horse at Panamint was heard on paper only and Bodie's little Bodie & Benton never achieved actual connection with any other line and for its short lifetime remained a railroad essentially between nowhere and nowhere. The heavy Nevada winters, as depicted here, often slowed operations on the narrow gage Eureka & Palisade.

Life Was Cheapest Of All In Wicked Bodie

ITS WAY OF LIFE WAS WICKEDEST OF ALL

For nearly four decades the mining town of Bodie in California's Mono County hard by the Nevada line enjoyed the reputation of being the wickedest and most tumultuous city in the entire American West. Mark Twain's Western stories gave identity to "The Bad Man from Bodie." The *Sacramento Union*, a notable connoisseur of frontier commotions and repository of violent legend, early in the sixties reported to its readers that Bodie was an authentic "shooters' town, embracing the wildest, maddest scenes the West has ever known." When J. Ross Browne, probably the best of all early-day reporters of the West, visited Bodie for *Harper's* in 1867, the community's reputation for stabbings and powder-burning was already established and Bodie gloried in it. A decade later John Hayes Hammond commented that during his stay there shootings had averaged one an evening in Bodie with time out only for Sunday, and ten years after Hammond's time Wells Drury, who put up at the Windsor Hotel as a correspondent for *The Territorial Enterprise* up in Virginia City, found things unchanged. Even in the nineties the *Union*, which regarded Bodie as an almost personal property, was able to record murders, death in the mines and holdups of the Bodie-Aurora stage with gratifying frequency. In the seventies *The National Police Gazette* published this scene in the Parole Saloon with the caption: "'I've just carved off that ear; give me the drinks on it.'—An incident of barkeeping existence in Bodie, Nev." The lapse of assigning Bodie to Nevada instead of California was a routine error. All overt incidents of the era were assigned to Nevada by editorial convention.

J. Ross Browne on his visit to the diggings of Bodie and nearby Aurora made the sketch of Fogus's Mill (*top*), at which ores from the Tioga, Silver Bulwer, North Noonday and Red Cloud Consolidated mines were treated. Bodie's deep mines supported a populace of 15,000 amidst bedlamite tumults for more than thirty years while a total of $50,000,000 was recovered. An everyday scuffle (*center*) in Bodie's hundred-foot-wide main street usually ended with business for the town's most sumptuous hearse, shown at the bottom of the page. Such was Bodie's evil repute that when a miner left neighboring Aurora to seek employment there, his little daughter's prayer that night was, "Good-by God; we're going to Bodie." The *Bodie Free Press,* one of the town's three newspapers, acknowledged the quotation but questioned the punctuation. "Good! By God we're going to Bodie!" was the way the *Free Press* reported it.

## RETRIBUTION WAS SURE EVEN IN BODIE

Life in the shootingest town in the Old West was seldom dull. Tumult and lethal violence were on a twenty-four hour a day basis throughout the sixties, seventies and eighties. Bodie's most sensational horse-whipping, in a day when a buggy whip was considered more genteel for ladies than a revolver, was precipitated when Miss Florence Molinelli returned after school to her family hearthside with the tearful intelligence that one of the tough youths of the town had made her an indecent proposal on the way from classes. Armed with a stout horsewhip and with Dr. J. W. Van Zandt, a friend and the family physician, for reinforcement, Florence's mother set out to avenge the family honor. The head of the family was underground at the North Noonday and wouldn't be home for hours. Encountering the luckless youth, as the *Bodie Free Press* later chronicled, "near the scene of his detestable crime," which happened to be outside the doors of Wells Fargo, Mrs. Molinelli had at him with the whip. The malefactor fled screaming into the countinghouse pursued by avenging furies and was promptly banged over the head with a heavy double-entry ledger by Major Atlee, the manager. The *Free Press* reported him in no good case some hours later. A staff artist for the *Police Gazette* later drew the event at its climax with Dr. Van Zandt, in the gratifying role of champion of outraged virtue, looking on from under a curly-brimmed top hat of the prevailing mode.

In a single day in Bodie in the eighties, shown here as it appeared some years later, the *Bodie Standard* reported the funeral of George Watkins, who had made the mistake of killing a policeman, the shooting to death of John Hackwell, a miner, at the portals of the Windsor Hotel, the fatal shooting by John Rann of a man named Costello in Wagner's beer parlors and the robbery of the Belleville stage by two men who then went down the road a mile or two to Dalzell's Station and robbed another stage for good measure.

Tough and durable to the last, Bodie's day of doom didn't arrive until 1932. On that final morning James Cain, president of the Bank of Bodie and also its cashier and bookkeeper, hung his silk hat behind the teller's cage, opened the vault (*left*) and prepared to do business with depositors who would never enter his doors again. The Bank of Bodie had no business. It hadn't had for a quarter of a century, but Banker Cain still opened his books to accounts long since closed and prepared to do business with the ghosts of Bodie's yesterdays. When flames which destroyed the town swept down upon the Bank of Bodie, searing the neat paint on its false front and caving its windows with doomsday crashes, Banker Cain had just time to close the vault upon the records of depositors long dead. In a final gesture of communion with the spacious, the splendid, years, he closed the door as a last allegorical act in Bodie's long and furious melodrama. The masonry of the vault still stands, though the furniture is long gone, a monument to vanished times in the West that will not return.

There were those, inevitably, who said that Bodie's fiery doom was long overdue. The mines that once dotted the slopes of Silver, Middle and Last Chance hills, the Homer, Black Hawk, Champion, Oro, Bodie Tunnel and Boston Con, had long ago produced their last car of paying ore, its last bullion sent over the road to the long-closed Mint at Carson City. With hounds at their feet, or some with their feet on lions, its residents rest in the cemetery at the edge of town. There are those, too, who know that though the false fronts and the bars and bagnios are gone beyond recall, Bodie is secure forever in the legend of the West. It was wickedest of them all.

IN BODIE THE WICKED WERE LIKE A TROUBLED SEA—

The brisk interlude of bad feeling depicted above was regarded as an everyday occurrence in Peters & Aldredge's Saloon and Billiard Parlors just off Bodie's main street. J. Ross Browne drew the encounter at lower left for *Harper's* from his memories of Bodie. Groups of feuding miners frequently fought near-military engagements (*below right*) upon meeting, a circumstance which justified the district correspondent of *The Territorial Enterprise* in writing that "the smoke of battle hardly ever clears away altogether in Bodie."

BEDLAMITE BODIE WAS THE SUNDAY EDITOR'S DELIGHT

## —AND SALVATION WAS FAR FROM THEM

"Gospel truth on stony ground," was the caption of this picture in *The Illustrated Police News*. "Clergyman in Bodie City, Calif., finds an unpromising field for evangelical work."

Heroic was the consumption of strong waters in Bodie's Philadelphia Beer Parlor, "The Handsomest Saloon in Town and Patronized by All Classes," at the Bodie House, the Windsor and Peters & Eldrege's. Now and then teams of the more powerful drinkers were recruited from the nearby mining towns of Aurora, Belleville, Hawthorne and Candelaria to challenge the champion tosspots of Bodie, as shown in the contemporary drawing at the right. Ruin and dismay was their inevitable lot, and ignominious return to their constituencies in the boot of Wells Fargo's stages.

THE DISCOVERY.

"WHISKY GOES"

FREIGHT FOR THE DIGGINGS.

JUMPIN CLAIMS, IS YER?

THE MILL.

MAIN STREET.

THE PACK-MULES.

"JOHN"

SUNDAY AMUSEMENTS.

# THE SENTINAL WAS FILLED WITH COMMOTIONS

THE EXODUS TO WHITE PINE.

OFF FOR WHITE PINE.

PROSPECTING AT TREASURE HILL.

Located in the White Pine Mining District of central Nevada, the town of Eureka enjoyed as commotional a reputation as any of its bonanza contemporaries. The conventional activities of its miners were depicted in *Harper's* and are reproduced on the page opposite. Its unconventional ways of life achieved even greater notoriety in their time. When a reporter for the *Eureka Sentinel*, one of the most articulate of all pioneer newspapers, made disparaging remarks about the legs of a prominent citizen, her irate husband (*above*) shot and dangerously wounded the newspaperman in the town's main street before he could discharge his own weapon in self-defense. When the inevitable "Great Fire" swept Eureka in 1879, the staff of the *Sentinel*, swathed in wet blankets, were just able to get an extra on the street with news of the disaster before the roof fell in about their ears. Eureka, as is suggested in the sequence drawings to the right, was a typical boom-or-bust mining community of the West that, for a brief span, attracted prospectors from everywhere with the all-compelling report that it was "greater than the Comstock." It was not.

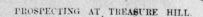

DISAPPOINTED WHITE PINERS HOMEWARD BOUND.

## The Finest Funeral

Eureka's most spectacular shooting was on the occasion (*above*) of the murder of Gus Botto, the town's leading gambler, by Jesse Bigelow, the cause being free tickets for the opera house. Wells Drury recalled his funeral as the finest ever seen in northern Nevada, high-lighted by the appearance of Botto's mistress, Hog-eyed Mary Irwin (*below*), attired in fashionable mourning, riding a Kentucky thoroughbred in the funeral procession. Hog-eyed Mary was soon afterward involved in the fatal stabbing of Bull-dog Kate Miller, a rival for the title of queen of Eureka's underworld.

A sad chapter in the history of the Nevada frontier was the fate of vast trains of camels, imported to carry salt from Austin to the Comstock, and eventually abandoned to die in the desert.

The Austin Flour Sack, auctioned repeatedly throughout Nevada to raise funds for the Sanitary Commission during the Civil War, gained fame for Raoul Gridley (*below*), originator of this high-pressure promotion device of early times.

Austin, Eureka's more tranquil neighbor and scene of the Reese River "excitements," was famous among other things for its narrow gage short line railroad, the Nevada Central (*above right*), which connected with the far-flung Central Pacific (*below*) 100 miles to the north at Battle Mountain. Near there on the C.P.'s main line was "The Maiden's Grave" (*above, center*), where railroad construction workers had erected a monument to mark the grave of a young girl buried there from one of the pioneer wagon trains which crossed Nevada long before the coming of the steamcars.

# PANAMINT,

# A SUBURB

# OF HELL

Throughout the sixties, as the incredible fortunes of the Comstock soared, Los Angeles hoped for a bonanza of its own which would make the Old Pueblo wealthy even as Virginia City's mines were making San Francisco a city of archmillionaires. In the midst of the depression of 1873, as banks, railroads and commercial houses failed throughout the land, Los Angeles fancied it had discovered its own golconda high in the ramparts of the Panamint Mountains, which formed the western rampart of Death Valley. Five miles up from the desert floor of Panamint Valley through an inaccessible gulch called Surprise Canyon, the discovery of rich surface outcroppings of silver brought prospectors streaming from all over the Western continent to Panamint City, here depicted by the distinguished artist, E. S. Hammack. Temple & Workman, the Los Angeles bankers, were interested; so was Trenor Park, patrician San Franciscan already many times a millionaire from the Pacific Mail Steamship Company of which he was president.

From Ballarat in Panamint Valley, Surprise Canyon leads for five miles, some of them seemingly straight up, to the site of Panamint City. So handy was this only access to traffic for stage robbers that Wells Fargo's all-powerful superintendent, John Valentine, flatly refused to establish a branch in Panamint City and characterized the place as "a suburb of Hell." Panamint gloried in the phrase.

Moving spirits in the promotion of Panamint were two bearded experts who had learned the technique of exploiting mining properties on the Comstock itself, Senator William Morris Stewart, and Senator John Percival Jones, both of Nevada. Both wearers of the toga were vastly influential in Washington and had the best connections in San Francisco. Both took keen delight in the exhilarations of mining gambles. The august names and peerless personal appearances of the pair put Panamint shares in the news and boomed them on the mining exchanges of the world.

Great wains such as these, which had seen service a decade previous freighting merchandise into the Comstock and were once more to be in requisition at Tonopah a quarter century in the future, were loaded with mahogany bars, crystal chandeliers, billiard tables, roulette wheels and the other properties of a progressive camp at Lone Pine, Independence and San Bernardino and headed for Panamint.

An early arrival in Panamint aboard one of Jack Lloyd's Lone Pine stages was Martha Camp, visible in the interior of Lloyd's Concord, accompanied by a troupe of hand-maidens. Martha was a madame well and favorably known in many parts of the West including Virginia City and her arrival furnished the booming diggings with almost every convenience. "All we need now is a shoemaker," said the *Panamint News* in reporting the event.

The most epic shooting of Panamint's brief but exciting emergence from obscurity took place shortly after the opening of Madame Camp's establishment in Maiden Lane. Edward Barstow, night watchman for the *Panamint News*, and W. N. McAllister, proprietor of the Snug Saloon, were suitors for the favors of one of the inmates. Barstow, intruding upon the trysting bower and discovering his rival in possession, was shot three times with the conventional self-cocking English bulldog revolver, and not even the combined *expertise* of Dr. Wells and Dr. Bicknell, hastily summoned from Dave Naegle's Oriental Saloon, could save him. Barstow's funeral in Sour Dough Canyon was the town's most elaborate to date and Bruce was adjudged in self-defense. A few weeks later their encounter was subject for a picture in the *Police Gazette*.

# Panamint's Night Life Was Cheery and Lethal

Panamint's boom was largely based on the stock-promoting activities of Nevada's peerless senators, Stewart and Jones, and the Los Angeles banking firm of Temple & Workman. Ten million shares of Panamint mining stocks found a ready market; a railroad, the Los Angeles & Independence, was chartered to connect it with civilization, and bad men, speculators, gamblers and hard characters by the score converged upon a town so tough that even Wells Fargo was afraid of it. Centers of Panamint's cheery night life were Fred Yager's Dexter Saloon and the Oriental of Dave Naegle, who was to achieve even greater subsequent celebrity by shooting California's notorious Judge David S. Terry in the capacity of bodyguard of Justice Field. The two recreational centers were prudently separated not only by the conventional wooden walls but by sheets of boilerplate to prevent stray slugs from breaking the costly glasses in each other's premises. Panamint's genius for chaos is suggested by the above scene at the Dexter when a group of gentlemen in wine differed over their cards. Seventy-five years after Panamint's great hour all that is left to mark its site is the tall stack (*below*) of its long silent stamp mill.

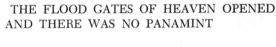

## THE FLOOD GATES OF HEAVEN OPENED AND THERE WAS NO PANAMINT

Panamint subscribed to all the conventions of the boom-or-bust diggings of the West except in the manner of its taking off, which was unique in the annals of such matters. Other mining towns perished by fire; Panamint, with no Noah in its population, was destroyed by flood. Five years after the first claimants of its ledges and outcroppings had ascended Surprise Canyon, a flash flood inundated the western ramparts of Death Valley. Warned by the stamp mill whistle of the presence of doom, most of the inhabitants escaped to higher ground, but one and all the establishments that made Panamint what it was were washed down-canyon and their remains next day were distributed over several square miles of Panamint Valley. Casualties included Naegle's Oriental, its neighboring Dexter Saloon, Harris & Rhine's general store, the bagnios of Maiden Lane and more than a hundred assorted structures of commerce, residence and convenience. Carried away on the waters were the Snug and Arcades saloons, Jack Lloyd's Stage office and every other structure of consequence. The mill, located on higher ground, escaped, but when the waters subsided there was no town left to support it. The only fatalities were among a family caught, as shown below, in Surprise Canyon, where a frontal wave twenty feet high drowned them all.

The deerstalker cap, single eyeglass and weeper whiskers were the hallmarks of the English dude in the American West. In Santa Fe town he got tossed in a blanket, at least in the imagination of the artist depicting the event for an Eastern periodical.

# XI

# *Dudes*

## The Dude or Tenderfoot Was a Classic Property of the Frontier, An Innocent Source of Merriment to the Waddies and Cow Pokes

IN SONG AND STORY and folklore and ultimately in the cinema, the softy from the East, the elegant Englishman or the Bostonian in a tall hat was the archetypal fall guy in the regions west of the Missouri. He was subject to hazing and rough treatment, but no actual harm, although in *The Texas Border* Robert J. Casey recounts that as it was pulling out of the El Paso depot an Easterner was lassoed from the observation platform of the *Sunset Limited* for wearing a monocle and quilted smoking jacket and was somewhat damaged in the process.

Dudes swarmed in the Far West from the very earliest times, like Francis Parkman, who doubted he would survive it and barely did. Valetudinarians and health seekers who might be classed as dudes since they were strictly alien to the time and place rode to Colorado in carriages over the Santa Fe Trail almost as soon as Zeb Pike had finished his survey of the region. They laid the groundwork for the movement that was to end up with Colorado Springs being known as "Little Lunnon" from the number of Englishmen who held out there.

The rest of Colorado absorbed a rich sprinkling of other Englishmen, largely younger sons sent out to engage in the cattle business. An Englishman was automatically a dude even if appropriately attired and speaking the idiom of the frontier. A vestigial trace of the English invasion of Colorado stands to this day in the once glittering Windsor Hotel in Denver's Larimer Street, named for a reigning queen and once populated with Oxford accents.

The most notable dudes of the early frontier were both British subjects on safari: Sir St. George Gore, whose mighty anabasis against the Rocky Mountains is depicted elsewhere in this brief chapter, and Sir William Drummond Stewart of Murthley Castle, Scotland, who between 1834 and 1843 made six overland trips from New Orleans to attend the annual rendezvous of the fur traders in the vicinity of Green River. Stewart traveled with a fabulous entourage not the least notable member of which was the artist Alfred Jacob Miller, whom he retained to paint the American West for the walls of Murthley Castle. On one of his trips Stewart presented Jim Bridger, the celebrated scout, long hunter and Indian fighter, with a suit of ancient Scottish body armor, which made Bridger into a dude of sorts, too.

As a variation on the theme of Old England the West once encountered a very exalted Russian dude in the person of the Grand Duke Alexis, who went out for buffalo along the North Platte with Buffalo Bill Cody as a guide and a full military escort of U.S. Cavalry.

Latter-day dudes of strictly American origins were Frederic Remington, who was destined to be the most celebrated painter of Western subjects in the record, and Theodore Roosevelt, who retained his memories and affection for the West even in the White House.

An almost forgotten dude, save in regional folklore, was the debonair Frenchman, the Marquis de Mores, who arrived in Little Missouri, Dakota Territory, in 1883, and created a neighboring township called Medora in honor of his wife, the Marquise. The De Mores set up housekeeping with a French chef, butler, footmen and housemaids, but four years later the great blizzard of 1887 wiped out the French outpost of empire and the De Mores returned to France forever. Today their memory is kept green by a statue of the Marquis cast in bronze in full cowboy attire gazing down the main street of Medora.

In time the dude became as much a property of the West as the gambler, the cattle rustler, the cow puncher, Wells Fargo agent and other stereotypes, and his translation to the immortality of pictorial representation is shown here in a few examples of this hilarious art form. Today in the New West, a dude is any Easterner or foreigner in temporary residence, in Nevada specifically for six weeks in search of a divorce. In the American lexicon "dude" is obsolete in sartorial connotations.

## CURLY WOLVES HOWLED ON SATURDAY NIGHT

Dudes and frontiersmen alike enjoyed themselves on festive occasions in the pioneer West. This lively scene depicts "A Dude and a Waitress" taking the prize for dancing "Bull Calves' Medley on the Grand Piano" at a Saturday night entertainment near Billings, Montana. A scene of less innocent merriment greets the eye below, where a group of waddies from below the Red River prove that everything is indeed up to date in Kansas City including their city attire and low way of life in one of Kaycee's night-life spots. The Texan on a toot as a rule found a high silk hat better adapted as a wine cooler than to be worn on the head, a stage which is obviously in the immediate offing here.

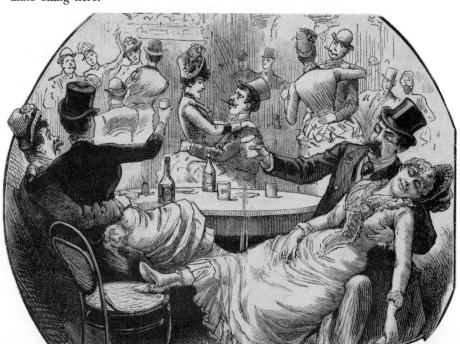

## DUDES CAME IN ALL SHAPES AND SIZES

At Wallace, Kansas, it was reliably reported that in the eighties the locals made a practice of shooting a dude's profile into the wall of any handy saloon if he were so incautious as to get down from the steamcars for an innocent glass of beer.

The *Police News* was delighted to report that during the seventies a young millionaire of Kansas City, Missouri, hired a cowboy champion to act as his bodyguard and plug-ugly in saloon brawls for the sum of $10,000 a year, payable in gold.

In the booming night life of Henry Yesler's Seattle a stranded road company in a music hall had no difficulty in raising the fare home when the troupe's pretty dancing girls made a personal touch among the open-handed men of Washington in the auditorium.

## THE OLD WEST HAD ITS OWN BRAND OF HOSPITALITY

"You will get off and have a parting drink," was the salutation to Eastern tourists attempting to ride through Miles City, Idaho, without patronizing the Cowboy's Rest, the Switch Key and Hurry Back, which constituted the major portion of the community's business. The natives didn't like to see a man leave their town in thirsty case.

"Having the old pontoons touched up by one of the royal family" is the caption to this scene of democratic indoctrination in the Little Missouri Valley when a member of visiting royalty on tour of the West was induced to black "Bad Man Bill Hennessey's" riding boots. The dim view which Westerners took of Englishmen was not infrequently changed by the remarkable drinking achievements of visitors from Albion like Oscar Wilde.

A group of Eastern tourists who descended from the stagecoach at Tucson, Arizona, in the late eighties found the nearest refreshment oasis in the hands of "two hustlers on a hurrah" who had taken possession and for three days allowed no one to pay for his drink. They enforced hospitality on all comers .at a pistol's point and almost everybody seemed to enjoy it.

## "NOBLEST ROAMER OF THEM ALL"

"The Noblest Roamer of Them All" is Forbes Parkhill's description of the eccentric Irish sportsman, Sir St. George Gore, who once made an offer to the United States to recruit a private army to exterminate the Indians and who mounted the greatest of all safaris in the West of the nineteenth century. Gore's hunting expedition cost more than $500,000 in the hard money of the fifties, lasted three years, covered 6,000 miles of the largely unexplored West and bagged 2,500 buffalo, 1,600 elk and 125 bears. Gore was the archetypal English sportsman of the period with Dundreary whiskers and monocle, and was given to deer-stalker caps and suits of exclamatory pattern. The Gore expedition moved grandly westward out of St. Louis in 1854 in twenty-one two-horse crimson *charettes* such as is shown in the above drawing, a personal carriage and a variety of express wagons, oxcarts and freighting wagons. Every night Gore's brass bed and iron washstand were set up in a green and white striped tent. The party's armament included seventy-five rifles, two wagon loads of fishing tackle under the direction of an expert trout fly tier, and fifteen shotguns. When he had shot enough after three years in Colorado and Wyoming, Gore offered to sell his entire equipment to the American Fur Company at Fort Union and when the factor for that august corporation tried to swindle him on the price he built a gigantic bonfire of all his wagons and boats and burned them in full sight of Fort Union. To this day Colorado's Gore Mountains, Gore Pass and Gore Canyon memorialize the valiant roaming and spendthrift ways of the eighth baronet of Manor Gore.

## VARIOUS ARTISTS REPORTED THE WEST VARIOUSLY

Nothing could have been more up the alley of *The National Police Gazette* than the cold-blooded murder in the restaurant of the Texas & Pacific Railroad at Marshall, Texas, of Benjamin C. Porter, a member of Maurice Barrymore's touring company playing *Diplomacy*. The encounter took place when a drunken Texas ruffian took exception to the presence of Northern "dudes" and Barrymore himself, father of John and Ethel, was wounded before the bravo could be disarmed.

No state in the West attracted to its mines and later its ranches more Englishmen than Colorado, where their clothes, manners and speech were a never-ending source of amazement to the red-neck pioneers. Late in the seventies *Harper's* sent W. A. Rogers and A. A. Hayes, an artist-and-writer team, to depict life in the Centennial State, and under the title "The Colonel Investigates the Humboldt (Mine)" Rogers sent back this caricature of English milords in tweeds, bowler hats and toppers going through a mine. For additional internal laughs, "The Colonel" is a likeness of Hayes while Rogers pictures himself standing by in a rat-catcher suit and leggings.

## JOHN L. TOOK A DIM VIEW OF SUCH FRIVOLITY

When John L. Sullivan was in New Orleans training for his fight with Jake Kilrain in 1889 he chanced to stop briefly in a Rampart Street saloon with the intention of obtaining a cooling glass of soda water. While there he witnessed a distressing episode in which a Texan who gave police his address as Fort Worth destroyed a number of bottles of fine liquor in a fit of pique, as shown in this contemporary drawing. Although obviously a dude, Sullivan himself was not molested or it would have gone hard with the fellow. The great John L. since earliest times in Roxbury, Massachusetts, had esteemed saloons as places to drink in and not shooting galleries and his disapproval of such irresponsible ways is evident in his profile.

### "YOUR SENTIMENTS DO NOT BECOME YOU, SIR!"

The "reverse dude" was noisily depicted in the *Police News* of 1890 when a brace of cow pokes from Omaha stepped from the cars of the Burlington Railroad in Chicago and started on a tour of the Canal Street saloons. Under a misapprehension that it was another joy joint they intruded on a temperance meeting and promptly expressed their sentiments in the matter with gunfire. Chicago was breezier then than it has ever been since.

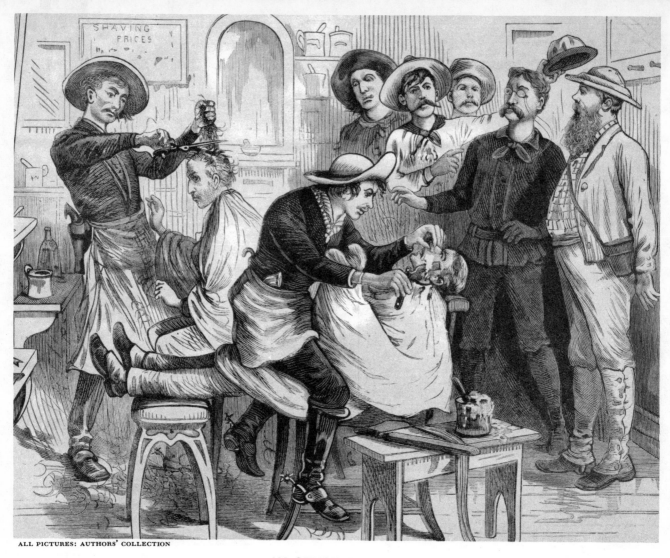

## AN OUNCE OF PREVENTION

The *Police News* was always happy to tell its readers of minor tumults and outrage in the Far West. Here it depicts "tenderfoot tourists in Montana being barbered by the boys so that they will not be scalped by hostile Indians."

In Eldorado County in California's Mother Lode, scene of Hangtown and much history, State Senator Maguire was found to be wearing striped socks and underdrawers and the constituency debated whether he was too dudish to hold office.

## NOT THE VICTIM TYPE

At Laramie, Wyoming, a stranger got down from the steamcars of the Union Pacific as they paused to wood up and the professional gamblers handy to the depot decided to take him. He turned out to be a professional from the Mississippi River steamers bound for rich pickings on the Comstock, and the whole thing was a terrible mistake. The stranger left with the house bank in his pocket and its personnel in shopworn shape on the floor.

### MAKE IT A BOILERMAKER, YOUR LORDSHIP!

An English milord and his body servant on the way through Arizona made the mistake of pausing at the Crystal Palace Saloon, a favored resort of Wyatt Earp, and asking for a pint of bitters to wet their whistles. Such temperance fare engaged the unfavorable attention of the regulars at the bar and they were "told to take straight whisky or we'll make a hole in your head and pour it in." In American periodical illustrations of the period no English milord but sported a curly bowler hat, Dundreary whiskers and a single eyeglass. The costume was *de rigeur* and any variation from it would have been esteemed a breach of trust on the part of the visiting foreigner.

## TRUE WESTERNERS WERE UNINHIBITED BY CITY WAYS

A generation that took pleasure in the legend of the dude among the he-men of the open spaces also de-lighted in the reverse of the medal which showed a cow poke in society or the Bad Man from Bodie in Delmonico's. In the above drawing a plainsman from the Kansas prairie dismays the patrons in the bar of Chicago's high-toned Sherman House with a playful pistol. Below at the left a "cowboy on a hurrah in St. Louis" emphasizes his democratic sentiments by ventilating the coat armor on the carriage of an aristo-crat, while at the right a cheerful customer from Cheyenne causes a distinct sensation in Boston while purchasing city finery on the premises of Hewins & Hollis, the Hub's old established firm of shirtmakers to the best people from Commonwealth Avenue.

IN LITTLE LONDON, TOO, THEY HAD HORSES IN THE SALOONS

### "AND ONE FOR MY HORSE"

The most notable dude in Colorado history was beyond all doubt Spencer Penrose, a younger brother of Pennsylvania's Senator Boise Penrose and many times a millionaire in Cripple Creek gold and Utah copper. Handsome and a dashing sportsman, Penrose's lasting monument is the fabled Broadmoor Hotel at Colorado Springs, one of the celebrated hostelries of the world. Legend maintains that Penrose built it because he was refused a drink in the rival Antlers Hotel (*below*) when he rode a horse into the bar. "I'll damn well build a hotel where they'll serve me and the horse, too," he vowed, and the artist here shows him making good his boast surrounded by admiring sports the day the Broadmoor opened. This is a part of the legend of the horse in the saloon under de luxe management.

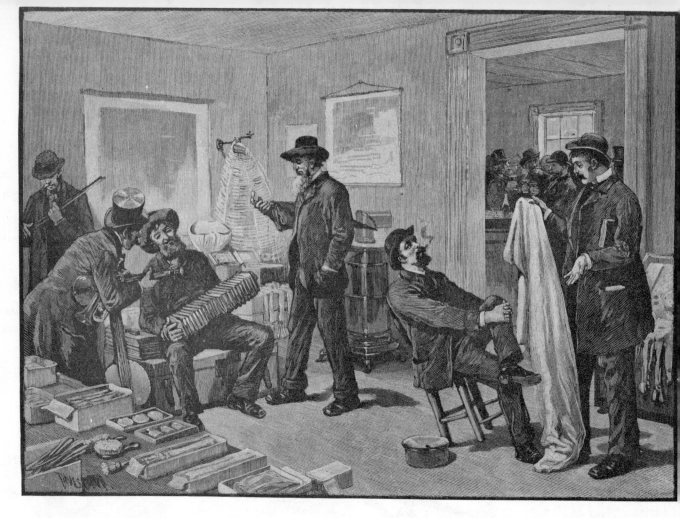

Theodore R. Davis, a Western artist who delighted in drummers and their folklore, drew "The Drummer's Room" somewhere along the line of the Kansas Pacific Railroad in the late sixties.

# XII

## *Drummers*

### After the Civil War a Generation of Travelling Salesmen Sold the Nation a Bill of Goods That Pointed to Distant Commercial Horizons

THE TRAVELING SALESMAN, or drummer as he was familiarly known in other years, was by no means an exclusive property of the West, but it was among the newly risen cities of the plains and aboard the vintage Pullmans that rolled smokily out of Chicago, St. Louis and Kansas City that he was at his most picturesque. An ambassador of empire on the move and prophet of the manifest Westward destiny of commerce, he came into being on the rising tide of industrial

306

manufacture in the East that followed the Civil War and, along with the political Colonel, the cowboy and the Shakespearean tragedian of the theatrical road, he soon became a stock character of the American scene.

He represented the great mail order houses which were coming into being along the Chicago River, or firearms manufacturers in Hartford and Bridgeport, saddlers in Kansas City, the designers of Levis in San Francisco or whisky distillers in Frankfort. When he represented steel mills marketing barbed wire, mining machinery or locomotive works outshopping steam engines in Taunton and Schenectady, he was big business.

The personality of the drummer became part of the American legend along with his anecdotes, persuasiveness and "twofer" cigars, so-called because they came "two fer a nickel." He was very apt to be a Jew and, inevitably, along with the frock-coated conductor, the merry news butcher and the brave engineer, he passed into the folklore of rail travel.

When the drummer left the main lines of continental railroads he fanned out into the cow towns of West Texas or mining centers of Nevada aboard the narrow gages and connecting coaches. He set up his pitch in sample rooms at the local hotel or took his catalogues and order book with him by buckboard to remote and lonely ranches.

The annual arrival on the distant ranges of Montana or Colorado of the representative of a big Kansas City merchandising firm was an event.

For the first day or two at the ranch house no matters of business were discussed. The drummer was treated as an honored guest, taken on quail shoots in the surrounding countryside, quiltings and Saturday night hoedowns at the county seat. Sometimes he introduced new and scandalous dance steps at these, such as the Rochester Wriggle and the Syracuse Shake. His status was ambassadorial and the neighbors gathered from miles around to hear his highly colored news and stories from the great world.

Finally the departmental heads of the ranch gathered on an appointed day, the ranch manager, clerk, bookkeeper, division foremen, cooks and hands. Requisitions were made out for the coming twelvemonth: saddles, ropes, branding irons, tinned foods, salt pork, coffee, working clothes, veterinary's supplies, ammunition and assorted hardware, all the artifacts not available to home manufacture in the simple economy of the frontier. A few weeks later the supplies arrived at the railhead or nearest connection and were freighted in by wagon train. The Western drummer's order book might show requisitions mounting into hundreds of thousands of dollars a month.

Somewhat removed from the homely destinies of drummers in whisky and patent washing machines were such tycoons among salesmen as John W. (Bet-a-Million) Gates and George Mortimer Pullman. Gates, whose florid way of life at Saratoga and Long Branch could be partly attributed to advertising and publicity, rolled grandly through the West in his private railroad car and sold millions of dollars' worth of barbed wire on the ranges of Texas and Oklahoma. Pullman, a supersalesman for the railroad car which bore his name, rode in a gaudy succession of his own private coaches, each more sumptuous than its predecessor, to demonstrate their wonderments and conveniences to a generation which was building railroads and riding them wherever steel could be laid.

## THE HAZARDS OF DRUMMERS
## WERE MANIFOLD

In the years following the Civil War when representatives of the great mercantile firms of the East were scouring the newly opened regions of the West for orders, their occupational hazards included train wreck, catastrophe to river steamers, highwaymen, the elements, primitive eating houses and fire. Hotels of wooden construction in an age innocent of any fire protection whatsoever burned with alarming frequency and, for some reason, almost always at night. Even great metropolitan hostelries were not immune to holocaust, as witness the terrible Windsor fire in New York, the burning of the Southern Hotel in St. Louis and the destruction of the St. Charles in New Orleans. Hotels in outland places burned like tinderboxes and were. A consensus in the matter disclosed that while a salesman caught in a burning hotel at night might abandon his frock coat, congress gaiters and even his gold watch and Albert chain, he almost invariably saved his most treasured of all belongings, his silk top hat. The drummer in this picture is doing just that in a fire identified as being in Leavenworth, Kansas. Below, Theodore R. Davis drew what is probably the first interior of a railroad club car ever to be sketched. He identified it as being on the Galveston & Houston Railroad and among its occupants are Northern drummers trying to establish friendly relations with hostile Secessionists still smarting from Appomattox with the toast, "Here's Jeff, fellows."

## THE SALESMAN LIVED A HAND-TO-MOUTH EXISTENCE

In the vast and as yet unpopulous regions of the West, the drummer was often obliged to abandon the steamcars in favor of the overland stage. Until late in the nineteenth century short lines and branches connecting the main lines with remote interiors were uncommon and the Concord coach went every-where the railroad did not. Occasionally salesmen were obliged to pack their sample cases into the wintry mountains of Colorado or New Mexico (*below left*) on muleback. They were always glad to get back to a station platform (*below right*) with its promise of Pullman comfort, limitless hot water, smiling porters and wonderful meals.

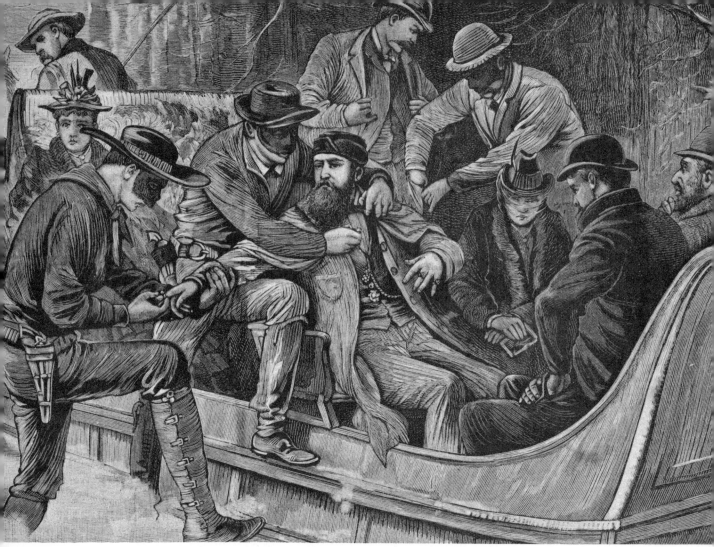

## MONTANA NEVER WAS ALTOGETHER LAW-ABIDING

Road agents near Missoula, Montana Territory, made a fine haul when they stopped a sleigh and took $18,000 in gems off the person of a drummer in Chicago gents' suits named "Diamond Ed" Huntley, evidently an early-day salesman with Diamond Jim Brady ideas of elegance.

While in Arizona, at an unnamed town on the Southern Pacific, ruffians forced a drummer in ladies' lingerie to part with his samples when they found he carried no stock other than these in his Gladstone. It was episodes like this that gave a city man pause and caused him to wonder if falling into the hands of Geronimo could be any worse.

HE DANCED FOR ALL HE WAS WORTH

### HIGH-HANDED DOINGS ON THE CARS

The *Police Gazette* kept its readers posted on all train robberies in the West and made the most of it, pictorially speaking, when a Burlington train was held up near Broken Bow, Nebraska, and a number of drummers made to contribute along with the other passengers. This sort of thing got the railroads a bad name.

A salesman in grain and feed arrived at the wrong time at Clayton's General Store near New Braunfels, Texas, and encountered there "the Wancho gang of train robbers" out for a good time between assaults upon the express cars of the Missouri-Kansas-Texas Railroad. They made him dance until he fell exhausted and laughed hideously as they made off with his watch and wallet.

Colorado highways in the seventies were a-crawl with brigands. *Leslie's* devoted a full page to this scene of banditry with the caption: "A Recent Robbery by Road Agents Near Leadville, Colo.—Searching a Commercial Traveler for Valuables."

## MONOCLES IN DURANGO REQUIRED BACKING UP!

From the pictures reproduced on this page, the reader might well imagine that of all the states and territories where the drummer of the Old West took his sample cases, Colorado was the most perilous. Perhaps it was. The scene below depicts one of the great moments in the history of Durango in the remote and desolate San Juan region when a nameless but immortal drummer, fresh descended from the narrow gage cars of the Rio Grande Railroad, made this splendid entry into the Nose Paint Saloon attired in a single eyeglass and top hat and carrying a Colt's equalizer to back them up. "His Style Was Dudish," said the impressed *Police Gazette*, "But He Had Nerve: 'Has Anybody Anything to Say About My Clothes?'"

## LIFE ABOARD THE STEAMCARS WAS SELDOM DULL

Few veteran drummers of the West's roaring seventies and eighties could boast they had never been in a train wreck. Many lost their lives in the cataclysmic crashes of the era and others were maimed for life, but the train in the ditch or through the open drawbridge were hazards of the occupation. Old-timers, schooled in the lore of travel, asked for sleeping space in the precise center of the middle car of the train, a vantage point from which either head-on or rear-end collisions might most likely be survived. This cornfield meet between two trains, each double-headed, of the Missouri-Kansas-Texas and the St. Louis, Kansas City & Northern took place near Orrick, Missouri, June 20, 1873. When not climbing out of the wreckage of Pullmans on such melancholy occasions, drummers aboard the cars were merry fellows (*below*) who ransacked their sample cases for props for an impromptu baseball game in the aisle.

## "EVERYTHING'S UP TO DATE IN KANSAS CITY"

Whatever privations the drummer might suffer when he departed from the main arteries of travel were compensated when he arrived in the great cities of the West: St. Louis, Kansas City or Denver. Here he encountered his friends and peers of the road in wonderfully ornate barrooms and famous restaurants, smoked two bit cigars and lied grandly about the orders he had taken. Here T. de Thulstrup has depicted the lobby of a Kansas City hotel in winter, where elegant women in evening dress and gentlemen in top hats mingle with men of the plains and ranchers with their overcoats worn fur-outside.

## WHERE NO GENTLE BREEZES BLOW— THE WESTERN WINTER

In the days before locomotives of 5,000 horse-power and rotary plows, drummers with territories in the Far West in winter often spent uncomfortable and enforced stops for days at a time aboard trains stalled in the snowdrifts of Idaho or Wyoming. The prudent salesman, in addition to a long, knotted rope to serve as fire escape in hotel fires, carried a quart bottle of Medford rum or the best bourbon in his carpet-bag against these emergencies. He could expect hardly greater luxury in the country hotels of the frontier in these primeval times. A contemporary drawing, reproduced at the right, depicted the sufferings of a pair of drummers caught in a Dakota blizzard: "Forty Degrees Below, Washing with Ice—Two Drummers Blizzard-bound at Childstown, Dakota, Without Fire or Water for a Week." Readers with memories long enough will recall that in the savage winter of 1951 the entire plains division of the Union Pacific was storm-bound for a similar period and passengers from transcontinental varnish trains sought shelter in bars and billiard rooms in Sidney, Green River and Rawlins for days at a time.

## IN AN AGE WHEN TYCOONS WERE ALSO DRUMMERS

In their time and generation the three well-upholstered gentlemen shown on this page would have been respectfully addressed as captains of industry rather than drummers, but they were nevertheless salesmen in very exalted brackets indeed. At the left above in a steeple-crowned top hat is the greatest extrovert of his age, James Buchanan ("Diamond Jim") Brady, whose Pressed Steel Car Company made the first all-steel freight cars to roll over the rails of the growing West. He also sold railroad tools worth millions, haunting tool sheds in top hat and morning coat with friendly foremen and presenting purchasing agents with a full list of their needs. Above, another great salesman of the frontier, George Mortimer Pullman, explains the excellence of pressed paper wheels on the trucks of his Pullman Palace Cars which revolutionized continental travel, and below another gaudy character, John W. ("Bet a Million") Gates holds aloft a grandchild at a demonstration of the strength of the barbed wire whose sales netted him many bettable millions and put an end to the old cattle ranges of the West forever. Each of them multimillionaires, these men represented the aggressive drive and force which carried a nation Westward through the agency of salesmanship on a scale hitherto undreamed of. As much as the long hunters, the cow pokes and the prospectors, they were pioneers in the Old West.

## "YOU GOT MY WIRE?"

When the overnight cars from St. Louis rolled into Kansas City or Fort Worth or Omaha the reception clerks at the recognized commercial hotels were fellows it was well to know. In towns where business was seasonal, sample rooms were at a premium and a five-dollar gold piece judiciously expended could do wonders. The commercial traveler didn't always live high on the hog, but with the coming of the Harvey Houses (*below*) with their crisp linen, pretty waitresses and incredibly fine food things in the Southwest were notably different. Wherever Fred Harvey opened a new restaurant, at Florence, Kansas, Dodge City, or La Junta, Colorado, there the drummers asked to be assigned. Harvey hired chefs away from the Palmer House in Chicago with the abandon most restaurateurs hired a bus boy, and the word got around among the drummers. Fast.

## A NEW ERA DAWNED WITH THE COMING OF FRED HARVEY

The arrival of Chinese immigrants imported to help build the Central Pacific Railroad at the San Francisco customs was drawn by Paul Frenzeny for *Harper's*.

# XIII

# *The Heathen Chinee*

## Chinese Labor Provided the West with a Source of Trouble, Persecution and Unrest for Three Decades

THE FIRST CHINESE in the West, two men and a woman, disembarked from the brig *Eagle* in San Francisco in the summer of 1848 and made tracks for the gold camps of the Mother Lode, where they disappeared almost instantly. They were, however, but the forerunners of a flood tide of Chinese to wash against the California coast, which raised the Celestial population of the state to 71,000 by 1870, more than half of whom were in San Francisco.

From the very beginning the Chinese brought trouble with them. The race prejudice of whites in California which had hitherto been directed against Mexicans and Indians was extended to include the yellow race, whose members soon found their properties in the diggings expropriated by white miners and in some

318

instances were murdered or run out of town. Barred from participating in mining bonanzas, the Chinese assumed the roles ever since associated with them in the public mind, as washhouse proprietors and restaurateurs.

Race riots directed against Chinese in San Francisco assumed the proportions of insurrections throughout the sixties and seventies. Their manners, habits, language, religion and personalities incited popular prejudice, but their greatest crime was economic: they would work harder for longer hours and less wages than any white man and for this their lives were made miserable for decades.

But if labor unions and incompetent whites generally disapproved the Chinese, there were corporations entirely willing to take advantage of their superior qualities of docility and frugal living. Even while its president, Leland Stanford, as Governor of California was denouncing the yellow menace, the Central Pacific Railroad was importing coolies by thousands to build its high lines over the wintry Sierra and across the Nevada deserts.

Political demagogues attributed all the ills of the day to cheap Chinese labor. Spellbinders and professional friends of the people demanded their deportation. Hoodlums, hooligans and labor unionists attacked, beat and occasionally murdered Chinamen of the most innocent and innocuous occupations. Chinese stores, laundries and dwellings were attacked, pillaged and burned. In 1877 race riots assumed such ferocity that the California National Guard was called out to patrol the streets of San Francisco and there was talk of reviving the Vigilantes of pioneer times. A volunteer organization known as the Pick Handle Brigade which was actually armed with rifles and revolvers augmented the forces of police and military to put down the rioting and order was gradually restored.

After the completion of the Pacific Railroad great numbers of Chinese found themselves stranded or remained by choice in the mining towns of Nevada, Utah and Wyoming, where they assumed the familiar occupations of porters, laundry-men and restaurant proprietors.

In Nevada full-grown Chinatowns appeared in Carson City, Virginia City and at Dayton and Candelaria where coolies briefly found employment in the building of the narrow gage Carson & Colorado Railroad through the southern deserts. But again the familiar pattern of abuse and persecution appeared. Labor unions protested against the Chinese willingness to labor long and hard for minimum wages, and in Carson City a full time boycott of all Chinese businessmen was inaugurated by the entire community. It promptly collapsed for economic reasons and until fairly recently Chinatowns still flourished in the Nevada capital and on the Comstock.

Further to the east, notably in Rock Springs, Wyoming, and in Denver, organized uprisings of hoodlums and worthless labor elements continued as late as the eighties with attendant indignities and occasional bloodshed, but with the enactment of the various exclusion acts and consequent abatement of the tide of immigration feeling subsided and the Chinese were largely absorbed into the economy of the community.

Feeling against Chinese and race riots continued sporadically, however, until after the turn of the century in such widely separated Rocky Mountain towns as Butte, Anaconda and Missoula in Montana and in Cripple Creek and Silverton in Colorado.

## SAN FRANCISCO BOUND

To build the Central Pacific over the High Sierra Charles Crocker first considered the possibility of Mexican labor, but the plan fell through and Crocker took a long look at his personal body servant, Ah Ling, who was a marvel of endurance and willingness. He decided to give the Chinese a try and as an experiment fifty were hired in Sacramento's flourishing Chinatown and taken to the end of track. Their extraordinary record for docility and faithful endurance at laying track impressed the railroaders tremendously and word was sent to China that 2,000 more laborers could find employment at once. The scene here depicted is aboard a trans-Pacific vessel crowded with immigrants bound for Colfax, Immigrant Gap and Blue Canyon.

## LOOKING FOR OPIUM

The well-known penchant for opium on the part of the arriving Chinese laborers caused immigration and customs officials to go over them with a fine comb when they arrived at San Francisco.

## WAITING FOR THE CARS

At Oakland Mole the coolies were transshipped directly from their vessels at the pier to the waiting cars, as shown above, and hurried up to the end of track in the Sierra foothills.

## TIPCART AND MULE

Passengers rolling swiftly across the Sierra today aboard the *City of San Francisco* or *San Francisco Overland* pass over this same fill in Blue Canyon photographed during its construction by Charlie Crocker's industrious and frugal Chinese. No earth-moving machinery other than mules and tipcarts was available and in many places cuts and fills were largely the product of carrying earth in baskets and in barrows.

## THE CHINESE THRIVED IN THE HIGH SIERRA

The Chinese labor at work on the Central Pacific relieved American workmen of pick and shovel work and released them for duty as powdermen, teamsters and foremen. At the end of the day the coolies boarded work trains back to their base camps or hitched a ride, as shown above. Everything possible was activated by gravity in the Sierra, as is shown below. Ties cut at high altitudes were shot down to the right of way in flumes. Note their marking as property of the Central Pacific. This sketch was made several years after the completion of the road through the Sierra by a member of the Leslie expedition, so that the ties shown were replacements and not the first to support the light iron of the continental railroad.

## THE HOODLUMS MADE LIFE MISERABLE FOR THE COOLIES

Rioting against the Chinese in San Francisco was started by the Hoodlums, a gang of youthful cut-throats, during the fifties and continued for nearly twenty years. Cutting off the queues of the Chinese and other forms of outrage were favored and in 1865 during a riot at the Rope Walk, as depicted here, several orientals were murdered.

## BURNING POWDER ON THE HEATHEN CHINEE

One of the weekly issues for 1865 of *The California Police Gazette*, no relative of the famed periodical of similar name in the East, carried this woodcut with the brief caption, "Summary Vengeance on a Mongolian Ravisher." There was no news account attached. The *Gazette* is now one of the rarest of all items of early Californiana, a few precious issues being preserved in the vaults of the Bancroft Library at Berkeley.

## DENVER SAW RIOTS

In 1880 anti-Chinese feeling reached its peak in the Cherry Creek Diggings and bands of white ruffians toured the Chinese section of Denver beating the inhabitants and looting their homes and places of business. One Chinese was saved by white friends who nailed him in a packing case and carried him through the mob. The only white man to defend the Chinese was a gambler and gunman of established local fame who defied the rioters with a gun in each hand, roaring "If you kill Wong, who in hell will do my laundry? Get out, you sons of bitches." Similar riots occurred throughout the Rocky Mountain regions, and in Montana all Celestials were finally expelled from the mines.

## TACOMA WAS CLEANSED

In Tacoma, Washington Territory, white vigilantes decreed that "the Chinese must go" and armed bands of settlers in primitive Tacoma enforced the ban, loading the Celestials onto wagons and bidding them set out for nobody knew where.

## EVERY HAND WAS TURNED AGAINST THE CHINESE

As in Tacoma (see page opposite), there were disturbances in Seattle, in which hastily sworn bands of white men had to preserve the peace with rifles. In the drawing at the right Seattle's oriental population was escorted under armed guard to the courthouse for protection while menaced by the mob. Below are shown the tumults in which a number of Chinese were killed at Rock Springs, Wyoming, a coal mining center on the Union Pacific. They had originally come in with the completion of the railroad, but their willingness to work for reduced wages made them intolerable to organized white labor in the lean year of 1885 when many native Americans were out of work in the West.

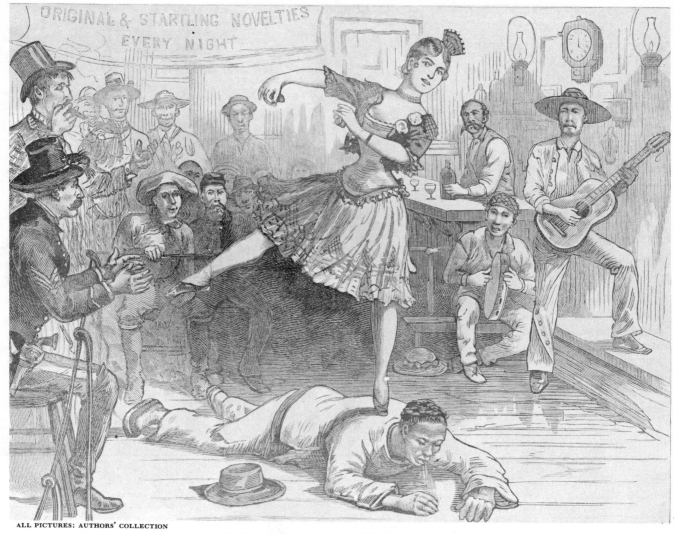

## THE SUPREMACY OF THE WHITE NORDIC WAS IMPLIED

in this spirited scene purporting to have taken place in Canyon City, Colorado, and recorded for posterity in the *Police News* with the caption: "The Greaser Has the Chinaman Under Foot—A Mexican Dancing Girl Scores a Hit With the Miners."

## ONE FOR THE ROAD

In Tombstone, Arizona, the cow pokes cut cards to determine to what points of the compass the local Chinese population should be dispersed, according to the *Police News,* with loud Christian shouts of "Start the heathen over the range." It was their evident intention that the heathen should not start on their journey in entire sobriety.

## THE *POLICE NEWS* WAS
## FOR THE WHITE RACE

As far removed from the plains and mountains of the West as Boston, where it had its headquarters, the *Police News* was as violently anti-Chinese, at least vicariously, as any know-nothing in the ranks of Western labor goons. It delighted in depicting the outrages against the Chinese everywhere in the West and regarded murder, torture and vandalism as something hilarious when it applied to orientals. The picture at the top of this page was entitled, "Whooping the Celestial Citizen Out of Washington Territory."

Elsewhere in the West, armed riders harassed the Chinese until they relinquished their property and got out of town. An anti-Celestial demonstration by waddies in Missoula, Montana, caught an innocent dude as it swept the town.

When cow pokes in Tucson tied a Chinaman to the back of a Texas steer and rode him out of town with Rebel yells, the *Police News* termed the victim "A Mongolian Mazeppa in Arizona." One of the purging committee, however, seems to have come to grief in the county ditch.

## VIOLENCE WAS THE LOT OF CHINESE IN THE OLD WEST

If they were not the victims of race prejudice and mob violence, the Chinese of the West were pillaged by Indians or outlaws. Near Laramie, Wyoming, as the railroad advanced under guard of Sherman's troopers, Chinese camp servants on the Union Pacific pay roll were set upon by thugs and tortured to reveal the whereabouts of their savings, as shown in the above drawing. They were also subject to intraracial violence, as is suggested by the below sketch of a mutually fatal encounter between two orientals in the Chinatown of Carson City, Nevada. After the completion of the Pacific Railroad, populous Chinatowns sprang up in Carson, Virginia City, Dayton, Candelaria and elsewhere throughout the desert reaches of the Silver State. Carson's Chinatown was celebrated until recent years for, among other things, possessing what was believed to be the only two-story outhouse privy in the West.

## SOUNDS OF STRIFE

J Ross Browne portrayed a quarrel between Nevada Indians and Chinamen in his "Washoe Revisited" under the title, "Digger Indians Collecting Taxes," and described the pandemonium that ensued as "absolutely gorgeous."

## "NOW IN THIS CORNER—"

The sporting element of Deming, New Mexico, organized this glove fight between one of Geronimo's braves and a local Chinese laundryman on which substantial side bets were wagered and which evidently aroused a good deal of enthusiasm for the manly art at the Bullwhacker's Rest. The outcome of the epic encounter was not recorded by the *Police News*. It is conceivable that such embattled episodes existed only in the imagination of Eastern editors, but they reflected the frontier as the world wanted it to be and in this role are actually a part of the mythology of the Old West.

## "PICK YOUR CARD"

Indians and Chinese alike were fair game to the three card monte throwers of the frontier if they ran shy of white suckers. Here a sharper from Cheyenne, a notable rendezvous of professional gamblers in the days following the advent of the Union Pacific, has set up his pitch at a "cross roads near Missoula, Mont." and is instructing the gullible in the fine art of being greenies.

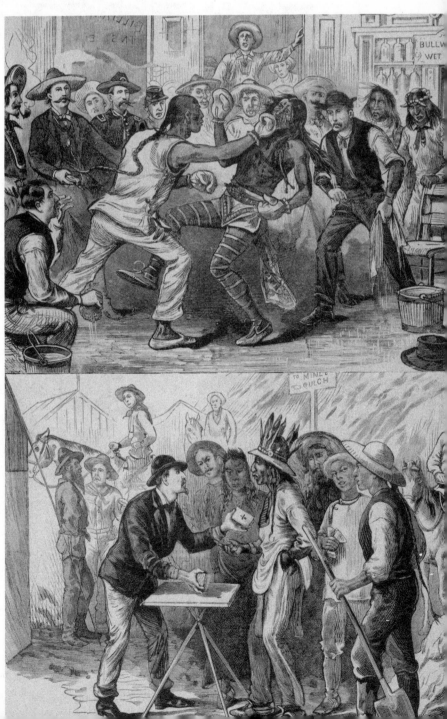

## COMPANY FOR DINNER

The utmost in social recognition that visiting Americans could hope for in San Francisco's Chinatown in an age before commercial tourism was an invitation to dinner with the heads of the Six Companies, overlords of the city's commercial and political destinies. Here Celestial merchants in flowing robes of ceremonial garb clinked glasses with nabobs in broadcloth and ledger-ruled trousers who had difficulty with chopsticks but agreed that the rice wine of the country laid right hold on a man after the first few cups washed down with Napa Valley claret and the best French champagne. The Six Companies lived high and entertained handsomely.

## "FIREMAN, SAVE MY CHILD!"

For many years the Chinese Hose Team was a celebrated unit of the fire department at Deadwood, Dakota Territory, and one of the show pieces of the Black Hills. The knee pants and golf hose were generally agreed to be picturesque in the extreme but there were those who wondered if straw hats were ideally suited to their wearers' occupation in times of crisis.

## GOOD OLD SUMMER DAYS

This scene in Grant Avenue in the late nineties is evocative of profound nostalgia for the San Francisco days when police wore high helmets, blue in winter, gray in summer, and dinner with six courses and a bottle of the best California claret was seventy-five cents at the Palace of Art Restaurant. The Chinese still clung to the picturesque blouse of tradition but the pigtails were gone and black Homburg hats had about them a flavor of the occident. When, no longer ago than 1950, the last faithful Chinese houseboy who had spent his entire lifetime in the service of a Nob Hill family died in his seventies, San Francisco newspapers were filled with wistfulness for the days that were gone and good times that would not come again by the Golden Gate.

## THE FRONT WAS RESPECTABLE

The first resident embassy of the Chinese Imperial Government arrived in San Francisco in 1878 and was received aboard the steamer *City of Tokio* by representatives of the powerful Six Companies with ceremonial dignity. In the sketch below Paul Frenzeny shows the Chinese Merchants Exchange in San Francisco where all Chinese business in the city had its seat. Despite such a façade of respectability, the real power in San Francisco's Chinese population were the underground tongs. The tongs were overlords of the vast commerce in opium, gambling, prostitution and the import of slave women which for many years was a considerable industry among the orientals. Each of the twenty or more tongs which flourished in the sixties and continued in power until the turn of the century maintained a standing army of *boo how doy* or fighting men who became known as hatchet men from their favorite weapon. Tong wars raged in San Francisco's underworld on a lurid scale with assassinations, feuding and sometime open battle involving half a hundred participants.

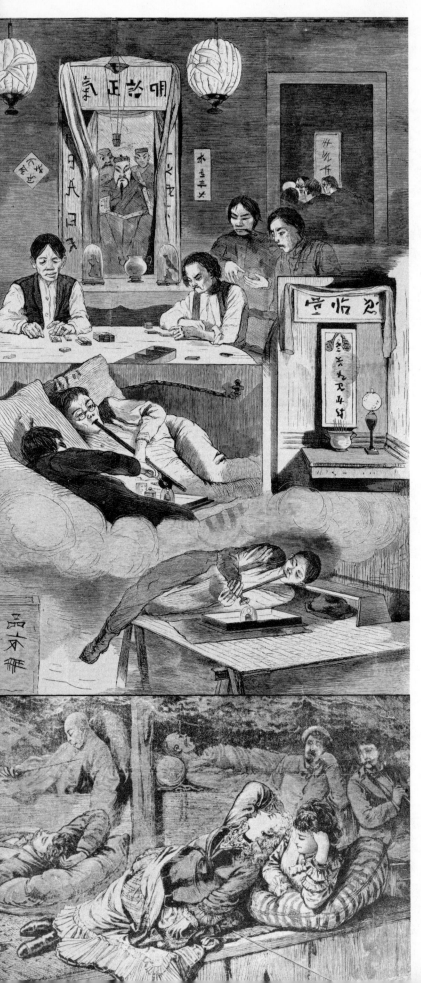

## A SNIFF OF POPPY

Always interested in novel vice and of an enquiring turn of mind where wickedness was concerned, nothing about the Chinese population of the West so fascinated nineteenth century Americans as their "opium dens." In large cities such as San Francisco tours were organized for out-of-town visitors to explore in escorted safety the subterranean resorts of Hop Alley, and in such remote desert fastnesses as Sodaville, Nevada, a favorite Saturday night excursion of the rough miners from nearby Belleville was to come to town to take a sociable pipe with the Chinese inhabitants. Bohemians found opium esthetically exciting, more hardened characters found it a pleasant variation on a steady diet of forty rod whisky. Even so respected and respectable a periodical of 1874 as *Harper's* catered to public interest in the matter with this drawing by Winslow Homer. No tour of San Francisco's tenderloin was complete without at least a tentative sniff at the poppy.

## SOMETIMES LILLY COIT—

Excursions into the realm of narcotics were by no means confined in the San Francisco seventies to the town's lower element, of which there was a plenty. Society from Nob Hill found it exciting to explore the vices of Chinatown and Lilly Hitchcock Coit, the celebrated society fire buff and scandal of conservative circles in which she moved, sometimes adventured into the sin dens of North Beach with a friend or two.

## OUT OF THIS WORLD

Always atmosphere-conscious, white patrons of the poppy seemed to prefer the more depraved and dubious resorts of Chinatown and San Francisco's Barbary Coast. Depravity was more delightful if the surroundings, too, were debased. In 1885 a special committee of the Board of Supervisors found twenty-six opium dens in Chinatown where whites were welcomed, with a total of 320 bunks for patrons. A few of the places where tourists were taken by the members of the Chinatown Guides Association were spurious, the mere fakements of immorality. By far the greater number were the McCoy with opium as the main attraction and Chinese prostitutes and gambling as side shows for the nocturnal thrill seeker.

### FRENZENY WAS HERE

The Chinese population of San Francisco far preferred resorts where opium might be smoked in attractive surroundings without overtones of tourist-bait. Many of their opium dens were luxuriously furnished with evidences of oriental good taste and large retinues of servants. Occasionally, as in the scene below, virtue would briefly raise its head and the police would raid premises in arrears with their graft payments, but in nine cases out of ten business as usual was under way the next morning. The Chinese opium smokers at the right were drawn by Paul Frenzeny, to whom no aspect of the life of the West was ever dull.

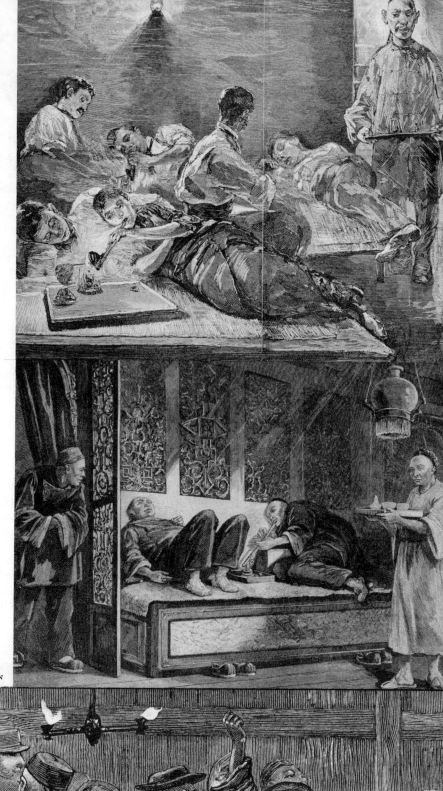

Not all the annals of San Francisco's Chinatown were bloody or sensational. Some were sentimental and heartwarming as when, during a reunion of the veterans of the Grand Army of the Republic in the eighties, "the moon-faced damsels of Grant Avenue gave the old vets a rousing reception," as the *Police News* put it.

## EVERYBODY'S CHINATOWN

In a generation before the song, "My Chinatown," San Francisco's district of oriental shops, resorts and residences was one of the show places of America. Far more picturesque and less sordid than New York's Pell and Mott Streets, it still had enough suggestions of gang warfare and secret sins to fascinate respectable visitors from Dubuque, Rahway and Cincinnati.

## BACKSTAGE INTERLUDE

Wealthy Easterners and residents of Nob Hill alike fell under the spell of the highly symbolic ritual of the Chinese theater in San Francisco and the *Police Gazette* for August 12, 1882, played the more romantic aspect of the cult of Chinese admiration with this drawing of stage-door Johnnies pressing their suit upon a popular actress after the performance in a Chinatown playhouse.

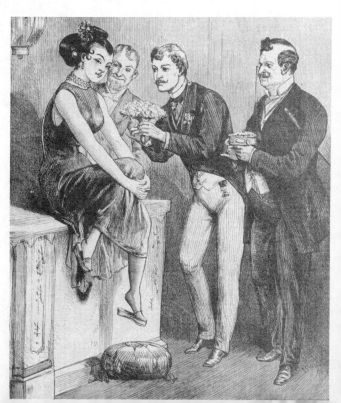

## LIFE AND DEATH WERE NOISY IN SAN FRANCISCO'S CHINATOWN

Firecrackers were the inevitable accompaniment of all Chinese festivals in the years of the West, including weddings, births and the celebration of Chinese New Years. And the Chinese took their departure for far places with ceremonial elegance and ritual, as is suggested by the Paul Frenzeny drawing of a Chinese funeral being solemnized at Lone Mountain Cemetery.

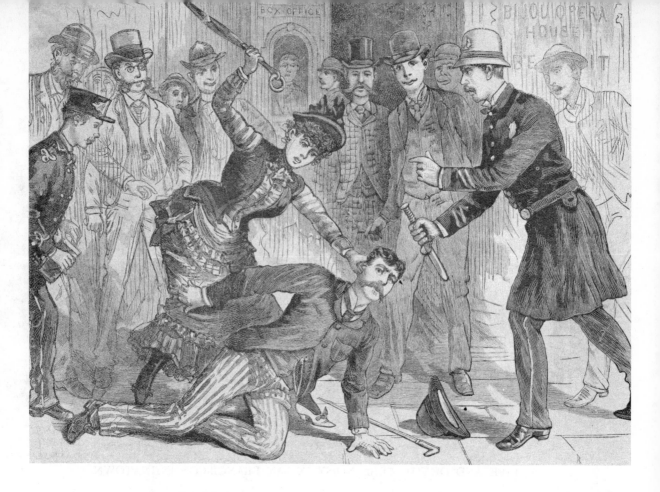

Upon one occasion still recalled with awe by Denver, Mattie Silks, Queen of the Tenderloin, severely beat her solid man, Corteze Thompson, in front of an admiring crowd of spectators in Larimer Street when she discovered that Thompson had been a customer at the love store of her hated rival, Madame Jennie Rogers. What was worse, he had begged the money for the excursion from Mattie.

# XIV

# *Pistol-Packing Madames*

## In Its Time and Place the .41 Caliber Derringer Carried in a Reticule Was as Deadly and Universal as the Colt's Navy

THE RECORD of the pistol-packing mamas of the old West is not altogether easy of access. Folklore endowed a good many belles and madames with gun-toting proclivities who, in proper fact, never so much as secreted a dainty derringer in their reticules, let alone swaggered through Tombstone, Alder Gulch or Bismarck with six pounds of Colt's patent hardware strapped to their waists.

Folklore to the contrary, too, it is doubtful if many women even among those known to affect firearms as ornaments were particularly competent to use them. There is no record that Calamity Jane Canary was able to hit the proverbial barn door even when she was sober, which was infrequently. Mattie Silks, who engaged in the only known formal duel between women in the bad old days in Denver, although she constantly carried a gun in a special pocket of her dress, was so bad a shot that she hilariously hit her lover in the neck when he was standing among the bystanders. Or was it accident? At this remove, one wonders.

Another swashbuckling woman who affected the identical "De Medici look" made fashionable by Mattie Silks, and proved to be an only slightly better marksman, was Verona Baldwin, who claimed to be a cousin of Lucky Baldwin and, cousin or not, lodged a .38-caliber slug in the millionaire's arm as he was leaving his private dining room in Baldwin's Hotel in San Francisco. Verona Baldwin claimed to be a member of the ruling family of Britain and was tall and stately and complemented her De Medici costume with a jeweled tiara and a shoulder-high staff with which she made dignified entrances to Denver's parlor houses in the nineties. She ran one herself, for that matter.

"I shot Mr. Baldwin even though we are related by blood," she said haughtily to the police after the scuffle in San Francisco. "He ruined me in body and mind."

Still another pistol-packing mama of the old frontier was Belle Starr, a Dodge City resident in the spacious days of the cattle drives from Texas to the loading pens at Dodge, where Wyatt Earp was at the moment marshal. Belle, an accomplished horsewoman whose vocabulary achieved fame even in a time and place of great freedom of expression, had a personal interest in other people's livestock which kept her in constant hot water. When her husband, an Indian named "Blue Duck," lost $2,000 in a brace game of faro in Dodge, Belle, according to Forbes Parkhill, held up the gambling establishment and recovered not only the original $2,000 but interest to the tune of $5,000 more, "proving that a pair of six-shooters beats a pair of sixes." On another occasion Belle was leading a band of horse thieves near Fort Smith, Oklahoma Territory, when her hat blew off. Nobody did anything about it and Belle pulled her Colt. "Get down there and pick it up, you ignorant bastard," she screamed at Blue Duck. "Haven't you got any manners when you're with ladies?"

Of all the women in the gun-fighting record, Mattie Silks is incomparably the most enchanting figure. Queen of the Denver tenderloin and the most celebrated bagnio proprietor of her time, Mattie, although nobody would call her exactly a connoisseur, had an eye for effect. Somewhere she had encountered a reproduction of Rubens' portrait of Marie de Medici dressed in a cloak with a long velvet train worn over a tight-fitting bodice with a high turned-up collar encircling the back of her neck. Mattie's working attire as the Queen City's ranking madame was a precise duplicate of the outfit, with two special pockets in the skirt, one for gold coins, for Mattie never acknowledged the existence of paper currency, and one for a pearl-handled six-shooter of modest dimensions.

Mattie's duel with Katie Fulton was for the favors of a Denver tout named Cort Thompson and took place on the banks of the Platte at a resort known as the Olympic Gardens, owned by the Denver Brewery. Every no-gooder in Denver's half-world was on hand for the event: shills and shell men, monte throwers, cappers, roulette dealers, con artists, pimps, bartenders and sports promoters. The disputants were armed with revolvers and marched to their appointed positions as thousands cheered. The guns blazed simultaneously and there was an outraged scream from the spectators' gallery. Cort Thompson had caught Mattie's slug just behind the ear. The next day *The Rocky Mountain News* ran a stern editorial calling on the Denver Brewery to prevent the repetition of such sporting events on its premises.

Then there was Big Nose Kate Fisher, inamorata of the elusive Doc Holliday, himself a handy man with a sawed-off shotgun, as he was able to demonstrate when he and the Earp Brothers shot the tripes out of the Clanton gang at the O.K. corral in Tombstone.

Kate and Holliday met up in Fort Griffin, Texas, where, shortly after this star-crossed event, Holiday had occasion to cut a man's throat during a friendly game of poker. While Holliday was being held in a hotel room a mob gathered and there was talk of lynching. With admirable presence of mind Big Nose Kate set fire to an adjacent livery stable and when the mob, its interest momentarily deflected from murder, went to put out the flames, she entered the hotel, covered the sheriff with a brace of Colt's Navy revolvers produced from under her skirt, and together with her rescued lover galloped off to Dodge City, a hundred miles away. "We laughed about it all the way," Doc afterwards told Wyatt Earp.

Some of the lady gamblers of the Old West carried firearms, others did not, relying on frontier chivalry in the event of unpleasantness. Poker Alice Ivers, perhaps the most nerveless professional dealer ever seen on the frontier, went armed, and on occasion used her long-barrel Colt's to persuade reluctant customers. There is no record that she ever discharged a revolver.

Eleanor Dumont, better known from Colorado City to Lead as "Minnie the Gambler," never was known to have a weapon in her hand although she dealt stud for Charlie Utter up and down the West until the close of her professional career in El Paso in 1904. Madame Moustache, who operated faro games all the way from San Francisco to Bannack and Eureka, was reputed to be a dead shot with hand arms, and the record contains at least one instance of her having ventilated a brace of tough customers.

All of which brings us to Rose Dunn, the "Rose of the Cimarron," who married "Bitter Creek" George Newcomb, one of the last great outlaws, and herself participated in the Battle of Ingalls, certainly the last of the great pitched battles between the forces of law and those of horseback crime which marked the passing of the old frontier.

One night in the spring of 1893 Bill Doolin and his mobsters robbed the Cimarron National Bank of Cimarron, Kansas, and then went into hiding in a veritable robber's roost at Ingalls, a tiny township and crossroads near Stillwater, Oklahoma. Rose was being wooed by Doolin's lieutenant, Bitter Creek, later described by E. D. Nix, the Oklahoma marshal, as a "fine specimen of manhood," when five months later the Federal marshals converged on Ingalls. The lay had been well spied out and they came in force, twelve or fifteen strong, with arms and ammunition for a protracted campaign.

The Battle of Ingalls, the greater part of which was waged on the premises of Mrs. Pierce's Hotel, was one of the epic encounters of the even then vanishing Old West. Perhaps its peer among pitched engagements can be found in the Battle of Northfield, where an embattled citizenry forever put the James boys of action. Its approximation can be found in a score of the better film spectacles of our own time. Driven by a hurricane of lead from Pierce's Saloon, Doolin, Bitter Creek, Bob

A noted gunslinger amongst the ranks of the lady gamblers of the West was Madame Moustache, who followed the hell-on-wheels towns that accompanied the Union Pacific's end of track across the continent. Eureka, Nevada, Bannack, San Francisco, Corinne, Utah, Nevada City and Grass Valley all knew the quick hand of Madame Moustache. Finally she drifted to Bodie, wickedest city of all, where two imprudent footpads, as shown here, attempted to hold her up on the way home one night with the house bank. She killed one and the other escaped. In 1879, still at Bodie, Madame Moustache's luck ran out with unalterable finality. She killed herself with prussic acid.

Dalton, Tulsa Jack Blake and Dynamite Dick Clifton sought refuge in the stable, firing as they crouched and ran with rifles and revolvers. With them, loading and firing and laden with cartridge belts and spare Colts, went the Rose of the Cimarron, archetype of all the pistol-packing heroines of romance, cinema and stage. When Bitter Creek went down with a bullet in his leg in the inn yard and his gun flew out of reach, Rose braved a storm of lead to rush a fresh gun and cartridge belt to him. Chivalrously, the marshals held their fire.

When twilight fell, Rose, Doolin and Bitter Creek, the latter badly wounded, made their escape. For weeks while Rose nursed her lover the three of them took it on the lam, hiding out deep in the Creek Nation. For nearly four years they lived in bandit hideaways while Bitter Creek and the remnants of Doolin's gang made occasional ineffectual safaris against remote banks or ranches. The marshals were closing in and one winter afternoon Bitter Creek and a companion were ambushed and shot from the saddle.

The Rose of the Cimarron married a blacksmith and faded from public sight, but not before she had entered the valhalla of legend as one of the authentic pistol-packing women of the riding years.

While Madame Moustache and Minnie the Gambler and other famed female dealers of the West almost invariably carried as heavy a personal armament as their masculine counterparts, Poker Alice Ivers never secreted so much as a Remington derringer in her reticule. Neither would she ever draw a card on Sunday. Born in England to an accent of refinement and with the manners and appearance of a gentlewoman, Poker Alice had nerves that contemporaries described as being fashioned of vanadium and played for stakes which Professor H. E. Briggs in his *Frontiers of the Northwest* reported as "formidable." She cut a wide financial swath in Leadville, Central City and later at Creede, having achieved the friendship and admiration en route of such frontier notables as Jim Masterson, Bat's brother, and Bill Tilghman, last of the shooting marshals. A white-haired old lady of seventy-five in Deadwood, where she spent her last years, Poker Alice was fond of recalling games played for stupendous stakes aboard the cars of the Union Pacific with Eastern men of money as they rolled through Cheyenne and on to Corinne and Promontory, as shown in the accompanying picture. In 1930, the last of all the great names in frontier gambling, Alice was faced with an operation where the chances were slim. According to James Horan, her last words to the doctors were: "It's all in the draw." Poker Alice, lost. Here she is depicted in better times skinning a "greeny" aboard the cars of the Burlington, a granger road that was one of her favorites because of the rustic origins of its passengers.

At Red Ledge, Idaho, according to a contemporary account, a miner named John Gump and his wife Effie had a falling out and settled the matter in the time-honored style of the frontier. "It's him or me and we don't want any help," ran the caption to a pictorial account of the ensuing duel in the *Police News*. The outcome was not stated.

In Omaha in the seventies the mistress of a respected married merchant, William Osler, opened fire on her lover's wife as they emerged from church services of a Sunday morning, to the great scandal of the community. The providential presence of an officer of the law prevented serious consequences.

In Arkansas Hattie Benton and her sister Hester made a good thing selling whisky "by the bottle or by the keg," as their sign proclaimed from a houseboat. The whisky, a local product, lacked the sanction of Federal stamp and a brisk gun battle ensued when the detested revenuers arrived on the scene. Hattie and Hester were lodged in jail and their stock confiscated.

Stage robbery (*above*) assumed new aspects of heroics in Colorado in 1878 when highwaymen attempted to stop the coach en route from Denver City to Idaho Springs. The passengers included a German baroness "wearing no less than $10,000 in matched diamonds and other precious stones" and two other females, both residents of Colorado. Undaunted by the masked miscreant, the ladies returned his fire with revolvers providentially handy and the robbery was foiled.

*The National Police Gazette* for January 28, 1882, failed to name the time and place in which the lady editor (*left*) warded off the ruffian who would have had at her with a bull whip, but that it actually transpired can scarcely be doubted. Wives of frontier editors temporarily incapacitated by minor shootings or other occupational mischance often took their husbands' places on the copy desk.

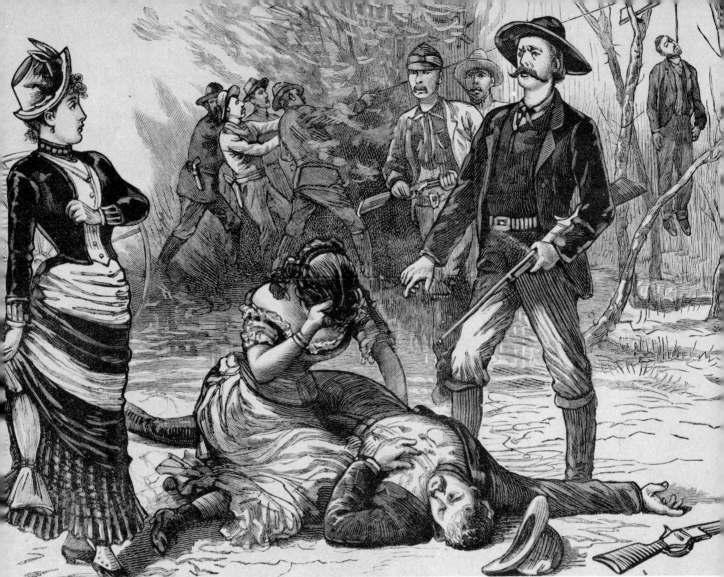

## A LENGTH OF ROPE ENDED A GREAT AFFAIR OF THE HEART

One of the accomplished and celebrated female gamblers of the westering frontier was "Madame Vestal," known to Denver in the seventies as the "Goddess of Chance" and whose staff of Fancy Dans kept case at the faro table or tipped the keno goose in a huge tent in Blake Street. When gold was discovered in the Black Hills, Denver was overnight depopulated of boomers and Madame Vestal joined the rush in a horse-drawn boudoir on wheels which was a forerunner of the modern trailer. Her solid man was Archie McLaughlin, who had been one of Quantrill's raiders in Bleeding Kansas and who found it hard to abandon ways of violence. Taken in stage robbery at Little Cottonwood Creek five miles out of Fort Laramie, McLaughlin and a companion were lynched by Vigilantes, as shown in this contemporary drawing, and the light of her life went out for Madame Vestal. She drifted to Las Vegas, Tombstone and finally San Francisco, where she died whisky-sodden and despised on Skid Road. It was only after her death that Madame Vestal, queen of the monte throwers, was identified as Belle Siddons, the famed Civil War spy whose services to the Confederacy had made her the most trusted agent of Generals Nathan Forrest and Sterling Price.

## MINNIE WAS NO FOOL

"Count the cards," cried Minnie the Gambler when she detected a cold deck introduced into a big-time game in Cheyenne by George Devol, a former Mississippi River boat sharper. An impartial arbiter discovered sixty-two cards in Devol's hand and the entire sum in play was awarded forthwith to Minnie the Gambler. Upon another occasion Devol was beaten up in Cheyenne by Wild Bill Hickok, who added insult to injury by walking out with all the money on the premises.

The informal lynching (*left*) of what the original caption in the *Police News* described as a "dastard miscreant" took place aboard the cars of the Texas & Pacific Railroad in 1891 and served as a warning to mashers not to molest the women of the Lone Star State in transit.

# A
# Bad End
# for
# Bad
# Cattle
# Kate

A grim episode of the Wyoming cattle wars which blazed throughout the eighties and nineties was the necktie party involving Cattle Kate Watson and her lover James Averill, who occupied small neighboring ranches on the Sweetwater River. Averill set Kate up as the proprietor of a bagnio frequented by the cow hands of the region and, as she was agreeable to accepting cattle in payment for her girls, Kate soon had a not inconsiderable herd, most of them stolen from big outfits in the vicinity. Kate's periodic shipment of beef critters over the Colorado & Southern to Denver soon attracted the unfavorable attention of the stockmen's association while Averill's attacks upon the large landholders in the columns of the *Caspar Weekly Mail* did him no good socially either. One day a group of determined men armed with Winchesters called on Kate and Jim and hanged them by the edge of the river. The lynching of a woman was something new to the West and the affair achieved national notoriety. The death of one witness and the disappearance of others obstructed any court action against the lynchers, many of whom were well known to have participated in the violence, and the case drifted into folklore, but not before bitter feeling had been engendered which was to contribute eventually to the "invasion" of Johnson County and the threat of actual civil war. The name of Cattle Kate Watson is still, according to James D. Horan, not mentioned in polite conversation in Wyoming.

Noted for her fashionable attire and fiery temper, Paris-born Eleanor Dumont, better known as Minnie the Gambler, was the sweetheart of Colorado Charlie Utter, also a celebrated dandy who astonished the frontier by bathing daily. Once in Colorado City Minnie took a cowhide whip to a gambler (*above*) whom she detected slipping a cold deck into a game with Utter. Below is depicted the attempt of a bandit queen of the eighties to hold up a Burlington train in deepest Iowa.

## PROPERTIES OF THE OLD WEST

One of the most amazing of all the pistol-toting madames of the old frontier was Mattie Silks, for many years undisputed queen of the Denver underworld. Mattie (*right*) ran a brothel of notorious dimensions and was celebrated for her De Medici gown into which were built two special pockets, one for gold and the other for a dainty revolver with which she enforced the respect and admiration due to a member of royalty in the wild night life of Larimer Street. Mattie's fancy man, a sprinter named Cort Thompson, spent most of her income for her. Not all the shady ladies of the old West carried firearms, as is evidenced by the scene below depicting two Cyprians who fought it out with bowie knives before the horrified gaze of a passer-by in Venice, Missouri. The elegantly engrossed pocket revolver also shown below sold in the eighties for only $3.00 complete with 100 rim-fire cartridges. Its makers, the Western Gun Works of Chicago, urged, "Everyone Should Go Armed," and from the record it would appear that a large part of the population in the time and place did just that. "Self-defense," said Western smugly, "is the first law of nature."

WESTERN COLLECTION

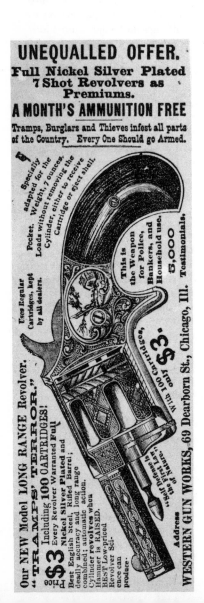

**UNEQUALLED OFFER.**
**Full Nickel Silver Plated 7 Shot Revolvers as Premiums.**
**A MONTH'S AMMUNITION FREE**
Tramps, Burglars and Thieves infest all parts of the Country. Every One Should go Armed.

Our NEW Model LONG RANGE Revolver. "TRAMPS' TERROR." Price $3 Including 100 CARTRIDGES! Every Revolver Warranted Full Nickel Silver Plated and Best English Steel, Rifled Barrel; deadly accuracy and long range combined; automatic action. Cylinder revolves when Hammer is RAISED. BEST Low-priced Revolver Science can produce.

Specially adapted for the Pocket. Weight, 7 ounces. Loads without removing the Cylinder, either to receive Cartridge or eject shell.

Uses Regular Cartridges, kept by all dealers.

This is the Weapon for Police, Bankers, and Household use.

5,000 Testimonials.

"Self Defense is the First Law of Nature."

With 100 Cartridges, only $3.

Address WESTERN GUN WORKS, 69 Dearborn St., Chicago, Ill.

## "PART OF THE OVERHEAD"

One of the Black Hills pioneers who eventually achieved the repository of folklore was Calamity Jane Canary, a boozy and disreputable hanger-on in border deadfalls from Billings and Cheyenne south to the Rio Grande, whom one of the chroniclers of her checkered career characterized as "part of the overhead" of the saloons she haunted. The consort of teamsters, bullwhackers and other hardened personnel of the staging stations and army posts, the Calamity wore men's clothing, swore men's oaths and became a property of Beadle's Pocket Library (*above*) in her lifetime. She claimed to have been a Pony Express rider carrying the government mails between Custer and Deadwood and after Chief Joseph's defeat of the Seventh Cavalry she tended the wounded as they were returned to Miles City. She also claimed to have been the wife of Wild Bill Hickok, near whom she was eventually buried at Mt. Moriah Cemetery in Deadwood. Almost everyone in the West knew Calamity Jane well and unfavorably although the record showed her to be something of a rough diamond in aiding the needy and destitute. She spent her latter years telling tall tales of the old days in Confederate Gulch, Lander and Livingston for anyone who would listen and was glad to pose in festive attitudes, as depicted above, for the primitive cameras of the age. Claiming friendship with most of the great of her era, she practiced a sort of primordial self-publicization and ended as a museum piece which gave her curators some trouble to classify. At one time she faced the footlights, shooting out property mirrors and telling audiences about life in Gilt Edge, Montana, and Deer Lodge, but her intemperate way of life caused her to miss cues and ad lib with bullwhacker's language and she soon lost the one legitimate employment of her life.

# Calamity

# Jane

Never one to assume a virtue if she had it not, Calamity Jane used to boast that she once was thrown out of a bagnio in Bozeman, Montana, "for being a low influence on the inmates." On another occasion (*above*), when she briefly maintained an address at a Tucson brothel, she repelled the advances of some customers who happened to be Mexican "greasers" with gunfire, thus establishing the white supremacy of American womanhood. At Fort Pierre, Dakota Territory, she caused a sensation (*below*) when she appeared in the role of Calamity Jane, the Girl Hawkshaw "on horseback and in man's clothing looking for cattle thieves." This role may have given rise to her billing by Kohl & Middleton as "The Terror of Evildoers in the Black Hills." That she was a terror everyone including Jane herself was ready to admit.

# Spelled

# Trouble

# Everywhere

In the eyes of history, Brigham Young, President of the Church of Latter-day Saints in All the World, was the incarnation of Mormonism.

# XV

## *Deseret*

### The Mormon Exodus from Nauvoo to Deseret, the Land of the Honey Bee, Was an Epic That Added a New Dimension to Western Legend

ROM THE TIME when in the deadly winter of 1846 they first set foot in Lee County, Iowa, a dozen miles above Keokuk on the Mississippi littoral as the first perilous stage in the journey to the far country of Deseret, as yet unnamed, unlocated and unidentified, the Mormons were a part of the West. They were also American refugees, fleeing American soil and homes before a mob of American terrorists. "She was persecuted to her death in a land of liberty," a Mormon youth was to write when he buried his mother later in the year on the Great Plains. Other groups of specialized people were to come Westward with a certain degree of cohesion of objective; all of them but the Mormons were drawn to the West. The Mormons were goaded.

Yet the flight of the Church of Jesus Christ of Latter-day Saints from Nauvoo, "The Beautiful Place," the holy city on the Illinois side of the river, was not without certain provocations. "We are a peculiar people," Mormons have said of themselves since the inception of the church. "From the beginning," wrote Bernard De Voto, "they had the complete smugness of a people on whom a monopoly of truth and virtue was conferred by Almighty God . . . further certified by God's assurance that they would dominate the whole world almost at once." In a frontier community predominantly Methodist and therefore intolerant, the revelations, semi-Masonic rituals, weird inspirations to hysteria, not to mention the polygamy of the Mormons, were direct incitement to explicit harassment. And most of all there was what Mr. De Voto has termed "a stream of associative communism." Mormon property and Mormon labor were held in common in the framework of the church. The Mormons were shifty in trade, as acquisitive as Jews and as cohesive as only religiosocial fanatics could be. Illinois had reason to distrust them.

Inevitably mob violence flared. Governor Lillburn Boggs, a Lucifer in the lexicon of Mormonism to this day, loosed the Missouri militia against Mormons in Carroll County. Night riders burned Mormon homes and farmsteads, expropriating their cattle and furnishings, and a long list of guerrilla outrages were attributed to Mormons and Gentiles indiscriminately. When the prophet Joseph Smith, in open and foolhardy defiance of all prudence, tore asunder the veil that had thinly shrouded Mormon polygamy and advocated plural wives for everyone, the Illinois mob simply made an end of Smith by murdering him.

Smith's murder was probably the salvation of the Latter-day Saints, for it cleared the path to leadership of a farsighted and completely resolute leader in the person of Brigham Young. Young knew that the day of Exodus was at hand, the going down out of Egypt assured. Total extinction loomed if the Saints remained, possible salvation lay across the Great Plains at some as yet undetermined far land. Brigham Young gave the word and the Mormons commenced to strike their tents.

Throughout the years that saw the rising tide of conflict between Mormon and Gentile in Illinois, Mormonism was part of the history of revealed religion in the United States and of the Middle West, but from the time the Saints loaded their families, corn mills, wrought iron plows and muzzle-loading rifles on the Mississippi ferries in the flight from Nauvoo, they were a property of Western legend.

The Saints were ill-advised in their Westward progress; they set out across the prairies a full sixty days before a Mountain Man would have considered the trip. Rain, sleet and snow retarded their teams and the grass of the plains was not yet green for forage for the cattle. The "divine handcarts" which were pushed by some for lack of mules or oxen broke down and there was nothing to repair them with.

The Mormon Exodus to Utah is as great an epic of movement as any in the record. When in July of 1847 Brigham Young looked down on Great Salt Lake and spoke the classic line, "This is the place," his words were as enduring as those of the soldiers of Zenophon at the end of the "Anabasis," "The sea, the sea," or the line in the journal of William Clark on seeing the Pacific at the Mouth of the Columbia, "Ocian in view! O! The Joy!"

## EPIC WAS THE SAINTS' PROGRESS ACROSS IOWA

The first 400 miles across the prairies of Iowa saw a steady stream of Mormon handcarts, ox teams, mules, horses and footmen for eight long months. The first arrivals at Council Bluffs came in June, the last in November. Those who arrived last made the best time from Nauvoo, as is suggested by the progress of the team and outriders shown below. By midsummer the prairie was dry, the grass tall and the weather clement. Those who came over the trail in summer passed many new-made graves of Saints who had perished there the previous winter.

## "AND SHOULD WE DIE
## BEFORE OUR JOURNEY'S THROUGH,
## "HAPPY DAY, ALL IS WELL!"

Later Mormon immigrant trains heading for Utah might travel with numerous wagons, oxen and cattle, as shown in a photograph taken at Coaldale in the sixties, but the first refugees from Nauvoo to cross the Great Plains in the winter of 1846 set out with fewer wheeled vehicles and most of those barrows known as "divine handcarts" (*left*). As the dreaded winter storms roared down from the Canadian border many of the handcarts became unmanageable in the drifts and their owners perished where they fell between the wheels. During the first great Exodus the Mormons took five months to cover the four hundred miles from the Iowa border to Council Bluffs on the Missouri River, a distance now covered by streamliners of the Burlington and North Western in seven hours. Six hundred victims of exposure to the elements, disease and hunger were buried at the First Winter Camp. "It is a time of deep affliction and sore lamentation for this people," wrote the Elder John Lee, who twenty years later was to be executed for his role in the Mountain Meadows Massacre. Mormon graves made a highway all the way to the Wasatch Mountains.

In July 1847, while the greater part of the Mormon immigrants were still on the trail behind, Brigham Young looked over the valley of the Great Salt Lake and saw the promised land. Legend holds that it was here he uttered the historic words: "This is the place!"

## MORMONS WERE EVER THRIFTY FOLK

The thrift, prudence and responsibility of the Mormons early impressed themselves on all travelers who visited Salt Lake. In the middle fifties a British reporter appraised as part of the character of the Saints "a spirit of energy that cannot be equalled in any city of any size . . . not a tippling house, not a gaming house, not a house of ill-fame," and he attended a ball where the good manners, fashion and gentility of the guests compared favorably with those in older and better established cities along the Atlantic. Perhaps the visitor was deceived in minor details. Mormons had long produced a beverage of certified potency known throughout the West as "valley tan," and prostitution held little charm in a community where multiple wives was the rule. But all agreed that the agricultural civilization decreed by President Young seemed more secure than the precarious social orders built on precious metals in Nevada and California a few hundred miles to the west. In the drawing above newly arrived immigrants and converts to the Mormon faith await transportation at Salt Lake to take them to homes and farms in the Utah countryside. At the right Mormons are shown paying tithes to the Church in the form of produce due to a scarcity of money while an elder in chin whiskers patterned after those of President Young looks on.

BRIGHAM YOUNG THOUGHT WOMEN BELONGED IN THE HOME

In 1859 when he passed through Salt Lake on the way to California, Horace Greeley interviewed Brigham Young in the presence of Heber Kimball and other dignitaries of the Saints. The most notable quotation from the Mormon President when the interview appeared in the *New York Tribune* concerned women in business and public affairs. "If I did not consider myself competent to contract a certain business without my wife's or any woman's counsel for it," said Young, "I think I ought to let that business alone." Young's stock soared all over the nation as a result of the sentiment.

Ten years after the Mormons had been dying in the snowdrifts of the Great Plains an artist for *Harper's Weekly* discovered this congenial social scene at a ball at Salt Lake. The Saints had always been fond of dancing.

The two sketches on this page, "Brigham Young's Wives at the Great Mormon Tabernacle, Utah," and "Mormons at the Communion Table," are unhesitatingly ascribed to the artists Frenzeny and Tavernier although they are unsigned. They appeared in *Harper's Weekly* in 1874 at a time when the Mormons were very much in the public eye.

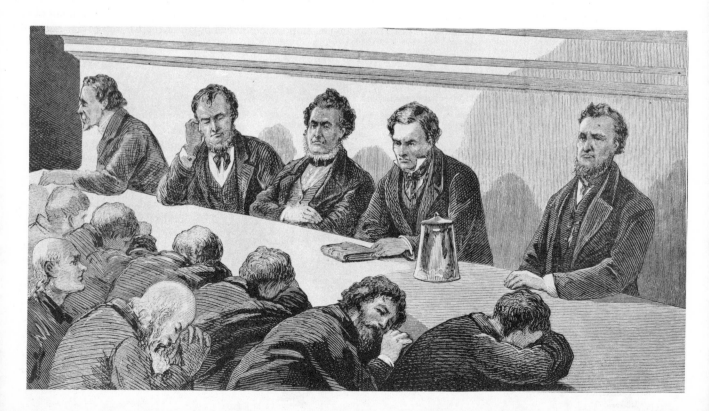

# A Voice for The Saints and The Honey Bee

A HAND PRESS AND SHIRTTAIL OF TYPE CAME IN COVERED WAGONS

One of the first concerns of President Young upon the establishment of Deseret—a word from The Book of Mormon meaning "honey bee"—was for a newspaper. The press and type for *The Deseret News* came across the plains in a wagon train, as shown above, and its first issue appeared while there was still sagebrush growing in the streets of Salt Lake City. It wasn't the first newspaper in the Far West, because four years earlier, in 1846, the *Californian* had been printed at Monterey, but it survived to be the oldest newspaper in the West in point of continuous publication and continuity of purpose and ownership as the official organ of the Church of the Latter-day Saints.

For a time *The Deseret News* was issued from a combined publication office and the mint in which the Saints' gold coinage was laboriously rolled by hand and was known as "Bullock's Money Mill." Later, however, it moved into a print shop in equally Mormon premises, the colony's Tithing Store, shown at the left where the compositors had more room to swing a type stick.

The original Ramage hand press from which, with the practical assistance of President Young himself, the first copy of *The Deseret News* was run (*above*) was "a little larger than a clothes wringer" and its maximum output under the most favorable conditions was two sheets a minute. The first copy of "The Voice of the West" is shown below.

The first copy of the Saints' newspaper was pulled in the presence of Brigham Young and Thomas Bullock, the mint master, on the afternoon of June 14, 1850, from type whose proof had been read by Willard Richards, its first editor. It contained a six-months-old news item concerning one of San Francisco's recurrent destructions by fire and a more recent account—it dated from February—of a Senate debate in Washington. The paper's prospectus, an overture to public acceptance dear to the heart of pioneer newspapermen everywhere in the Old West, advised "Travellers and Emigrants" that it would print their names, time of arrival and departure, for two bits and that subscriptions were available at $2.50 for six months *"invariably in advance."* In a short time *The Deseret News* was to be joined by the heroic company of such notable newspapers in the West as *The Alta California* in San Francisco, *The Weekly Oregonian*, *The Territorial Enterprise* in Virginia City, Nevada, *The Madisonian* in Virginia City, Montana, and *The Tombstone Epitaph*. Less rakishly secular than any of these by reason of its associations, the *News* was, as it still is, the most readable church-owned newspaper in the world.

---

**BY W. RICHARDS.   G. S. L. CITY, DESERET, JUNE 15, 1850.   VOL. I. -- NO. 1.**

LAT. 40° 45' 44"   LON. 111° 26' 34"

### PROSPECTUS.

### DESERET NEWS.

Motto—"Truth and Liberty."

We propose to publish a small weekly sheet, as large as our local circumstances will permit, to be called *"Deseret News,"* designed originally to record the passing events of our State, and in connexion, refer to the arts and sciences, embracing general education, medicine, law, divinity, domestic and political economy, and every thing that may fall under our observation, which may tend to promote the best interest, welfare, pleasure and amusement of our fellow citizens.

We hold ourselves responsible to the highest Court of truth for our intentions, and the highest Court of equity for our execution. When we speak, we shall speak freely, without regard to men or party, and when, like other men, we err, let him who has his eyes open, correct us in meekness, and he shall receive a disciple's reward.

We shall ever take pleasure in communicating foreign news as we have opportunity; in receiving communications from our friends, at home and abroad; and solicit ornaments for the *"News"* from our poets and poetesses.

The first number may be expected as early in June as subscriptions will warrant—waiting the action of 300 subscribers.

Terms, 6 months, $2,50; *invariably in advance.*

Single copy, 15 cents.

Advertising, $1,50 per square lines, and 50 each succeeding insertion.   $1 for half square, or 8 lines.

TRAVELLERS AND EMIGRANTS, 25 cents per copy, with the insertion of their names, place of residence, time of arrival and leaving.

Companies of 20, and upwards, entered at once, 20 cents each.

A paper that is worth printing, is worth preserving; if worth preserving, it is worth binding; for this purpose we issue in pamphlet form; and if every subscriber shall preserve each copy of the "News," and bind it at the close of the volume, their children's children may read the doings of their fathers, which otherwise might have been forgotten; ages to come.

### U. S. SENATE.

"Sketch of debate," in the Senate, for Feb. 6, 8, 12, inclusive, 1850, on the Right of Petition; represent Messrs. Seward, Hale & Chase as chief speakers. Mr. Mangum presented the proceedings of a meeting at Wilmington, N. C., denouncing the fanaticism of the North, threatening a dissolution of the Union, in a certain contingency, &c.—Laid on the table. Several petitions were presented by Mr. Hale, from various sections, "for promotion of the abolition of slavery; improving the condition of the free people of color; to prevent the increase of slavery by the non-admission of new States into the Union; for abolishing slavery in the District of Columbia; to prevent the introduction of slavery in the Territories: to prevent internal slave trade between the States; and respectfully ask Congress to propose, without delay, some plan for the immediate and peaceful dissolution of the American Union."

The Germantown ladies address Congress as "Dear Friends," and after an appropriate prayer, "we bid you an affectionate farewell." Many joined the above gentlemen in debate, which was generally warm, criminative and recriminative; somewhat dramatic, with some symptoms of the tragic. Query; If the people, the whole

people, want the Union peacefully dissolved, why not dissolve it? Why ask Congress to do a thing they have no power to do? Congress did not make the Union; the Union made Congress, and the people made the Union; consequently, on the principles of federal republicanism, the same power that makes must unmake, if unmade at all; and if the Union is ever peacefully dissolved, it will be by the sovereign people who alone possess the rightful power of dissolution within themselves, and not in their Senators or Representatives; and we hope we shall never again hear of any portion of the American people petitioning Congress to do what it has no power to do, even if it had the disposition. Let our Union remain forever, peacefully!

### TERRIBLE FIRE IN SAN FRANCISCO.

An appalling and destructive fire occurred on the 24th of December, which threatened for a time to reduce the famous city of San Francisco to a heap of smoking ruins. The fire broke out in Dennison's Exchange, and in two hours, nearly a million of dollars worth of property was destroyed. The Parker House was among the buildings burned. All the buildings, except the Delmonico Hotel, on Portsmouth square, and all on Washington street, commencing at the "Eldorado," and running to Montgomery street, were burned. The Parker House, U. S. Restaurat, Exchange, Eldorado, Merchant's Exchange, Car House, Central House, Washington Arcade, Pollard & Cos. Auction Room, Guerschard & Van Buren's Establishment, and many more valuable buildings were burned, or blown up, to stop the progress of the fire.

## MASSACRE AT
## MOUNTAIN MEADOWS

Seldom mentioned in the Mormon record and a closed chapter to discussion with Gentiles for many years was the massacre at Mountain Meadows, Utah, in 1857 of a party of Gentile immigrants on the way to California and the laying of the blame for the atrocity at the door of Utah Indians. The Mormon state at the time of the occurrence was in a condition of extreme hysteria and the events leading up to the massacre are so involved that its bibliography alone occupied ten full pages of fine print in Juanita Brooks's *The Mountain Meadows Massacre*. Certain it is that the Mormon Elder John D. Lee who was twenty years later to be held accountable for the slaying of the wagon train obeyed to the letter his orders of Brigham Young to "waylay our enemies, attack them from ambush, stampede their animals, take their supply trains . . . to waste away our enemies." It was many years before the truth about Mountain Meadows began to be noised abroad, so firmly closed were the lips of all members of the Church of Jesus Christ of Latter-day Saints about the matter.

## THE WHEEL OF RETRIBUTION
## COMES FULL CIRCLE

Twenty years later retribution caught up with John Lee. Nephi Johnson, an Indian interpreter, turned states evidence against him. Federal justice now obtained in Utah and Lee became a hunted man. Seized by United States marshals, he was brought to trial at Beaver, Utah, and eventually sentenced to death for his crime. At the right Lee is pictured as he awaited execution at Beaver State Penitentiary; below, his execution by a firing squad hidden in a covered wagon at Mountain Meadows itself. The scene of the massacre had been selected for the execution of justice with a nice sense of drama, and it was widely believed at the time that Brigham Young had been assured that the sacrifice of Lee would hasten Utah's admission to the Union.

A feature of Lee's execution was the presence to record its details of an official photographer who was instructed to give each of the doomed man's three wives a print of the picture he took as Lee sat on his coffin awaiting the firing squad. "Center on my heart, boys," he cried when the time had come. "Don't mangle my body," and he fell backward "without a cry or any twitching of the limbs."

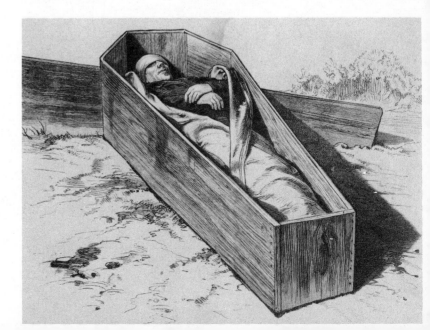

# Hypocritical Virtue Sniffed Audibly at Plural Marriage

Nothing about the Mormons unless it was their community of property in the framework of the church so outraged the sensibilities of an incurably pious generation as their practice of plural marriage. The opportunities for scandalized virtue were too numerous to be missed by magazine editors, many of whose private lives, like those of Frank Leslie and Theodore Tilton, were subsequently to be proved farragos of adultery and promiscuity, and the moist-eyed sentimentality of the two illustrations on this page, each of them entitled "The New Wife" and each of which appeared at different times in *Leslie's,* are typical of the editorialization of the time. A later generation would have found them either hilarious or clinically emetic.

## LESLIE'S ACTED THE ROLE OF A REFORMING WHORE

This cartoon conceived in a spirit of pursed-lips sanctimony appeared in *Frank Leslie's Illustrated Newspaper* in 1882 with the caption, "Woman's Bondage in Utah." Although the periodical was by now under new management, its founding genius, Frank Leslie, had been exposed only a few years previous by the Virginia City *Territorial Enterprise* as a libertine of gaudy dimensions and his wife as an opportunistic prostitute. Readers who recalled the background of *Leslie's* found provocation to coarse laughter in its highly moral indignation about the Mormons.

## MOUNTAIN MEADOWS ENCORE?

The distinguished cartoonist Thomas Nast, who had a low boiling point about almost everything, drew this picture for *Harper's* in 1882 with a caption which promised, "When the springtime comes, gentle Indian, much guns, much ammunition, much whiskey, much kill pale-face." The speaker was identified as "Polygamous Barbarian." Utah's jealous neighbors in New Mexico were busy spreading rumors, later proved altogether fictitious, that the Mormons were cementing an alliance with the Indians for a general massacre of the entire Southwest. Memories of the Mountain Meadows Massacre of 1857 lent the project a certain spurious plausibility in the Eastern imagination.

# As The Rails Converged On Promontory

The entire nation was sensible of dramatic tension as the rails of the Union and Central Pacific railroads converged from the East and West upon Promontory Point in Northern Utah close to the tip of Great Salt Lake for their rendezvous with Manifest Destiny. Above, a photograph taken near Elko, Nevada, shows the Central Pacific's construction gangs paralleling the line of the Overland Telegraph as they lay the rail. The sketch below by A. R. Waud shows the Irish tracklayers of the Union Pacific mingling with "Charlie Crocker's Pets," the Chinese coolies of the Central Pacific, during the last mile of construction. Ironically, although the rails met in Utah, Brigham Young would have nothing to do with the final ceremonies. He was vexed because the railroad had not been located to pass through Salt Lake City and was busy building his own connecting railroad, the Utah Central.

## THE EYES OF ALL THE WORLD WERE ON UTAH THAT DAY

From the West behind the Central Pacific's *Jupiter* came President Leland Stanford's private train filled with California dignitaries (*above*) and on May 10, 1869, the world learned that the rails had been joined and the American frontier was a thing of the past. The artist's sketch shown below depicts the Rev. Dr. Todd of Massachusetts invoking a blessing on the enterprise, a scene as frequently duplicated or paralleled in Western art as any save possibly the Custer Massacre.

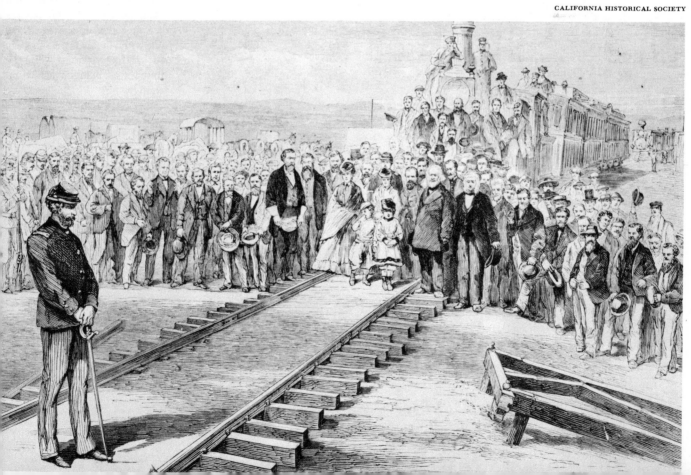

Col. Charles Savage of Salt Lake took the most celebrated and widely reproduced photograph in the history of the West as the engines *Jupiter* and *119* touched pilots at Promontory in 1869.

## FINALE!

A. J. Russell sketched the driving of the Gold Spike at Promontory from a photograph taken by Col. Charles Savage of Salt Lake, as shown at the left, while below is the off-stage side of the two trains while the drama was being enacted out front.

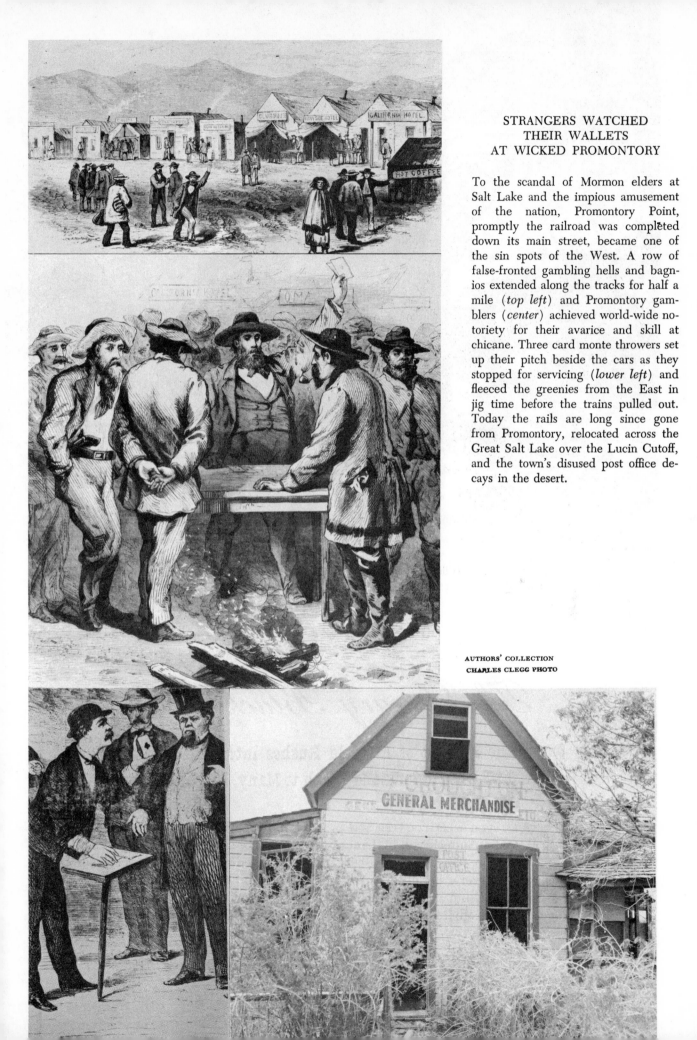

## STRANGERS WATCHED
## THEIR WALLETS
## AT WICKED PROMONTORY

To the scandal of Mormon elders at Salt Lake and the impious amusement of the nation, Promontory Point, promptly the railroad was completed down its main street, became one of the sin spots of the West. A row of false-fronted gambling hells and bagnios extended along the tracks for half a mile (*top left*) and Promontory gamblers (*center*) achieved world-wide notoriety for their avarice and skill at chicane. Three card monte throwers set up their pitch beside the cars as they stopped for servicing (*lower left*) and fleeced the greenies from the East in jig time before the trains pulled out. Today the rails are long since gone from Promontory, relocated across the Great Salt Lake over the Lucin Cutoff, and the town's disused post office decays in the desert.

At the height of the Black Hills gold rush, John Randolph drew this picture for *Harper's* and added to the already national excitement with the title, "Struck It Rich."

# XVI

## *The Dreary Black Hills*

### One of the Greatest of All Gold Rushes into Forbidden Lands Brought Riches to Some and Death to Many, Including Custer

UNLIKE SUCH WELL-LOCATED and precisely dated bonanzas as the discoveries of gold at Sutter's Mill by James Marshall and of silver at Tombstone by Ed Schieffelin, the gold of the Black Hills penetrated the national consciousness piecemeal and over a period of years. Father Peter John De Smet, S.J., knew all about it in 1848, but made no mention of the circumstance and warned friends among the Sioux that knowledge of the yellow metal among white men would

368

mean the end of their Dakota hunting grounds. Six years later a member of the entourage of Sir St. George Gore, the fabulous British huntsman, discovered yellow flecks in the trout-infested waters of the Belle Fourche, but Gore, who was interested only in sport and was a rich man already, warned him to keep his secret and took his party away posthaste before they might become involved in a gold rush. Throughout the late sixties there were well-authenticated records of the recovery of substantial quantities of gold by daring frontiersmen in small parties, many of whom were liquidated by the Indians after striking it rich, but news of their discoveries traveled remarkably slowly considering its message. All this time gold was being discovered and its discovery made a matter of public record only a few miles to the west in Montana at Bannack, Virginia City and Last Chance, but the Black Hills remained shrouded in gloom and mystery much as the Sioux wished they should.

Up to a point the white man was agreeable to leaving the Black Hills alone as the abode of the sacred Manitou of the Sioux, and the Federal government confirmed the willingness with a treaty declaring the region holy ground and sacred to the tribes forever.

The point at which a large number of adventurous men along the frontier and back in New York and Boston, not to mention along Wabash Avenue, began to consider this setup unreasonable was when a group of miners who had attached themselves to General George Armstrong Custer's Seventh Cavalry found some amazingly interesting specimens in French Creek in 1874. The discovery of gold was made official a year later by a government geologist, Professor Walter P. Jenney, and the secret that had been only surmised for a full generation was now a known fact. The news recapitulated all the shadowy legends that had slumbered in men's minds ever since the forties, it was authenticated by current fact and in no time it became gold rush.

By 1876 the rush to the Black Hills in flagrant violation of treaty and good faith was on in torrential dimensions. Communities such as Rapid City, Deadwood, Terraville and Keystone were served by a variety of entrepôts along the line of the Union Pacific, Julesburg, Cheyenne, Laramie and Sidney. Yankton, Dakota Territory, was even handier and hundreds of adventurous gold seekers holed up there for the winter of the centennial year waiting for the ice to go out of the rivers and what roads there were to become passable.

It was the Mother Lode, the Comstock, the Reese, the White Pine all over again, with improvements in the form of self-cocking firearms, the steamcars and the Sibley stove. The *Chicago Inter-Ocean* touched off the fireworks with an exclusive story about the discoveries, headed "GOLD—The Land of Promise—Glittering Treasure—Found at Last, a Belt of Gold Territory 30 Miles Wide," and in the Sherman House and Potter Palmer's Hotel strangers at the bar were thirty minutes later shaking hands as partners in assaying the new golconda. "The rush," opined the *Sidney Morning Telegraph* "is going to be a lallapaloozer." It was.

The firstcomers to French Creek were promptly dispossessed of their claims by General George Cook, who still cherished notions of the sanctity of the government's treaty with the Sioux, and sent packing back to the railroad where they took up residence, mostly in Cheyenne, and set about plotting how to get back to the diggings in spite of the Sioux and the soldiery.

Every gold rush in the West and to Alaska enlisted the presence of hard cases and no-gooders, but such was the index of worthlessness among the Black Hills pilgrims that it speedily became a legend in its own right. In May of 1876 the *Laramie Daily Sentinel* remarked editorially that, "judging from the number of boozy individuals around town, one would suppose that a delegation of Black Hillers had arrived." Fifty miles to the east of Laramie, "the roundhouse at Cheyenne," probably not the abode of the Union Pacific's locomotives but a flophouse of regional fame, became immortal in a ballad:

> The roundhouse at Cheyenne is filled every night
> With loafers and bummers of most every plight;
> On their backs there's no clothes, in their pockets no bills,
> Each day they keep starting for the dreary Black Hills.

Laramie and Cheyenne were not the only ports of entry to the diggings where the gold seekers gloried and drank deep. Sidney, Yankton and Julesburg, a community already established in evil repute since the days when old Jules Reni, the French Canadian founder, had poured a barrel of whisky into a barrel of flour to make whisky bread, shared in the tumults of the Black Hillers. "Julesburg had never had a lid," wrote Arthur Chapman. "If so it had been blown right into the sagebrush at the start and nobody had ever bothered to recover it." The Black Hillers did nothing to abate the legend of wicked Julesburg.

By the spring of 1876 most of the no-gooders and zip-cooners were back at the French Creek Diggings, having slipped past the cavalry of General Crook in small groups. The Army flatly refused to protect them and withdrew, for the time being, from the Black Hills adventure, leaving the prospectors to cope with the wilderness and the Indians on their own, which they cheerfully set about doing. Some lost their scalps but there was a powerful lot of gold recovered, too, and the wave of immigrants swarming off the yellow wooden coaches of the U.P. back along the main line assumed tidal proportions.

Late in the year a group of prospectors found gold-bearing sands of gratifying richness in the spring at a place known as Dead Tree Gulch, a site presently to become the cosmopolis of the region under the shorter name of Deadwood. By July 1876 Deadwood achieved precisely the population of Virginia City, a thousand odd miles to the west, 25,000 "if you can count people who are living in layers," as a contemporary wrote.

The year 1876 found an estimated 75,000 gold seekers making the dirt fly in the Black Hills and a newspaper dispatch from Fort Sully remarked, "The campfires of the teams at night would guide one to the Black Hills without any trouble, they are so close together."

All this time, as might be expected, resentment was mounting among the Sioux, whose leaders, Red Cloud, Spotted Tail and Little Big Man, had ridden into the West River country when they had been unable to negotiate with authorities to stem the rush. The struggle for the Black Hills involved five powerful Sioux tribes, the Sans Arcs, Hunkpapas, Oglalas, Brûlés and Miniconjous.

Events were rapidly shaping up for a showdown even as the tide of immigrants reached its flood in the spring of 1876. The Sioux federation was gathering for council which was to lead inevitably to open and organized warfare and General

George Armstrong Custer, who had started the whole matter when he rode into Floral Valley back in 1874, was heading for an appointment in Samarra, otherwise known as the Little Big Horn River.

## HO FOR THE BLACK HILLS AND THE GOLD!

The Black Hills excitement reached fever pitch at Yankton, Dakota Territory, a community of 3,000 permanent residents near the confluence of the Mississippi and the Dakota rivers. Here wagon trains outfitted for the interior and, as *Leslie's* put it in its issue of March 25, 1876, "hotel keepers find it profitable to keep up the excitement and marvelous stories of lucky finds are put into daily circulation. . . . The Yankton merchants are reaping a rich harvest from the numerous strangers arriving in town. . . . Woodchoppers along the Mississippi are going to the Hills in large numbers. Everything is now 'Black Hills' and should the present excitement continue a month or two longer, a stampede from the Atlantic states will set in." The scene below shows a train of 200 men and 57 wagons leaving Yankton for the diggings, a sight which was duplicated almost daily for many weeks. "Dealers in miners' supplies have made handsome profits," said *Leslie's*. "Fitting out trains has made business decidedly brisk."

# Black Hills Gold Was a Secret Twenty Long Years

CULVER SERVICE

The Black Hills gold rush might have been precipitated twenty years before its time if Sir St. George Gore, the English huntsman, had announced the discovery of gold in the waters of the Belle Fourche in 1854. Sir St. George had no intention of having his fishing party (*left*) turned into a gold rush and strictly forbade his retainers to mention the matter. The first organized expedition to explore the forbidding Black Hills, under the command of Lieutenant G. K. Warren, was stopped fifteen miles north of Sundance by outriders of the Miniconjou Sioux (*below*) who told him the white man's smell would ruin the buffalo hunting. A twenty-six-year-old medicine man of the Hunkpapas named Sitting Bull joined in warning the topographers off what had been promised as Indian land forever by the Laramie Council of 1851. Sitting Bull is shown here telling the white man to be gone, and Lieutenant Warren withdrew, although he shortly turned in a report and map showing the location of Harney Peak, named for his colonel and highest point in the Black Hills.

WESTERN COLLECTI

Remington painted "Miners Prospecting for Gold" in 1887 and didn't say where his scene was laid, but it might have been anywhere in the Black Hills of the seventies in the great gold rush of which the artist must have heard much during the years he was painting the Old West as he knew it at first hand.

## IN THE YEARS BEFORE THE HOMESTAKE

Like the Mother Lode, Pike's Peak and the Comstock before it, the Black Hills region soon swarmed with gold and silver prospectors. digging shafts and tunnels into the hillsides in the first primitive methods of recovering the rich ore they sought. Before the coming of the big operators every miner with a claim dug his own shaft with the aid of his partner and soon the Wyoming-bound stages of the Sidney & Black Hills Stage Line were reporting hold-ups and shooting all the way from Sidney to Custer City. The Black Hills were paying off and a notice appeared in the *Pioneer:* "NOTICE TO BULLION SHIPPERS: The spring cleanup will leave Deadwood for Cheyenne on the Regular Stage at 7 A.M. Monday. Wyatt Earp of Dodge will ride shotgun." No effort was made to molest Earp or the $200,000 in bullion that rode the boot of his stage. The mining scene depicted below was sketched by the celebrated team of Western artists, Frenzeny and Tavernier, for *Harper's.* In a few years more scientific methods were to characterize gold mining in the Black Hills.

THERE WERE HOMESTEADERS AS WELL AS PROSPECTORS IN DAKOTA

Not all the pioneers who began streaming onto the Black Hills in the mid-seventies were prospectors after precious metals. Many were homesteaders seeking small ranches and farms on which to raise families. Their first shelters were sod houses, cellars or one-story log cabins, and Charles Graham has portrayed one such hamlet on the bleak countryside in the above drawing titled "Banking up for Winter in Dakota." The lower sketch by W. A. Rogers shows winter immigrants making a shelter for the night on their way to the promised land of plenty.

## THE INDIAN THREAT WAS EVER PRESENT IN THE LONELY BLACK HILLS

The roving bands of murderous Sioux in the Dakotas posed a constant threat to homesteaders in lonely outlands and the menfolk seldom left their families unless urgently required elsewhere. The sketch at the left occupied the entire outside cover of *Leslie's* for May 20, 1882, and was in keeping with a widespread sentiment throughout the nation to round up the Indians and end their depredations once and for all. In the below drawing Frenzeny and Tavernier depict a settler's family, driven from their homestead by hostiles, fleeing southward to safety under military escort in dead of winter.

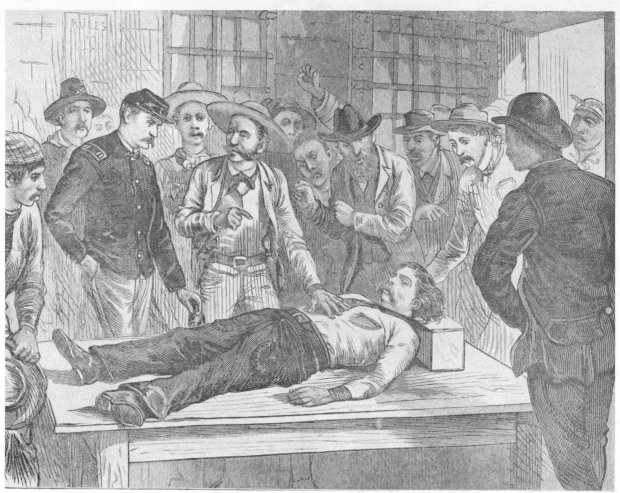

## "ARKANSAW JOE" WAS QUIET AT THE END

The village of Pierre is in the center of the lower half of the Territory of Dakota, at the junction of the Cheyenne an Missouri Rivers. (So read a dispatch in the special correspondence of *The Illustrated Police News* of Boston, Massachu setts, for December 11, 1880.) It is eight hundred miles west of Chicago and is the present terminus of the Chicago North Western Railroad which is destined to reach the Black Hills before many years.

Two hundred miles of the above road has been built in the past season. The village is of only a few weeks' growth, an consists of some forty or fifty houses, stores and saloons. Just over the river, in the Indian Reservation, is Fort Pierre, a sma place of shanties and log houses, but of considerable importance as being the shipping point for supplies for the Black Hill

A large number of men are engaged in the transportation of this freight, and some of them are of the worst class of de peradoes and outlaws found on the frontier. Two and three murders among the bullwhackers have been committed in th dance houses during the past four weeks, and the citizens becoming alarmed, formed a vigilance committee.

After giving proper notice to stop drunken brawls and shooting in the streets of Pierre, the committee were defied b the ringleaders and their lives threatened, and it was a question which party would control the town. For several days th river had been impassable on account of the ice, but on the evening of the 18th of November it froze over, and a delega tion of "Bull Whackers" went over to Pierre with all manner of threats. The vigilance committee were on the ground read for any disturbance, well armed with revolvers and rifles. Many of them have lived on the frontier and "knew their men. About 11 o'clock P.M. some fifty shots were heard within a half minute, and then all was still during the remainder of th night. In the early morning many people were in the streets inquiring the cause of the shooting during the night. At las some one observed an open door in a shed adjoining a saloon near the river, and inside was an old carpenter's bench wit something on it covered with a sheet.

On removing the sheet the body of "Arkansaw Joe" was found, the terror of the vicinity for the past two years. Th body was neatly laid out in a new suit of clothes, and as one person remarked, "Arkansas made a very quiet citizen." Som twenty bullet holes were found on his body, and one shot opened his skull some three inches. Four of his comrades wer wounded. Arkansas' real name was Parker, and report says he was from one of the best families in the East. A reward o $2,000 had been offered for his body for several months. He was quietly buried, and all felt a sense of more security to lif and property when the last sod covered his coffin. Such is life on the northwestern frontier.

# Something Queer

# Was Hid Behind The Mountains

# For Some, It Was Death

While the Chicago & North Western Railroad was still many hundreds of miles short even of the railhead at Pierre, Dakota Territory, mentioned in the vignette of violence on the page opposite, prospectors from the entire Rocky Mountain region were tightening the girths of pack mules and saddle horses, as shown in this drawing by I. P. Pranishnikopf for *Harper's Weekly*, and heading for the fabled gold of the Black Hills. Mostly the jumping-off places were along the line of the Union Pacific Railroad, at Sidney, Julesburg, Cheyenne or Laramie and, although the word Denver appears twice in signs on buildings in this drawing, it is unlikely that it was made in the Colorado capital. There were many "Denver Stores" on the frontier, just as there were "Boston Stores" in great profusion.

## THREE AGES OF DEADWOOD

When Deadwood, South Dakota, in 1876 became the metropolis of the Black Hills gold rush, it looked much as it does in the above sketch made on the scene by an artist for *Harper's*. The town was built between a towering canyon wall and a river which inhibited its growth any way but lengthwise. Later the same year it had achieved the estate shown in the photograph at the left below and was obviously in business to stay. The casualty lists were long in Deadwood's early days and the community achieved a cachet of badness which has attached to the name ever since. The Bella Union, named for San Francisco's wickedest dive in the fifties, was one of the really notable vice dens of the West. There was the Gem Theater, the Green Front sporting house and a saloon called the Bucket of Blood. Deadwood roared and seethed with mirth and iniquity as the wealth of the Black Hills was hoisted aboard the Deadwood Coach in Wells Fargo's treasure chests and headed for the railroad at Laramie or Cheyenne. The Burlington didn't arrive until some years later. The entire town was razed by fire in 1879 and partly carried away by a flooded creek four years after that, but, like Tombstone, the town was too tough to die.

BOOM TIMES IN A BOOM TOWN

When Deadwood was enjoying spacious times, as shown here, it was famous among other things as the scene of the shooting of Wild Bill Hickok and a great many lesser notables in the annals of pistol fighting. It also was, paradoxically enough for such a roaring sin spot, a good theater town. In the eighties Jack Langrishe, a player with fair notices in papers in London and New York, took a shine to the town, leased the Bella Union and gave the Black Hills several years of theater, including a production of "Uncle Tom's Cabin" that is still remembered. A later parallel to Langrishe's fondness for gold rush excitements was to be found at Tonopah, Nevada, twenty years after when Nat Goodwin was so fascinated with that boom town that he associated himself with it on a permanent basis as press agent and first citizen.

One of the notable frontier
papers of the West was the
*Champion,* which Charlie
Collins of the *Sioux City
Times* started at Gayville,
just around the corner from
Deadwood. The first type
for the *Champion* was lost
when the steamboat *Car-
oll* burned, but more was
obtained. Collins was in a
way responsible for the
first Black Hill gold rush.
He had written the editori-
als of the Sioux City paper,
set out of the cases as he
composed them, calling
the first attention to the
possibilities of gold in the
Black Hills.

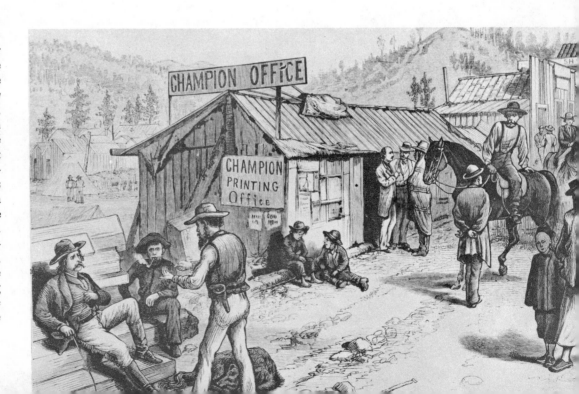

An Indian trading post in the Black Hills furnished the material for a typical frontier sketch for *Harper's* of July 1875 by the celebrated artist team of Jules Tavernier and Paul Frenzeny and illustrates admirably the Indian predilection for incongruous items of white man's attire. Most of the braves admired the silk top hat beyond all else and it was an almost universal article of trade and barter.

## HIGHWAYMAN WITH HUMOR

"Every few days there was another stage robbery," says Robert J. Casey of Deadwood's golden era. Mostly they took place at Robber's Roost or Canyon Springs and everyone was delighted when, instead of murdering everyone in sight, a jovial knight of the road gave a victim a chance to win back his valuables in a quick game of seven-up. The time was August 1888 and the scene Canyon Springs.

Keno, a primitive gambling pastime much in vogue in Nevada to this day, was a special favorite in Deadwood, and this admirable drawing by Theodore B. Davis shows a typical game and layout of the period with the keno goose at the dealer's right hand. The proprietor of the game when drawing numbers was said to "tip the keno goose." Presumably the word is an allusion to golden eggs.

## A TEN-GAGE INVITATION TO LEAVE

Barbershop and saloon patrons back in the effete East were delighted with such action pictures as this, which appeared in *The Illustrated Police News* with the caption: " 'My Finger Is on the Trigger—You Get or I'll Let Go'—A Concealed Shotgun in a Bank's Counter in the Black Hills Region." The *Police News*, published in Boston, was frankly an imitation of the venerated *Police Gazette* printed in New York and internal evidence indicates that in many instances the same artists drew pictures for both.

## CHEYENNE WAS TOUGH AND DURABLE

About the time it became the most notable of the jumping-off places in the Black Hills gold rush, William Henry Jackson, most celebrated of all photographers of the old frontier, exposed this wet plate shot of the town's main street. Cheyenne had come into being at the fiat of the Union Pacific Railroad and it was there the track crews had settled down for a quiet winter of drinking, stabbing and shooting before romping the advancing iron over Sherman Summit and on to Laramie. With this wild youth behind it, Cheyenne was of no mind to assume attitudes of civic rectitude for years to come and remained a town to reckon with right down to the Wyoming cattle wars of the nineties. Below is the U.P. depot at Cheyenne as seen by an artist for *Frank Leslie's Illustrated Newspaper.*

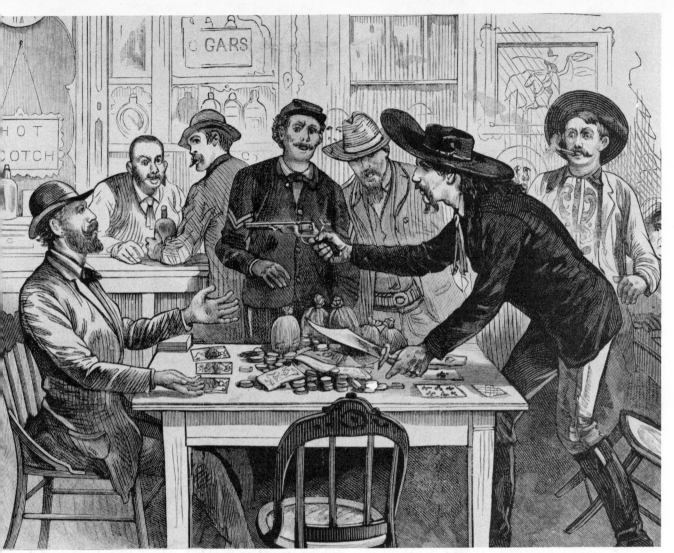

## HE PICKED THE WRONG GREENY TO TRIM

Most famous of all gambling establishments in Cheyenne's shooting years was the Greer Brothers' Gold Room where George Devol, a celebrated Mississippi River sharper, was dealer. The game prospered on the patronage of greenies and suckers who descended from the cars of the Union Pacific to take the air as the train was serviced. One imprudent day, however, Devol attempted to cheat Wild Bill Hickok, as portrayed above. Hickok made the dealer restore his losses, wrecked the premises and walked off with the contents of the cash drawer. Old-timers recalled the occasion with admiration for many years afterward.

Hickok bore the reputation of being one of the West's most skilled gunfighters until one August afternoon in 1876 in Deadwood he sat down to a poker game with his back to the door and was shot to death by a notoriety seeker. The cards he held as he died, aces and eights, were forever afterward known in the West as the "Dead Man's Hand."

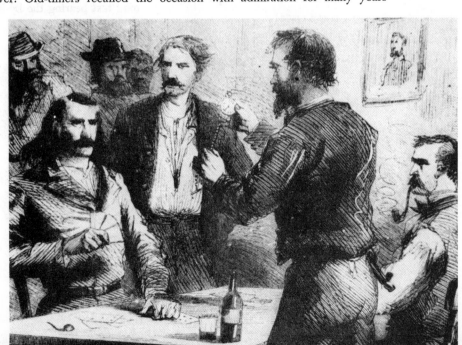

BAGS A BEARER OF DISPATCHES.

KILLS A FRONTIERS-MAN.

COUNTS COUP ON AN IRISHMAN.

A REGULAR DUEL.

SITTING BULL AS AN ARTIST.

In 1870 a book of original drawings in color crayon was brought into Fort Buford by a Yanktonai Sioux and traded for $1.50 worth of provisions with the innuendo that the trader had stolen it from Sitting Bull and that the fifty-five drawings traced on the blank side of printed rosters of the Thirty-first United States Infantry, each eight by ten inches square, were the pictorial autobiography of Sitting Bull himself. The authenticity of the book and its scenes was confirmed by Assistant Surgeon James C. Kimball and the original was deposited with the Superintendent of Indian Affairs in Washington. Six years later when Sitting Bull was in the public eye for his participation in the Custer Massacre they were reproduced in *Harper's Weekly* with a facetious running text bearing the by-line, "Porte Crayon."

STEALS A DROVE OF HORSES.

## CUSTER AND BLACK KETTLE WERE OLD ENEMIES

General George Armstrong Custer, dramatic and insubordinate Civil War cavalryman in charge of the Seventh Cavalry in the Black Hills campaigns, had not endeared himself to the South Dakota Sioux when in November of 1868 his troopers had raided one of Black Kettle's villages as shown above and killed many of the tribesmen. Many others were taken prisoner and led off to the reservations, as depicted in the below drawing by Theodore Davis for *Harper's*. The stage was set early for the final showdown at the Little Big Horn a few years later.

# The Plains Scout Carried a Passport to Romantic Legend

### ON THE LONE PRAIREE

The scout of the Western plains, of whom Buffalo Bill Cody was the romanticized archetype and whose true prototypes had been Jim Bridger, Kit Carson and Dan'l Boone, ranks second only to the hair-pants cowboy with his whisky thirst and gunpowder ways in the pantheon of national hero types. He came into being with the Rocky Mountain fur trade early in the century and lasted in personalized form as long as Buffalo Bill's "American Wild West" show, which is to say until the time of the 1914 war. No delineator of the West neglected him, and his fringed buckskins, long-barreled Sharps or Henry rifle, followed in due time by the repeating Winchester, as in the bottom picture, were immortalized as properties of the frontier by every artist of the time and place from Paul Frenzeny to Remington himself. De Thulstrup's "Reading Sign" appeared in *Harper's* in 1885 (*above*) while David Carroll sketched "One of Custer's Scouts Surrounded by Indians" during the Black Hills expedition of 1874. The odds against which Carroll's lone, surrounded fighting man will eventually prevail, betting to the contrary notwithstanding, are only conventional: about 100 to one.

WESTERN COLLECTION

## DRAWN BY ZOGBAUM

No artist in the field of the West, at least until the coming of Remington, presented readers of *Harper's* with more dramatic and detailed pictorial reports of cowboys, Indians, plainsmen and cavalrymen than Rufus F. Zogbaum. In these two pictures, "Sheridan on the Plains" and "The Discovery of the Village," Zogbaum brought to life both the formal military command of conquest and the romantic suggestions that clustered about the scout, the lone adventurer on a dangerous mission. As an artist he was, according to Professor Taft, one of the most untiring of all seekers after atmosphere and realism in his personal experience, so that he was informed by one admiring stage driver that he had no soft ways about him like some of them Eastern fellers that has been raised with lots of servants about them and think God Almighty's sun only shines for them. . . . Dignity will do very well for the East . . . but there ain't no room for it here, you betcherlife." Probably more than to any single artist, Montana owes a debt of gratitude to Zogbaum for his pictures of early life in the roughest of all Western states.

## EVERYTHING WAS "ARMY"

Frederic Remington's "Merry Christmas in a Sibley Tepee" may not be the master artist at his best, but it shows the national interest in the armed forces in the West at the time. J. Bower drew "A Sick Soldier on a Travau" at the height of the Indian campaigns of 1876, while Paul Frenzeny showed Army procurers purchasing cavalry mounts at a plains outpost at the same period.

# THE WARS WERE NOT UNIVERSAL

It would be a mistake to imagine all the Indians in the Black Hills on the warpath throughout the period of the troubles. At Standing Rock, William Rogers was able to sketch a Beau Brummel among the tribesmen having his hair done in stylish fashion by the post barber, enjoying the comfort of the latest thing in Koch's Patent Barber Chairs while a bear's pelt hung handy to supply bear grease, highly esteemed at the time as a pomatum.

At Fort Abraham Lincoln, Dakota Territory, an army sergeant got what for from a brawny squaw who claimed he took liberties not becoming a gentleman with a lady at the local roller skating rink. Less blood flowed than at the Little Big Horn.

While at Pierre, since the days of the Mountain Men a community with pretensions to sophistication and urban worldliness, a scout in straightened circumstances shoots craps for his Indian wife without attracting undue attention while her original husband looks on, presumably with an eye to a cut in the eventual transaction.

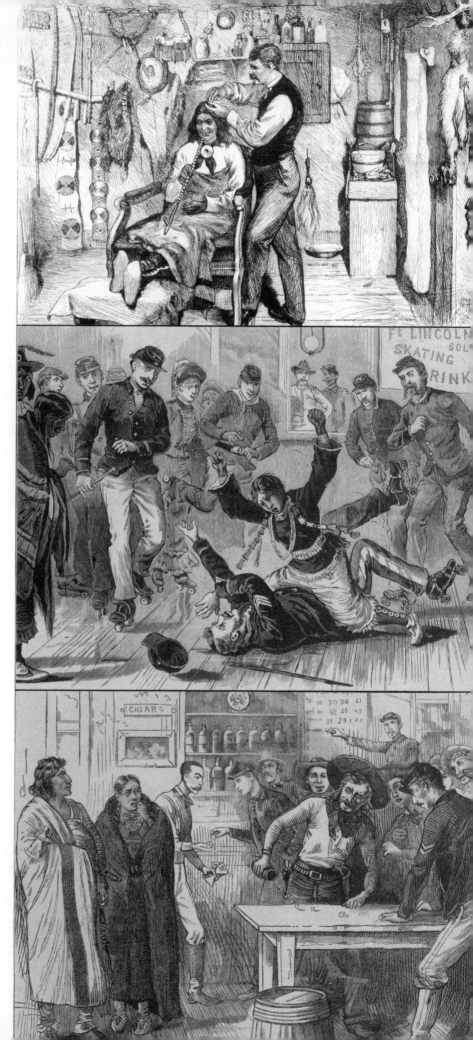

## THERE WAS A TIME LAG IN REPORTING THE CAMPAIGNS

Charles St. George Stanley sketched this picture for *Harper's* of a "grand council" held by General Crook's scouts at Goose Creek, Wyoming, during the course of the campaign that was to end in the Custer debacle. The reporting of the Black Hills hostilities, while as fully and intelligently covered by Eastern newspapers and periodicals as the Civil War had been, lacked facilities for transmission of news accounts and pictures and there was always a time lag, insufferable to editors in New York, between events and their appearance in print. News of the massacre at the Little Big Horn had to await the arrival at Bismarck of the steamer *Far West*, although newspaper legend maintains that a drunken night editor had an account of it in his hand and failed to perceive its importance five days earlier, as detailed elsewhere in this chapter.

## "BATTLE" AT THE ROSEBUD

Defeat or victory, save in such conclusive cases as the Custer Massacre, was largely a matter of the telling in the Indian campaigns. Indian partisans claimed that the "Battle" of the Rosebud River was a defeat for General Crook, but its military importance may be estimated by his casualties: eight dead and twenty-three wounded. Next day Crook's scouts accounted for several more Sioux, as in this picture from *Leslie's*, bringing their known casualty list at the hands of Crows and Shoshones to twenty dead.

## TWO ARTISTS IN EMBATTLED MOOD

The animated painting entitled simply "Nez Percé Raid," by F. O. C. Darley (*above*), is not identified with any specific episode in the hostilities of the Black Hills, but shows what was evidently an attack on an immigrant wagon train in the classic manner of the plains. One of the large staff of artists who worked for *Leslie's* largely in the field of the West was T. de Thulstrup, whose "Attack on the Village," reproduced below, is equally general but also equally graphic and representative.

# Alive or Dead, Custer Was the Stuff of Folk Legend

## TIME TOOK CARE OF CUSTER AND ALL OTHER MATTERS

General George Armstrong Custer, *beau sabreur*, *beau ideal* of a cavalry-conscious time, came out to take charge of the Seventh Cavalry. Perhaps the most dashing, glamorous and romantic, if slightly tarnished, figure to emerge from the Union ranks in the Civil War, his objective was a great and decisive victory over the plains Indians. His orders were to destroy all Cheyennes and Arapahoes, burn their villages and exterminate their warriors. Custer was fated to fulfill a romantic destiny in overwhelming defeat, achieving thereby an immortality he never could have won as the ally of whisky, bad leadership, native incompetence and the times against all the Indians of the West. Time took care of Custer at the Little Big Horn and of the Indian dream at Wounded Knee.

The expedition of the Seventh Cavalry into the Black Hills of South Dakota under General Custer was one of the most elaborately provisioned, well-armed and liberally equipped outfits ever to take the field against the Indians of the Western Plains. West of Bismarck until a few years ago, according to Robert J. Casey, the ruts left by his wagons on their way to a rendezvous with immortality at the Little Big Horn were still visible on the prairie. There were 110 wagons, six ambulances, two field pieces with their caissons, ten companies of the Seventh Cavalry, one each of the Twentieth and Seventeenth Infantry, a platoon of artillery, 150 white and Indian scouts and geologists, miners, botanists and assorted pedagogues sufficient to bring the entire company up to 1,200. They filled the prairie from horizon to horizon.

## CUSTER NEVER LEARNED

Custer's first experience with plains Indians was in
Kansas in 1867 where he pursued the Cheyennes
and Sioux so enthusiastically that his orders from
Washington couldn't catch up with him. As a result
a young dispatch rider, Lieutenant Kidder, and ten
of his men journeying from Fort Sedgwick on his
trail, were ambushed and killed by the hostiles.
Custer himself, as shown in the sketch at the bottom of the page by Theodore Davis, discovered
their bodies some time later. To a man given to
premonitions of disaster, the Kidder massacre might
have cast long warning shadows, but not to the im-
petuous Custer. Less than a decade later his own
body, surrounded by those of the faithful Seventh
Cavalry (*right*), was to be found under similar circumstances on a Montana upland, only here the roll
call of the dead was greater, the implications not
local to the Kansas frontier, but to the nation.

# General Crook Was the True Nemesis of the Sioux

## CLOSE CALL FOR CRAZY HORSE

General Crook's winter quarters for the campaign of 1875 were at Fort Fetterman (*above*) and it was on a foray from this stronghold that he drew first Sioux blood at Clear Creek, a branch of the Powder River. Here, all unknowing, he trapped Crazy Horse himself when he opened fire with a rifled howitzer (*below*) previous to charging the Indian encampment, but Crazy Horse retreated up the draw while Captain Anson Mills's battalion fired the teepees (*left*) and destroyed important quantities of the enemy's rifle ammunition in the flames.

THREE PICTURES: LIBRARY OF CONGRESS

## CRAZY HORSE'S DEATH WAS THE END OF SIOUX HOSTILITIES

The day of his surrender to General Crook at the Red Cloud Agency in May 1877, as shown above from *Leslie's*, was the saddest in the life of Crazy Horse, perhaps the greatest Sioux warrior of them all. Crazy Horse was shortly afterward killed in a riot at Fort Robinson which grew out of a misunderstanding. "As the grave of Custer marked the highwater of Sioux supremacy, so the grave of Crazy Horse marked its low ebb," said one officer who had fought against him. After that comparative tranquillity descended on the Indian wards of the government, such as those portrayed below by H. F. Farney at the Standing Rock Agency. The free Indians followed the buffalo in their disappearance from the plains of the West.

## TUMULTS AND ALARMS SIGNIFYING NOTHING

The Battle of the Rosebud, shown above in a drawing by Charles St. G. Stanley for *Leslie's,* engaged popular fancy more for its picturesque name than for its military or strategic importance. The casualties were negligible and the advantage to the Sioux microscopic, although General Crook was indeed forced to withdraw from the engagement. The same was true of the attempt, depicted by the same artist below, to surprise Crook in his encampment on the Tongue River. A full page in *Frank Leslie's Illustrated Newspaper* could lend Waterloo implications to almost any powder-burning.

## MAGAZINE READERS IN THE SEVENTIES LOVED A GOOD CRY

The Western artist Paul Frenzeny made a handsome and arresting group study for *Harper's* when he drew "Fresh from West Point—The New Lieutenant on His First Scouting Expedition," showing the clean-shaven youth in tailor-made blues among the grizzled scouts. More unabashedly a tear-jerker was the layout below with the caption, "Romance on the Hudson—Reality on the Plains." The arrow in the breast, the grieving battle comrade, the picture of the loved one fluttered from dying fingers, all were a piece of the sentimentality of the seventies.

# The Public Prints Followed General Crook with Avidity

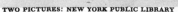

## WITHOUT RESERVATION READERS ADMIRED TO SEE THE U.S. CAVALRY

The proven circumstance that all wounded who fell into the hands of the Sioux died by torture made their removal from any engagement the first concern of cavalry officers and men alike and, if any were needed, provided added excuse for the extermination of the redskins under every condition in which they might be encountered. In this lively but improbable drawing in *Leslie's*, the Montana Sioux are shown attacking one of General Nelson A. Miles's sick trains as it was attempting to evacuate wounded along the Yellowstone. It is doubtful if a wounded man lying unlashed to a stretcher rigged between two wildly galloping cavalry mounts would have lasted for any great distance, but readers were uncritical when confronted with any heroic representation at all of the nineteenth century equivalent of Arthurian chivalry, the United States Cavalry in action against the enemy in the West.

Less romantic than the mounted troopers were the slogging foot "sodgers," the packmasters and the wagon train, and artists depicting these less glamorous aspects of Mars in the field seldom bothered to sign their efforts.

CROWS AND SHOSHONES GREATLY ADMIRED TO KILL THE SIOUX

Allied by their common hatred of the Sioux, the scouts recruited by General Crook from among the Shoshones and the Crows were invaluable allies in the skirmishes along the Tongue. More than 300 in all, the Crows under Alligator-Stands-Up and the Shoshones under Washakie were brought into camp by chief of scouts Frank Grouard, an old hand at Indian warfare and legendary figure of the plains. At Goose Creek the Shoshones performed a war dance for General Crook, as shown at the top of the page, to show their hearts were bad against their enemies, while, at the bottom of the page and not to be outdone in patriotic ferocity, a Crow warrior rides through camp crying for scalps. Albert Berghaus sketched the brave in full career among the teepees.

## THE END OF CUSTER: CASSILY ADAMS

Of Cassily Adams's painting, "Custer's Last Fight," Dr. Robert Taft, the ranking authority on the pictorial matter of the Old West, has said: "It has been viewed by a greater number of the lower-browed members of society—and by fewer art critics—than any other picture in American history." It is probable, too, that if a poll were taken among the millions who have seen it and have also seen reproductions of the "Mona Lisa," "Blue Boy" and the Sistine Madonna, "Custer's Last Fight" would rank immeasurably as the favorite work of art. It is conceivable that its only rival in popularity would be the parallel study of the final moments at the Little Big Horn, John Mulvany's "Custer's Last Rally." Between the two of them they have certainly attracted more conversational comment, speculation and admiration than all the paintings in Fifth Avenue's Metropolitan Museum of Art and the Frick Museum put together, if only for the overwhelming reason that for the past three quarters of a century one or the other of them has hung in almost every saloon, bar, taproom, beer stoop, rathskeller, and speakeasy in the United States. The Adams painting was lithographed by the Anheuser-Busch brewery of St. Louis in 1896 and more than 150,000 copies have since been distributed as promotion for the firm's product. It has long since passed into the realm of pictorial Americana and as such occupies a position of honor in the homes of rich men and collectors who wouldn't look twice at a Rembrandt or Titian.

## THE END OF CUSTER: THE PUBLIC PRINTS

Mystery and speculation have been attracted by Custer's final and losing skirmish with death more than by any other single episode in the saga of the West. Controversy has raged over who first published the news of the Little Big Horn and, to the satisfaction of everyone, the question has never been definitively resolved. Legend has it and was perpetuated by John Edward Hicks in his *Adventures of a Tramp Printer* that a mysterious account of the tragedy came over the night wire to the offices of the *Sioux City* (Iowa) *Journal* four days before the steamer *Far West* arrived at Bismarck July 5 with the terrible details. The account was believed to have been based on Indian smoke signals from the Montana uplands and the night telegraph editor held a beat of fantastic dimensions in his hand. Unhappily, he was in wine at the time and failed to realize the significance of the paragraph so that it got buried in a stick of state news where nobody saw it. On July 6 C. A. Lounsberry, editor of the *Bismarck Tribune* and Associated Press correspondent there, was roused from bed on the docking of the *Far West* and immediately filed a full dress account of the disaster which was printed throughout the nation the next morning. Mysteriously, however, *The Madisonian* of Virginia City, Montana, carried a correctly detailed story on July 6, a full day before the news was known in New York or San Francisco, basing its account on a telegram from Bozeman. The below drawing of Custer's final moments is by A. R. Waud, a Western artist with some knowledge of his subject.

# The Custer Saga

# Began To Gather Glory

# In His Lifetime

One of the last photographs of General Custer shows him, surrounded by a group of his scouts ostentatiously armed with Colt's then new Frontier Model six-shooters, seated in front of a tent whose stencils mark it the property of the Dakota Division of the advancing Northern Pacific Railroad. Although Pahaska was notoriously fond of animals, the dogs in the foreground from their ill-fed appearance were probably Indian dogs. At about this time the Sioux warriors under Low Dog who were soon to converge on the Little Big Horn were dancing the scalp dance (*below*) in realistic and bloody anticipation of counting many coups.

## "UNDER THE DEEP ROOTS OF THE VIOLETS"

After the debacle at the Little Big Horn which shocked the nation into activity against the Indians, a cairn of horses' skulls (*below, left*) marked Reno's Hill as long as the elements permitted. The remains of General George Armstrong Custer were interred at West Point with solemn military state (*above*) and a year later Lieut. Colonel M. V. Sheridan (*below, right*) and a detail of soldiers were ordered to disinter the bodies that had been buried where they fell on the Dakota prairie and bring them back to Fort Lincoln for shipment to national cemeteries or their families. All this time the great Custer legend was growing in the national folklore.

# Even in Afteryears the Black Hills Dreamed of Gold

## END OF THE LINE, ALL ASHORE

After the collapse of the Sioux confederacy, life and progress resumed their accustomed way in the Black Hills region. At Fargo, Dakota Territory, steamboats reached the head of navigation on the Red River of the North and prospectors, homesteaders and ranchers disembarked from the shallow-draft packets to be met by land speculators with glowing prospectuses. W. A. Rogers viewed the scene with approval and sent back the above sketch to his editors at *Harper's*. The continental conquest was nearing its final chapter.

At Fargo, too, tension between Indians and whites had so relaxed by the time Walter Young made this sketch of Indian boys in a snowfight that readers back East could view the scene without writing the editors of *Harper's* and lecturing them on subversion among the staff.

## COMMERCE RODE THE CARS TO THE DAKOTAS

Long after the initial rush to the Black Hills was over, the Union Pacific depot at Omaha still advertised lunch baskets for Black Hillers, but the pilgrims now were not exclusively prospectors; they included scientists, lecturers and substantial businessmen. Soon, too, South Dakota had its own railroads, such as the Fremont, Elkhorn & Missouri Valley, built to serve the Homestake Mine at Lead, shown in this old photograph where its Deadwood-Crown Hill branch met the main line at Blacktail Gulch.

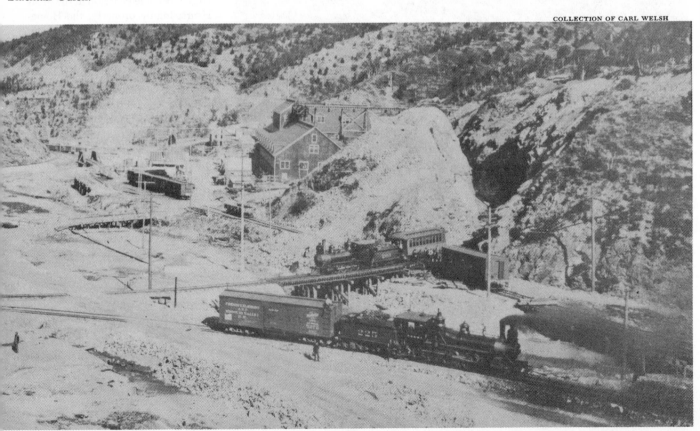

## HAPPY HUNTING

A decade after the first great gold rush had stampeded prospectors in tens of thousands for the Black Hills, the gold mining industry had largely become centered in the great Hearst family property, the Homestake Mine at Lead, South Dakota, and the Black Hills were becoming more famous as a hunting ground than as a source of precious metals. Above is a picture from *Leslie's* showing "The Product of a Day's Sport Near Webster, Dakota," while below is Rufus Zogbaum's drawing, "Hunting Wild Turkey by Moonlight" in the same general region. Most of the birds shot in the Black Hills were destined for the Chicago market, the primitive refrigeration of the time being insufficient to permit shipment further east.

## "CHANGE AND DECAY
## IN ALL AROUND I SEE—"

Although the railroads were closing in on
the river traffic, fine steamers still navigated
the Missouri, as is attested by the poster at
left. Morals and manners were changing,
too, in favor of what passed for respectability. At Helena, the *Police Gazette* told
interested readers in barbershops the whole
way from Portland to Portland, a posse recruited not from prospectors but the young
ladies of town horsewhipped Michael Rau,
"a tonsorialist, for talking too much with
his mouth." Aside from the invasion of the
immemorial right of barbers to bend the
ear of their captive audience, it was becoming apparent that domestic virtues or at
least their affectation were coming to the
West along with the new electrical light,
flush toilets and the bustle.

Rufus Zogbaum's "The Prairie Letter Box" might have had its inspiration anywhere in Montana or Oregon where distances are vast and regions lonely even to this day.

# XVII

## *The Big Sky*

### The Illimitable Distances of Montana, Oregon and Washington Merged in a Vastness Which Left Its Impress Forever on the Minds and Habits of the Pioneers Who Sought Them Out

WHEN STEWART HOLBROOK, who was to become the region's most notable historian and the champion of its way of life, first came to the Northwest in the second decade of the twentieth century, there were still available in Montana, Idaho, Washington and Oregon artifacts, attitudes and characteristics of the frontier. Elsewhere in the West, save in Reno, municipally sanctioned prostitution was largely in decline, but in roaring Butte he found a flourishing red light district complete with chatty inmates who read *Cosmopolitan* and *True Story* to keep abreast with things.

While there were cement sidewalks and eventually parking meters in Abilene and Dodge City, at Raymond, Washington, he found that wooden planks were still the accepted paving for the footways. At Wallace, Warder and Burke in Idaho he found rows of substantial false fronts on all the main streets and nary a glass brick façade or neon tube. In Butte, whatever obscenities of cocktail lounges might infest Denver and Cheyenne, there were nothing but men's bars where men stood up to drink men's booze. The once riotous Oriental Bar in Tombstone, Cochise County, Arizona, might install a soda fountain where Wyatt Earp had gloried and drank deep, but at Erickson's in Portland the grand manner of backwoods drinking prevailed and gouging was still an accepted aspect of combat.

In a word, Holbrook found not merely archeological traces of a way of life vastly superior to anything known to the age elsewhere in the United States, but actual participation in and acceptance of that way of life. Men drank whisky, prostitutes sold their favors for hard currency, the Great Northern's trains ran by steam as God intended them to and strong fellows when they were cross at each other beat their brains out instead of whistling for a cop.

Holbrook, who lives today in a mansion that has an elevator in it in a fashionable section of Portland, would be the first to admit that the Northwest has changed, infinitely for the worse. But he maintains that, comparatively speaking, the region retains more of its atmosphere of yesterday than any other part of the West, and probably he is right.

For the purposes of American history the Northwest came into being with the acquisition of the Louisiana Purchase, an event which Henry Adams remarked was too portentous for contemporary measurement or evaluation. Some notion of its portentousness, however, was possessed by President Thomas Jefferson who, at Monticello, had drawn for him a hypothetical map of the Western continent which he was eager to fill in with appropriate symbols of geography, and the material for the fulfillment of this project was supplied by the epic explorations of Lewis and Clark from the mouth of the Missouri all the way to Astoria. William Clark and Meriwether Lewis put the seal of authenticity on the concept of Manifest Destiny when they sighted the Pacific Ocean across the tumbled waters of the Columbia River and Clark wrote in his diary, "Ocian in view! O! The Joy!"

It is possible to conceive that from that moment on everything in the history of the Northwest was anticlimax, but it is a philosophical concept which would hardly have been shared by, say, Marcus Whitman, Henry Yesler or James Jerome Hill.

In 1842 Whitman, for instance, started adding to the commotional nature of Oregon's mythology if not its factual history by his supposed raising in the East of a vast train of wagon immigrants who were to journey to Oregon and settle its lands beyond all possibility of their seizure by the rascally British who were hiding in the underbrush. That the Oregon Trail had become a well-defined wagon road almost a decade previous and that Oregon was tolerably safe from British encroachment through the agency of Daniel Webster's ability to outdrink Lord Ashburton, the British Ambassador to Washington, is seldom mentioned in the regional folklore of the Northwest.

Only a little less commotional were the doings in Montana come two decades after Whitman "saved Oregon" and got himself murdered by Walla Walla Indians. There in the vicinity of Virginia City, Alder Gulch and Bannack flourished the greatest and most murderous gang of organized bandits and stage robbers ever to operate in the West's gunpowder years, not even excepting the energetic James boys or the cutthroats who gathered around Frank McLowery and Ike Clanton in Tombstone and had to be eliminated by Wyatt Earp some time later.

At Bannock the renegade sheriff, Henry Plummer, until a group of Vigilantes took him out and hanged him, was overlord of an integrated and highly organized dynasty of highwaymen whose murdered victims numbered literally hundreds and whose loot from pillaged stages ran to millions. Montana was in the business of producing gold a full ten years before its discovery by miners attached to General George Armstrong Custer's Seventh United States Cavalry in French Creek, Dakota Territory. Why they were so slow about uncovering gold in Dakota remains one of the mysteries of the Old West and unlikely of solution at this remove.

In any event, the Montana Vigilantes perfected an interstate organization for the punishment of crime which antedated the F.B.I. by three quarters of a century. When they discovered that numbers of Montana's more prudent desperadoes were taking it on the lam to the Cherry Creek Diggings at Denver City, they organized a corresponding chapter of Vigilantes in Colorado to whom they sent photographs and descriptions of the wanted men. The Denver branch quietly and expeditiously lynched the criminals without the bother and expense of trial or extradition and the chapter at Bannack promised to do as much for Colorado some day.

Nor does the anticlimax theory hold much water in the case of the Black Hills along the Montana-Dakota boundary where, just 100 years after American independence, more than 75,000 assorted roughnecks, bummers, drunks and a few expert prospectors joined a gold rush which for sheer numbers if not actually recovered wealth eclipsed both the Mother Lode and the Comstock bonanzas. The resultant hard looks between the prospectors and the Sioux in no time flat led to an all-out Indian war which spilled over into Montana and the Custer Massacre at the Little Big Horn, June 25, 1876.

And then, while assorted Sioux, Kiowas, Cheyennes and Nez Percés were making life a trial for the troopers of General Nelson A. Miles and General George A. Crook, came the greatest tumult of all: the railroads. Before even Custer met immortality at the Little Big Horn the Northern Pacific was building westward out of St. Paul-Minneapolis and a one-eyed King of Get named Jim Hill was clapping acquisitive hands on a baling-wire railroad known as the St. Paul & Pacific which would one day become part of the amazing and irresistible Great Northern.

No prudent historian would call James J. Hill an anticlimax to anything. If he was, then so was Ghengis Khan.

Hill took a look at the Northwest all the way from Minnesota to Puget Sound and wanted it. His gaze took in the millions of acres of rich black arable land that stretched all the way across the prairies of North Dakota and Montana until they reached a land of mists and rains in Washington where there grew in incredible profusion the densest growth of timber available to logging anywhere in the world. He dreamed dreams and saw visions of corn and wheat in the Dakotas and wheat and corn in Montana and pigs and cows in both and passenger traffic to populate all of them and of lumber in hundred-carload trains coming out of the Blue Mountains and the Cascades and he saw commerce with the Orient through the seaports of the Pacific, and Commerce as emptying an inexhaustible cornucopia of riches into the pocket of James J. Hill. The way to tap all of them, including the cornucopia of Fortune, was, of course, flanged wheels rolling on steel rails behind engines that burned not wood, which Hill considered not fuel so much as revenue freight, but coal.

It all ended of course in the Great Northern, or perhaps ended isn't the proper word, for from the Great Northern, Hill went on to control the rival Northern Pacific and the far-flung Burlington, which gave him a real railroad empire and made him incomparably the most powerful man in the entire Pacific Northwest. He was a man to whom power came naturally and he liked to use it. Few men ever opposed him, none successfully, and communities that crossed his whims simply found themselves no longer in existence. He ran his railroad around them and the communities perished.

Some trace of all these briefly rehearsed excitements is still discernible in Montana, Idaho, Oregon and Washington. Happily, where they have disappeared in their entirety there exist histories, legends, folklore and pictures. Some of their pictures are reproduced here.

## MONTANA RELIGION WAS BACKED BY COLT'S GUNS

Religion on the Montana frontier was characterized by overtones of muscular Christianity if the artists of the time and place are to be credited. In the scene above, "The Cowboy Evangelist" gives a snoring worshiper what for with a six gun in the tabernacle at Deer Lodge, while below is a heartening episode in which a minister in Missoula assured attendance at divine worship by buying the rival saloon across the street and closing it on Sundays. The pretty waiter girls and keno dealer are obviously inconvenienced by this strategy, especially when its terms are enforced by the sheriff, who has drawn a gun in defense of the Ten Commandments.

## CHEERFUL TIMES IN VIRGINIA CITY

This lively scene in a hurdy-gurdy house in Montana's early camp, Virginia City, has sometimes been mistakenly placed in the more celebrated Virginia City on the Comstock Lode in Nevada. Girls, bottles and music all seem in plentiful requisition and a cheerful time in progress for all. In the scene below masked varmints are in progress of levying tribute on the roulette game at Virginia City's Old Montana Club. Conceivably they could be associates of the infamous Sheriff Henry Plummer, although no such occasion was listed in the bill of complaints which finally hanged them all.

At the time of the Montana Vigilantes' night riding, the future city of Helena, shown here at about 1870, was known by the more picturesque name of Last Chance Gulch. A roaring resort town for the cow hands, gamblers, cattle barons, highwaymen and assorted frontier characters of the territory, Last Chance Gulch boasted a red light district that is still legendary in the West. Its sporting houses, located in a thoroughfare still known by the town's first name, Last Chance Gulch, remained operating institutions into the second half of the twentieth century and only closed their doors by edict of a reform administration in 1953.

## PERIL RODE THE HIGHWAYS OF MONTANA TERRITORY

The first staging line to connect the tumultuous diggings of Bannack, Virginia City, Nevada City and Last Chance Gulch was Oliver's, with a weekly through coach to Salt Lake which was usually heavily laden with gold. After Oliver's came the Concords of invincible Ben Holladay, the bearded King of Hurry everywhere West until the coming of Wells Fargo. In 1883 the *Montana Post's* Bannack correspondent wrote, "The road between here and Rattlesnake is nearly impassable; the Overland Coach arriving tonight was five hours coming over the mountains, a distance of eight miles, and overturned five or six times." By 1865 stage robberies on the Montana roads, as depicted below in *Harper's,* were a commonplace. Guards and drivers were shot from the box without warning and large sums of bullion were lost never to be recovered. In the holdup at Pontneuf Canyon below Rattlesnake $100,000 in "clean dust" was looted from the strong box.

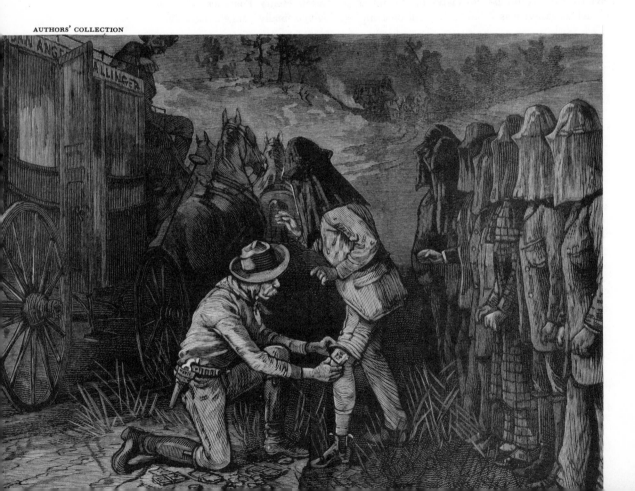

For reasons not altogether clear at this remove, the Montana Vigilantes adopted the mystic numbers 3–7–77 as the symbol of their fearsome activity and a warning containing the dread numerals nailed to his cabin door (*above*) caused many a desperado to leave the territory. When five road agents including Jack Gallagher, Plummer's lieutenant, were hanged (*below*), several thousand townsfolk of Virginia City witnessed the execution at the corner of Wallace and Van Buren streets. One of the Vigilantes was afterward asked: "When you put the rope around that fellow's neck didn't you feel for him?" "Yes," replied the rancher, one of whose friends had recently been murdered by highwaymen, "I felt for his left ear!"

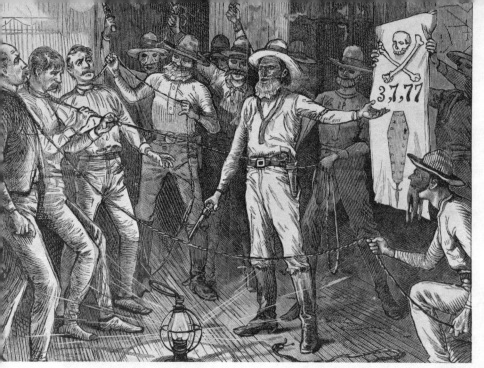

A MIDNIGHT CALL FROM THE BOYS

In the case of less desperate or merely suspected outlaws a committee of masked strangers called on them at midni
(*upper left*) and displayed the mystic symbols of the Vigilantes. The more prudent left town next day but a few reca
trants (*upper right*) who defied the edict ornamented the Montana landscape in attitude of permanent suspense.

In some of the earlier Vigilante executions at Bannack
and Virginia City, women purporting to be the wives of
the victims accompanied by weeping children attempted
to prevent the hangings by making scenes of grief and
pleading with the captors. When most of these were
found to be local prostitutes enacting a role of respectable domesticity their presence was thereafter forbidden
and the necktie parties were conducted on an altogether
stag basis.

## RETRIBUTION SOMETIMES CAME IN THE MAILS

Flight from Montana Territory in some cases failed to save the objects of Vigilante attention. Frank Williams, one of the participants in the Pontneuf outrage, fled to the Cherry Creek Diggings in Colorado, but the Montana Vigilantes maintained correspondence with a similar group in the future city of Denver and when Williams was identified by mail he was seized in an Adams Express office (*above*) and hanged to a handy cottonwood on the margin of Cherry Creek. Retribution had arrived by post. Back in Bannack three more desperadoes were apprehended (*below*) and hanged on the outskirts of town, bringing the total number of executions to twenty-four since first the Vigilantes had organized.

The early sixties in Montana Territory were so wild and lawless as to compare with the violence and abandon of San Francisco a decade earlier. Leader of a band of outlaws operating out of Bannack, Alder Gulch and Last Chance Gulch, which at the zenith of its operations numbered more than 100 highwaymen and maintained an elaborate system of espionage in stables, stage houses and taverns, was Henry Plummer, who occupied the office of Sheriff of Bannack. Hundreds of murders and the robbery of scores of treasure-laden stages on the Virginia City-Salt Lake run were laid at the door of the Plummer gang and its leader began to attract suspicion to himself with his wealthy ways. When the down stage of the Overland Company was held up at Pontneuf Canyon (*left*) and five men murdered, public sentiment was crystallized and the Montana Vigilantes came into being.

# THE VIGILANTES OF MONTANA

A Vigilante group was organized at Virginia City under the same articles (*left*) that had governed the San Francisco avengers in the fifties. The oath pledged members to secrecy, law observance and loyalty to each other and their standard of frontier justice, and additional members were recruited from Nevada City, Lewiston and other important communities in the territory. A reign of terror began for evildoers in all walks of life and morning after morning found bodies dangling from ridgepoles, treetops and other improvised gallows. In six weeks twenty-four outlaws died violently and many others took their congee in dead of night and without the formality of saying good-by. Among the last to be executed (*page opposite*) was Sheriff Henry Plummer. Only a few days previous he had entertained, all unknown to him, members of the Vigilantes at dinner off a turkey sent from Salt Lake via Ben Holladay's Overland Stage at a cost of $60 in gold later identified as having been stolen in a holdup in which two stage messengers had been murdered. The Vigilantes enjoyed Plummer's hospitality and three days later hanged him with a minimum of bad feeling all around.

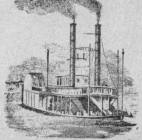

## I. G. BAKER & CO.

### FORT BENTON, MONTANA.

| | |
|---|---|
| I. G. BAKER, St. Louis. | W. G. CONRAD, Ft. Benton. |
| C. E. CONRAD, Ft. McLeod. | J. H. CONRAD, Ft. Benton. |

**PROPRIETORS OF THE BAKER LINE STEAMERS,**

## Finest and Fastest Steamers

*ON THE UPPER MISSOURI.*

# RED CLOUD

*AND*

# COL. MACLEOD.

*Will contract Freight from all Eastern Cities to all points in Montana.*

**EASTERN OFFICE, 219 OLIVE ST., ST. LOUIS.**

## BANKERS, FREIGHTERS

### INDIAN TRADERS,

Dealers in General Merdhandise.

**THE HIGHEST CASH RATES PAID FOR FURS AND ROBES.**

PROPRIETORS OF

### BAKER & CO.'S BONDED LINE.

*Will insure Goods via the Missouri river.*

**S. C. ASHBY, Agent, HELENA.**

## COMMERCE CONVERGED ON BOOMING HELENA

At the time it was known as Last Chance Gulch, Helena, as pictured here, was the center of the freighting industry which was the lifeblood of Montana Territory. Vast quantities of incoming freight and outgoing furs traveled, too, via the upper reaches of the Missouri River whose steamboats, represented by the advertisement at the lower left, provided one of the romantic chapters in Montana's frontier saga. Wagon trains in and out of Helena during the Indian wars of the middle seventies traveled (*below*) heavily armed, but generally speaking Montana's white criminal element was more dangerous to life and property than the braves under Crazy Horse.

## FORT BENTON WAS A TOWN WITH HAIR ON

The Grand Union Hotel at Fort Benton, Montana Territory, named for similar establishments at Saratoga Springs and in New York's Forty-second Street, was a respectable house, as its façade (*below*) might indicate. It was understandable, therefore, that the night manager should take exception to a cow hand who insisted on riding his horse upstairs to his bedroom on a wager in the bar. Fourteen .44-caliber slugs in his person, according to a contemporary account, all of them lodged there by the indignant night manager, prevented his winning the bet. Even in later years, when riding horses upstairs had gone out of vogue in Fort Benton, the *Police Gazette* (*right below*) indignantly reported that sports played poker there during a tedious sermon at the Baptist Church.

GRAND UNION HOTEL

PITZLEY & TRAVERS
PROPRIETORS

## THE NORTHERN PACIFIC FIRST BROUGHT THE CARS TO THE WILDERNESS

The Northern Pacific, whose president was cultured and highly intelligent Henry Villard, a newspaperman who had covered the Civil War for the *Cincinnati Commercial Enquirer* and come west with Horace Greeley during the Pike's Peak excitements, was the first transcontinental road between Puget Sound and the Great Lakes. Much of the territory it traversed was worthless; it was badly financed and in places hastily built, but it was a beginning and when in 1886 its rail ends met at Bullock, 700 miles east of Portland and 1,200 from St. Paul, the entire West cheered lustily. Four trains with forty-five Pullmans, diners and club cars came together for the event, as sketched above, and oratory and champagne flowed in uninhibited Niagaras. Back in St. Paul similar scenes were enacted in a more urban setting and a grateful citizenry cheered as the road's backers and builders passed under a triumphal arch. Within a decade the N.P. had gone into bankruptcy and its control passed into the hands of J. J. Hill, the Empire Builder himself. Below is a Chinese construction camp along the right of way.

For all its troubles and unsound financing, the Northern Pacific contributed a mighty epic to the legend of railroading in the Northwest when it drilled the tunnel at Stampede Pass high in the Cascade Mountains. Excepting the Hoosac Tunnel in Massachusetts, no railroad tunnel on the American continent presented such engineering difficulties. Climate, weather, geology and distance from supplies all were against the builders. Only twenty-eight months were allowed by contract to the brothers Sidney and Nelson Bennett to complete a task which other engineers estimated would require a decade. Lives were lost, costly machinery rolled down mountainsides, blasts exploded prematurely. When the line was finished the N.P.'s cars rode a right of way that soared above the clouds, as suggested in this contemporary sketch by Charles Graham, leaped across bottomless canyons on spidery trestles, and skirted microscopically narrow ledges above perpendicular canyons. The coming and going of the cars represented the nearest thing to flying on the approaches to the Stampede American travel was to know until the age of the airplane.

## THE NORTHERN PACIFIC HAD ITS TROUBLES

At Billings, Montana, this shameful scene was enacted when the Northern Pacific's *North Coast Limited* stopped on schedule in 1888 and Conductor Clark was forced to dance the can-can on the station platform by unidentified ruffians whose attire proclaimed them cow punchers from the surrounding region. The railroad's scholarly President Henry Villard, when apprised of the indignity worked on his employee, exclaimed, "Confound it, that's no way to run a railroad!" On the page opposite, the *Police Gazette* for July 7 of the same year recorded another breach of operating decorum when masked brigands held up and robbed another N.P. express between Big Horn and Meyers Station, Montana Territory. Shortly thereafter the affairs of the Northern Pacific became so demoralized that it passed into the hands of one-eyed old James J. Hill, who had planned it that way anyhow.

EMPIRE BUILDER WITH HANGOVER

No living person has been able to explain this photograph which turned up in recent years in the archives of the descendants of the great J. J. Hill, the Empire Builder of the Northwest. Left to right are Governor Merriam, a Mr. Upham being apparently rebuked by a Mr. Gotzian for aiming a blunderbuss at him, and Jim Hill himself, with what seems to be a severe hangover, resting on the back of a stuffed buffalo led by the first colored coachman in St. Paul. Nor can Louis Hill, a grandson, explain why Governor Merriam is beating a recumbent animal with a bludgeon.

### JAMES J. HILL LOOKED TO HORIZONS INVISIBLE TO LESSER MEN

No estimate of James J. Hill, most powerful single architect of the destinies of the Northwest, can transcend that of Stewart Holbrook: "the greatest curse of all—James Jerome Hill, Jim Hill, the Little Giant, the Devil's Curse of the northern plains, the prince of the Great Northern, king of the N P, emperor of the Burlington, the man who made the Pacific Northwest, the Empire Builder, the man who wrecked Minnesota, wrecked the Dakotas, Montana and all Puget Sound, the Prophet of Northern wheat, the Evil One of the Homesteaders—aye, Jim Hill, the barbed wired, shaggy-headed, one-eyed old son-of-a-bitch of Western railroading." A legend alive, a legend dead, Hill's Great Northern Railroad alone is a monument and an immortality such as a monarch might envy and his vision encompassed a realm that crossed the Pacific and embraced China and Japan. Agriculture for the Northwest, trade with the Orient were his obsession.

GREAT NORTHERN RAILROAD

## THE GREAT NORTHERN IS PILLAGED

Ephrata, Washington, on the main line of the Great Northern between Spokane and Wenatchee, in the early nineties consisted of half a boxcar which served as depot and telegraph office, a siding and water tank. Once Ephrata made headlines when near it armed brigands held up and robbed a Great Northern passenger train, as shown below, to the profane indignation of James J. Hill.

## WHY DISPATCHERS TOOK TO DRINK

Few Western themes so unfailingly caught the fancy of the artists of the time and of magazine readers who viewed their work in the seventies and eighties as the train caught in a snowdrift. From Maine to Oregon readers shivered vicariously as the laboring locomotives ground to a halt, the snow drifted under the stalled trucks and finally banked around the platforms against all possibility of resuming progress. The railroads of the Northwest, the Northern Pacific and Jim Hill's still building Great Northern, were particularly vulnerable and the artist here has shown an N.P. express near Bismarck. The giant airplane of today downed in some inaccessible mountain solitude where rescue parties must strive for days had its counterpart in the transcontinental cars lost someplace between nowhere and nowhere.

## THERE WERE OTHER HAZARDS

Self-styled bad men and lunatics sometimes attempted liberties with the train crews, but usually came out second best. During his travels in the Northwest Rudyard Kipling was witness to an encounter between a belligerent passenger and one of Henry Villard's conductors "who neatly cross-buttocked him through a double plate glass window off the train." The conductor "guessed he would die and allowed there was nothing to be gained by monkeying around with the Northern Pacific Railway."

ONE TOOK LIBERTIES WITH FRONTIERSMEN AT HIS OWN RISK

When Jim Hill's tracklayers reached Whitefish, Montana, one of them identified as "Ben White, boss iron layer" made the lamentable discovery that he was participating in a brace game at a local casino. The artist depicted for the *Police News* Ben's initial annoyance just before he flattened the premises like a collapsed opera hat. Below, in an Oregon ranching community unspecified, "Solomon Cohen, Custom Misfits" has to cancel a transaction in which he hoped to sell a bill of shoddy to Jim Norton, just in town for the week end. Like Indians and "greasers," the Wandering Jew of the West was on the bad books of the *News* and was invariably depicted on the losing end of an argument.

## BUTTE'S GALENA STREET WAS KNOWN EVERYWHERE FOR FUN

In wicked Butte, Galena Street was "the line" in the town's wild days and the *Police News* was pleased to report a raid there on "a den of infamy surrounded by a stockade and guarded by bloodhounds." Reform was only temporary, however, and soon thereafter the public prints were chronicling the wedding of Molly Demurska, queen of Butte's female seminaries, to Jack Jolly, the town marshal. The happy couple were married in the Clipper Shades Saloon and drawn through the streets, as shown below, on the town fire engine. Jolly was shot and killed a few years later by Soapy Smith on his way from Creede to the Klondike where he himself came to a bad end.

## LAST CHANCE GULCH GLORIED AND DRANK DEEP

Antedating Butte, however, was Helena, first known as Last Chance Gulch and also a citadel of sin whose red light district survived almost intact until the fifties of the twentieth century when it was forced underground by a reform administration. Shooting was so commonplace in Last Chance Gulch as hardly to achieve space in the newspapers, but the miners and teamsters who populated its saloons insisted on fair play, as shown above, where a disarmed disputant is given a chance to pick up his weapon before becoming ventilated. The first barbershop in Last Chance was alfresco, as shown below at the left, while miners on Saturday night admired to clean out saloons in the hearty manner suggested at the right. Saloon owners took a dim view of shooting up the French clock, however, as it tended to impede its practical value.

## SALMON TO EAT

Long before the ocean catch of salmon for canning became one of the great industries of the Pacific Northwest, early settlers along the Columbia River set up wheels which ingeniously caught the salmon and deposited them in a handy tank to await the primitive tinning methods of the time and place. In a few years the homely domestic source of revenue was to become a vast scientific industry conducted on the scale of big business. This pastoral scene on the Columbia was drawn for *Harper's* by A. C. Redwood in 1883. Eventually the salmon wheels were banned by law, but along the riverbanks of the Northwest to this day can be seen ruins indicating where they once had turned, scooping up gleaming fish for the dinner tables of the nation.

## DUCK FOR DINNER

Ever since Puritan times in the Massachusetts Bay Colony when a contemporary chronicler recorded that in Boston the citizens were so well fed that at dinner time "each man did have a duck upon his plate," wild duck has been a favorite American food. In the neighborhood of Klamath Lake in southern Oregon in the early eighties, wildfowl were such a menace to agriculture that patrols were maintained to attempt their extermination. Fortunately they were largely ineffectual and northern California and Oregon today provide perhaps the most populous hunting grounds in the world for wild duck, geese and pheasants.

## CYRUS McCORMICK MOWED DOWN WHEAT AND THE COMPETITION, TOO

The technique of reaping in the Northwest had improved a good deal between the time of the appearance of this advertisement for Manny's Patent Combined Reaper and Mower in leading farm periodicals in the sixties and the late eighties when seemingly endless vistas of Cyrus Hall McCormick's reapers moved over the vast grain fields of Montana and the other wheat states. McCormick's harvester (*below*) was the invention of a Virginian with a Yankee turn of mind and it revolutionized scientific grain farming in America. So successful was the McCormick reaper that its manufacturer soon set up nineteen assembly and distribution plants in strategic places in the West. He also revolutionized farm credit and refused to intimidate farmers who were unable to pay for their machines with legal see-here-nows. His prestige in the West on this account alone was enormous. The McCormick family eventually married into the family of Joseph Medill, opinionated editor of the still opinionated *Chicago Tribune*, and the rich and powerful Medill-McCormick dynasty of the Middle West resulted. When shown forty-two mechanical binders at work on the vast Dalrymple Farm in the Red River Valley where he had once ridden with cavalry and Indian scouts, Frederic Remington said, "The immensity of the wheat fields of Dakota is astonishing to a stranger. . . . We drive all day and are never out of them. They stretch away as far as the eye can travel."

## THE LOGGERS CAME WESTWARD TO "LET DAYLIGHT INTO THE SWAMP"

The year 1890 saw the great migration of loggers from the Lake States to the Pacific Northwest well under way. Land-lookers for the timber barons had come on ahead of them, purchasing fantastic tracts of woodstand from San Francisco Bay to the Canadian line growing Douglas fir that was twelve feet in diameter at the ground and grew 300 feet tall, not to mention redwoods whose dimensions defied measurement. Overnight California, Washington and Oregon became timber crazed and the greatest timber kingdom of all time came into being at the command of Frederick Weyerhaeuser of St. Paul. What the fabled King Ranch of Texas was in the hierarchy of cattle barons, the Weyerhaeuser colossus was to the business of cutting trees. It totaled 2,000,000 acres of woodland in Washington, Idaho and Oregon alone. On this page some of the early operations of this era are shown at top and left while at the bottom are some of the log brands of the period which indicated the ownership of felled trees just as a cattle brand identified the owner of a steer. In 1878 Frank Leslie's London correspondent sent on a picture (*page opposite, upper left*) of a steam saw that was expected to revolutionize the lumber industry being inspected by Mr. Gladstone, Queen Victoria's prime minister, but nothing came of it in America. Trees continued to be felled by hand until long after the turn of the century. About this time *Leslie's* was able to show its readers some of the perils of a logger's life (*upper right*) entitled "Cutting the Key Log." At the bottom of the page J. MacDonald drew for *Harper's Weekly* a study of "A Loggers' Camp at Night," where nocturnal activity seems to have been a far cry from its more frenetic evidences when the loggers reached town on one particular night of the week, namely Saturday.

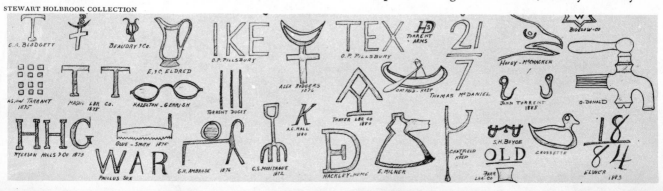

# Most Profane Calling in North America Was the Bullwhacke

The three pictures on this page from the collection of Stewart Holbrook, accepted historian of the lumber business and the Northwest, show bull teams at work hauling felled logs over the skid road at Satsop River, Western Washington, in 1893. For half a century, according to Holbrook, bull teams did most of the logging west of the Cascades. The teams hauled the logs over a skid road of felled trees half buried in the forest floor to form a sort of track, one end of which was in deep timber, the other at a sawmill or waters over which the logs could be floated to one. Most important man of a woods crew was the bullwhacker. "His profanity long ago became legendary in the Western woods," writes Holbrook. "When he raised his voice in blasphemous obscenity, the very bark of the smaller fir trees was said to have smoked a minute, then curled up and fallen to the ground. No sailor, no truck driver, no logger who hadn't driven bulls could hope to touch its heights of purple fluidity. And when both goadstick and profanity failed to rouse the plodding oxen to their best, the bullwhacker might leap upon the animal's backs and walk the entire length of the team, stepping heavily with his caulked boots and yelling like all the devils in hell."

THREE PICTURES: COURTESY STEWART HOLBROOK

THE SHAY LOCOMOTIVE WAS A CLASSIC PROPERTY OF LOGGING

Bearded like Moses and tough as a logger's steak, Ephraim Shay was logging in Michigan in the eighties when an open winter, with no snow and consequently no sledding, left his timber on the ground where it fell, hundreds of miles from market. Shay swore that never again would he be dependent on the whims of weather and he devised forthwith the geared locomotive, slow of speed but of enormous tractive force, that still bears his name and under Lima manufacture became the classic logging locomotive everywhere in the United States. In the middle left is shown a Shay geared locomotive, photographed by Charles Clegg, in operation on the Camino, Placerville & Lake Tahoe Railroad in the California High Sierra. At the bottom: many loggers in the Northwest recalled the old days when the Lakes States had been the center of the logging industry and every outfit with any pride at all in Wisconsin and Minnesota had to sport a so-called "Champeen Load" which took its logs over the ice roads to the river. The load here shown behind two fine white horses is white pine.

Although no such loss of life was ever involved in forest fires in Washington, Oregon or Idaho, old-timers who had come west from the Lake States in the last decades of the nineteenth century to "let daylight into the swamp" recalled with a shudder the conflagration that had entirely wiped out the lumber town of Peshtigo, Wisconsin, in 1871. Both Chicago and Boston were consumed in monster holocausts within a year of the Peshtigo fire and it received little enough attention from the world at large, but it survived in the memories of loggers for years to come and its details were rehearsed around bunkhouse stoves along the Skykomish River and around Puget Sound for decades. More than 1,100 persons were burned to death within half an hour in Peshtigo in a forest fire that approached the town without warning and at express train speed on a hot October morning. Some of the few survivors of the Peshtigo disaster were saved (*below*) by immersing themselves and their families in a nearby swamp. Even the worst forest fires in the Northwest such as the great Tillamook Burn outside Portland, for all the destruction of woodland, took but a microscopic fraction of the lives lost at Peshtigo.

PESHTIGO PERISHED IN FLAME AND SMOKE

## MOST OF THE WAY, THE LOGS FLOATED ON THE WATERS

To get his logs from the Columbia River to his sawmill at San Diego, California, Simon Benson, boss logger of all Oregon, made them up into monster seagoing rafts, breaking up log jams in the upper river such as is shown above at the left, and chaining them together in the vast rafts shown at the right, ready for the open Pacific. At the extreme right of this old photograph is a cradle being prepared for such a raft as shows in the foreground. Below are shown sailing ships at Bainbridge Island, Washington, forty minutes by ferry from Seattle, ready to set out for far ports of the world, while in the foreground huge logs from the deep woods of the Cascades are waiting for the dinkey engine and capstan to haul them to the sawmill floor.

## DEEP WOODS CHRISTMAS CHORUS

In a sentimental age when everyone was interested in what everyone else did at Christmas Paul Frenzeny sketched this picture for the Christmas Number of *Leslie's* with the title: "Christmas in the Oregon Mountains—The Backwoodsman's Christmas Frolic." If the entertainment seems naive, that was a shortcoming that would be immediately rectified the next time the boys hit the Skid Roads of Portland, Tacoma or Seattle.

ERICKSON'S WAS THE CATHEDRAL OF THE WORKING STIFF

Of all the communities with hair on them in the West that claimed mile-long bars, the nearest to achieving this dimension, according to Stewart Holbrook, was Erickson's classic lumberman's rest on Portland's Skid Road in the eighties. Erickson's mahogany measured 684 lineal feet. At Erickson's, too, the beer schooners were the largest—sixteen fluid ounces—the bouncers were the biggest, 300 pounds being par, and the free lunch the most celebrated of any west of Wabash Avenue. It was the proprietor's whim to describe this mighty collation as the "Dainty Lunch" of the house. The bread was sliced an inch and a half thick, the daily special was a quarter of roast steer and there was always available a millstone-size Scandinavian cheese which Erickson was pleased to call "Gude ripe." August Erickson catered almost exclusively to the working stiffs, timbermen, railroaders and river-boat men, but allowed no discussion of politics or religion at his bar. When the *Telephone* or *Harvest Queen* made the pier at Portland, anywhere from 300 to 500 wage slaves, the phrase is Holbrook's, made for Erickson's in a concerted rush. Old-timers said they would rather attempt to stop a buffalo stampede on the Great Plains. Burnside Street, which was Portland's world-famous Skid Road, was sometimes invaded by temperance workers (*below*), but they fared badly at the hands of the inhabitants and usually retreated in disorder.

## FLASH FLOOD AT HEPPNER

One of the worst disasters in the annals of the Northwest was the flash flood which destroyed Heppner, Oregon, a county seat for a rich sheep-grazing and wheat-growing region. The cloudburst which wiped Heppner almost off the map on an August afternoon at the turn of the century overflowed Willow Creek so suddenly that 225 persons, nearly a quarter of the population, were drowned, proportionally a far greater number than the victims of the Johnstown flood in Pennsylvania. Best remembered episode of the Heppner disaster was the remark of Dick Neville, Civil War veteran and bartender at the Belvedere Saloon, who shouted as the customers ran out in panic: "I'll stay with her till she floats."

## JOSEPH PEAVEY HAD A SHREWD YANKEE NOTION

The most important single property of the lumberman's calling, not even excepting the bullwhacker's goad, was and still is the peavey, a patent cant dog such as most of the men in this group carry, invented back in 1858 by Joseph Peavey, a blacksmith at Stillwater, near Bangor, Maine. When the peavey was invented, writes Holbrook, "the tool was born that would in years to come roll untold billions of feet of logs into the many rivers that run between the Penobscot and the Pacific, and from Hudson's Bay to the Gulf of Mexico."

## "TWO HANDED EUCHRE FOR A WIFE"

Perhaps apocryphal, possibly true, the scene here depicted from the pages of the *Police News* shows "Bill Warner, A Columbia River Gambler out of Funds, Plays His Wife as a Stake Against $1,200—A Losing Wager the Wagered Woman Refused to Honor." Like much of the folklore of the West, such an episode may have scant foundation in fact, but it represents the popular concept of life in the deep woods as the rest of the country liked to think of it.

No movement save the achievement of its own continental destiny has ever laid so compulsive a hold on the American imagining as the surge of the trail herds toward the Kansas railheads of the sixties and seventies.

# XVIII

## *Beef Critters*

### Until Spindletop, Texas Wealth Had Been Alive on the Great Cattle Ranges, Its Legend a Saga of Distance, Space and the Great Trail Herds of Yesterday on Their Way to Kansas

**P**URISTS IN THE FIELD of Americana like to point out that a full century before either Texas or Kansas existed as a geographic fact there were cowboys herding beef critters around in Georgia and parts of New England. Probably they are right. People ate beef in the eighteenth century. Steers needed herding. The best way to herd them was on horseback. And it is all beside the point.

The first American cow poke of popular conception was, for better or for worse, a product of the State of Texas and, like Minerva in this respect if in no other, emerged full-blown into the American awareness and survived without much modification or mutation of type as long as the great ranges and the huge cattle herds of the West lasted. What modification of character he did sustain was as much as anything the result of his portrayal in the art and literature of his times. The waddies learned things about themselves from the illustrated periodicals that they had never known before and, being obliging fellows, were agreeable to living up to the pattern set for their behavior, character and appearance in *Harper's, Leslie's* or the *Police Gazette*. So, to a certain extent, it may be remarked, did other types in the West: gamblers, madames, peace officers and outlaws. They saw themselves in the public prints and began to live up to their billing.

The background of the Texas waddie was purest Spanish. The cattle that were his business came to the Western hemisphere with the Spaniards; six heifers and a bull of Andalusian stock landed at Vera Cruz in 1521 for Gregorio de Villalobos, the first cattle rancher on the American continent. The cow poke's horse was the descendant three hundred years later of the mounts of the followers of Hernando Cortez. His lexicon was in generous measure derived from the language of Spain: lasso, corral, rancho, chaps, la riata, sombrero, quirt and remuda. The entire heritage of the man on horseback in the Americas derives from the caballeros of the Spanish ascendancy in the New World.

The first Texas longhorns to show the way of the great cattle drives three decades later were driven overland to Shreveport and New Orleans in the forties, but the possibilities of a vast Northern market for steer beef did not make themselves apparent until after the close of the Civil War. When the Texas regiments were disbanded, defeated but unbowed, after Appomattox, the ranchers found that during their absence at the wars the longhorns, wandering wild and free on the illimitable ranges, had increased fantastically. "The Civil War ended just in time," one Texan remarked. "In another year the whole south end of Texas would have sunk under the weight of the cows."

What to do with the beef critters was a problem. The Louisiana market of postbellum days could absorb the merest fraction of the supply and the project of driving herds all the way to the slaughterhouses, then located largely in Cincinnati, St. Louis and Chicago, was out of the question. Even if they survived the distances the steers would have no meat on them after such a trek.

But by 1867 word reached Texas that a railroad, the Kansas Pacific, was building westward out of Kansas City, to bisect the state with the eventual goal of Denver City, as the Cherry Creek Diggings were coming to be known. Already the 136th milepost had been planted at Fort Riley and the twin ribbons, not of steel at this time but of wrought iron, were being laid down with astonishing speed across the level prairie. The news gave imaginative Texans ideas.

In 1868 the iron of the Kansas Pacific reached 164 miles west of Kansas City and here it achieved a rendezvous with destiny at a place named by its founders, for no particular reason, Abilene. To beef-poor Texans down Corpus Christi way the railhead represented a solution of most of their economic difficulties. The management of the railroad was induced to build a few dozen primitive livestock cars, the first of many thousands, and up from Texas straggled the first trail herds, which were to make history. As the railhead moved westward and for other reasons, Abilene was to be superseded as the cow town of the West by Hays City, Ellsworth, Dodge City and Newton, but it had set the pattern for life and death at the end of the trail and even though Dodge City eventually claimed to be Queen of the Cow Towns and offered credentials to verify the claim, Abilene remained in the American consciousness the archetypal stamping ground of the Texas cow poke.

Abilene's whisky and gambling profits soared to unimagined heights. The clattering wooden open-platform coaches of the primitive railroad were arriving jammed to capacity with prostitutes, three card monte throwers and bourbon salesmen, its head-end revenue cars crammed with roulette wheels, barrels and case goods, music boxes, frame dwellings, crystal chandeliers, mahogany bars and .41- and .44-caliber revolver ammunition from the far-off factories of Bridgeport and Hartford. Times were brisk, and at the Alamo, most spirited and ornate of Abilene's twenty sluicing spots, two dozen bartenders (the figure is Robert Casey's) and three orchestras operated 'round the clock, keeping the waddies alternately steamed up with forty-rod and gentled with fashionable airs on the fiddle and trumpet.

The big operators paid off the hands at the end of the drive in minted gold and the hands in turn were mined with enthusiasm bordering on avarice by the madames, girls, procurers, gamblers, saloonkeepers and bunco steerers. A hard-boiled city marshal named Wyatt Earp was imported to maintain what law and order were desirable, which wasn't much either from the standpoint of the resident population or its transient Texans. Texas Street banged with gunfire and roared with orchestrions twenty-four hours a day and the town's once modest boot hill assumed proportions of a high pressure real estate development.

All this uninhibited hurrah was distasteful to the rest of Kansas, which was largely populated with sod pushers and other primitives who viewed the fornication and whisky guzzling of Abilene with Methodist frowns and eventually pushed a law through the Kansas legislature forbidding the loading of cattle at Abilene. Although the law was patently discriminatory and could have been set aside with no great legal fuss, the cattle shippers found it easier to move on to Hays City down the railroad line a spell, and presently, in 1872, no fewer than 1,000,000 longhorns were prodded aboard the cars at Hays and started on their way to becoming porterhouse steaks in Baltimore and Pittsburgh.

Thus it came about that Kansas, for all the individuality it had established for itself as a border state in the troublous times before the Civil War and for all its indigenous and often dubious regional character in the years following Appomattox, was for a full decade following the first cattle drive to Abilene in actuality a suburb of Texas or a suburb of Hell, depending upon the point of view.

It wasn't the number of Texans or their density so much as it was the noise and disorder that accompanied their arrival, tenure of foothold at the bar and ultimate departure. A good many of them stayed on in Kansas as permanent residents of the boot hills at Dodge and Newton and, as somebody was to remark in a poem that achieved fame at a somewhat later date, here and there under the cottonwoods there was a spot which is forever Texas. The waddies tangled with Wyatt Earp or Bat Masterson or Charlie Bassett or internecine strife raised its head over the comparative merits of Lampasas or El Paso, and friends took their saddles back to the

446

folks and left them alone on the wide prairee. Texas had a sentimental stake in Kansas as well as a commercial and social foothold.

The important fact about Abilene, Wichita, Caldwell, Hunnewell, Dodge, Hays, Ellsworth and Newton, all Texas border towns with a moral and personal code as foreign to its setting as English jurisprudence in Singapore, was that they produced a generation of Texans even more emphatically sons of Sam Houston in their temporary exile than they ever thought of being along the banks of the Trinity or the Brazos. Texans retain the trait to this day, and ordinarily conventional and circumspect bankers from Houston and vice-presidents in oil from Longview who seldom appear at home in anything but blue serge suits and bowler hats suddenly blossom with Alamo screams and rodeo raiment when they hit the lobby of the Waldorf Astoria.

The conduct of the primal cowboys in the railheads of Kansas was to have disastrous results when the Methodist counterrevolution began to gather momentum in the late seventies and early eighties and Topeka was to become a citadel of bone-dry temperance and other austerities, but this was a merely regional calamity and possessed of no implications in the grand design of American folklore.

What is important in the chronicle of the West is that the prototype and pattern for generations of cow hands yet unborn (he was a cowboy or waddy until the necessity for keeping the beef critters on their feet in the stock cars arrived with the railroads and the cow poke was evolved) was in process of evolution among the Texans-in-Exile bellying up to the bar in the Alhambra Saloon in Abilene. All the properties of the cowboy person and cowboy way of life, the gun toting, extravagant gambling, loyalty to the outfit, the regional clannishness, hurrahing of main streets, riding horseback into the taverns, the free spending and free wheeling which came to obtain far from the main line of the Kansas Pacific, in Cheyenne, Bozeman, Billings and Belle Fourche, had their origins in the drives over the Chisholm, Old Shawnee and Red River Trails.

If, then, it is in fact true that, as Professor Robert Taft believes, Rufus Zogbaum's sketch "Painting the Town Red" in *Harper's Weekly* in 1885 actually set the pattern for the general concept of cowboy life, it can only be said that the American public was uncommonly slow on the uptake of an idea that was to become a national obsession. The mid-eighties were the age of Frederic Remington and Theodore Roosevelt on the range and the primal cowboys who had traded shots with Bat Masterson in the Alamo Saloon at Dodge City were either telling tall tales to their grandchildren in San Antonio or long since gathered up for fertilizer by the old bones man of the plains.

Somehow this would seem late in the game. Fifteen years after Promontory the West was filling up with dudes in ratcatcher suits and Albert watch chains. Everything was up to date in Kansas City and the flush toilet was in the foreseeable future. An up-and-coming surgeon in Tombstone was advertising an electromagnetic device for locating gunshot in the human person and the "derby hat, the smoking chimneys, the cord binder and the thirty day note" of Remington's classic lament were at hand.

The cowboy himself was by then very old Stetson.

# Longhorns Spelled Romance to All the World

Less concerned for detail than the later Remington, the artist team of Frenzeny and Tavernier sketched a mellow West where composition and warmth were predominant. These sketches of Texas trail herds on the way to Kansas appeared in *Harper's* two years before Remington, as represented on the page opposite, drew his first realistic cowboy devoid of sentimentality and attired in the cavalry trousers, rifle scabbard and canteen indicative of his background.

THE ARTIST AS A YOUNG MAN

One of the earliest of all published Remington cowboy pictures, "In from the Night Herd," appeared in *Harper's Weekly* October 9, 1886. It was the forerunner of scores to come which were to elevate the artist to the top rung of his profession and represent the cowboy in the universal imagination until the coming of the mandolin-plucking clothes horse of the films with his parody of Western attire, speech and manners.

# To an Entire Generation Hoofbeats Were a Symphony

## STAMPEDE!

Almost anything could stampede a cattle herd either on the range or on the trail, a calculated alarm by Indians or rustlers or an extravagance of nature such as the thunderstorm depicted above near Kerrville, Texas, by L. W. McDonald for *Leslie's* in 1881. Only infrequently, however, was a herd stampeded to destruction or partial loss such as was sustained when a herd threw itself over a cliff into the Pecos in New Mexico, as shown in the lower picture. It seems probable that many of the steers shown in their mad plunge were rounded up downriver or otherwise retrieved, for cattle could and had to swim to be brought to market, looking, as an old-timer said, like so many rocking chairs in the water with only their heads showing.

## "SO MUCH CARRIES AWAY THE WIND"

The New Year's blizzard of 1886 put an end to beef on the dinner tables of America for a long time to come. Hundreds of thousands of cattle perished; literally hundreds of cattle outfits were wiped out permanently. The trend toward fattening Texas steers in the Northwest had populated the ranges of Montana and the Dakotas with animals unaccustomed to severe winters and when the worst series of blizzards in the history of weather swept down from Canada, coating the grass with a carpet of ice and often freezing the cattle as they stood in their tracks, the vast herds were in many cases altogether obliterated. The following year was also a blizzard year and what was left of the grazing herds never saw spring. More than 80 per cent of the beef critters between the Canadian border and the Rio Grande were dead. Some of the big English outfits in Colorado simply closed their books and made no attempt to reopen and many cattlemen seriously doubted if beef could ever again be bred as an important industry. "The era of great cattle companies was gone," wrote Paul Wellman in "The Thundering Herd," "along with the wild extravagance, the toplofty ideas, overstocking, frenzied finance, mismanagement . . . their great flood tide was past." When the industry staged its comeback it was financed by conservative bankers from State Street and the packing houses of Chicago with their own ideas of economy and interest on their investment. The cattle barons with their standing armies, their limitless hospitality, their ranges as big as European states were gone into the realm of legend and the folklore of a vanished time. Charles Graham drew the sketch above showing cattle in a blizzard from a preliminary sketch by Henry Worrall.

## WICHITA HAD ITS SOBER MOMENTS OF COMMERCE, AS WELL

Wichita followed Newton as the center of the cattle-shipping trade over the rails of the Santa Fe which connected there with the iron of the Newton & Southwestern. While the waddies who had driven the cattle north from the Texas ranges were carrying on like crazy with the Calico Queens in Delano, Wichita's roaring red light district, more prosaic scenes were being enacted (*above*) in the back parlor of Keno Hall where drovers and representatives of Eastern packing houses were settling their accounts. Here the trail boss or owner of the beef critters, as the case might be, received gold and banknotes to pay off his hands and here the trainmaster figured his car loadings and tonnage ratings for the weeks to come. A few patrons got a shave and used the ice water cooler in the background, at least until the accounts were squared. In the scene below buying agents for Fred Harvey look over some merchandise at the stock pens.

## "EVERYTHING GOES IN WICHITA!"

A genius for outdoor advertising born before his time erected billboards on roads leading to town with the legend "Everything Goes in Wichita," and the Texas cow hands thirsty from the long trail drives were just the people to take up the offer. Wichita's Douglas Avenue was one of the celebrated thoroughfares of the West, its saloons conveniently displaying the likeness of barrels for those who couldn't read while its wooden sidewalks were at no inconvenient elevation from the gutter for a man in wine. A photo of Wichita (*above*) is supplemented by a Frenzeny-Tavernier drawing of Douglas Avenue at the right. Below the steers are being loaded on the cars of the Santa Fe for shipment to St. Louis and Chicago while the survivors of Wichita's whisky and gunfire head home to Texas.

## BEEF SOON BECAME BIG BUSINESS

The killing, distribution and eating of beef in the United States underwent a profound change after the Civil War. What had formerly been a small-time local operation involving only locally raised steers turned overnight with the shipping of great numbers of superior Texas cattle into a great national industry. Dynasties of packers in Chicago, Armours, Swifts and Cudahys, arose to match the dynasties of breeders, Adairs, Goodnights and Chisums of the Southwest. Steers arriving by rail from Kansas (*below left*) were processed in vast packing plants in Chicago and St. Louis (*above*). So great was the loss from maimed cattle in the primitive cars of the times and the rough handling of trains that a patent cattle car (*right below*) was shortly evolved by the Santa Fe to protect the beef critters in transit.

Inland navigation was safer for cattle than the high seas. Here they are being loaded upon a Mississippi River steamer at New Madrid, Missouri, for shipment to New Orleans along with a joint cargo of corn and assorted merchandise.

## CATTLE WERE POOR SAILORS INDEED

Cattle didn't take easily to boats. Their special handling, protection from maiming in heavy weather, feeding, cleaning and care generally made them a trial to shipowners and crew alike. Until the coming of refrigeration, however, Texas cattle were shipped in vast numbers to Europe from Southern ports and some of the difficulties of the operation are pictured below.

VIGILANTE COURTS IN SESSION WERE A FAVORITE THEME OF WESTERN ARTISTS

Frenzeny and Tavernier's "Vigilance Court in Session" (*page opposite*) is an accepted classic of Western portraiture because it embodies all the details of swift frontier justice on the cattle range where horse stealing and rustling of stock were capital offenses. A less discriminating but even more spirited study of the same subject was drawn for the *Police News* by an unknown artist whose readers demanded action and who captioned the drawing, "Mr. Thomas Polk of Copperas Cove, Texas, a Horse Thief, Has a Fatal Unpleasantness with His Neighbors." Copperas Cove is missing in today's atlas but had there been such a place, its Texan inhabitants would undoubtedly have reacted like this to such provocation.

The seizure by a Vigilante posse of a suspected horse thief or border criminal wasn't always fatal, but the chances were against the accused. Few innocent men were hanged and a vast number of the guilty stretched hemp they would never have achieved if the community had waited for the coming of more formal justice.

That ubiquitous manifestation of Western individualism and freedom from conventional restraint, the horse in the bar, was a commonplace in Dodge City's riding years. When a Texas cattleman rode into the Alamo, a premises curiously presided over by a reformed Quaker, and asked for a double toddy, the bartender knew it meant not a double for the rider but one each for horse and man. Every toddy consumed by a trail rider at the Alamo was reputed to increase the value of a Texas steer approximately $2.75.

## DODGE CITY MUSIC HALL SHOWS WERE ON BOTH SIDES OF THE FOOTLIGHTS

Eddie Foy was a stage favorite at Dodge City, playing several seasons there at the Comique and Alcazar music halls, both favorites with free-spending cowboys and their ladies of the evening. On one occasion Foy forgot to warn the young ladies of the chorus line that being lassoed from the audience was part of the routine and terror prevailed among the pretty things in tights until the matter could be explained.

# Whisky Fixin's Were Important to Everyone

LODGERS IN BOOT HILL MOVED OVER FOR A LADY

Undoubtedly deplorable were the morals of dainty Dora Hand of Dodge City's Alhambra Saloon, for whose smiles ten men were said to have died suddenly. Like all the fair but frail of the old frontier, Dora was endowed by legend with an aristocratic background, and old-timers asserted that she had been born in affluence in Boston's Beacon Street and educated in Germany. In any event she had sung on the stage of the Comique with Eddie Foy and been in Abilene and Hays before becoming the steady girl of Dog Kelley, first mayor of Dodge and owner of the Alhambra, where she remained aloof from the rougher customers if only through the agency of a table to stand on, as is suggested by the contemporary drawing. When Dora's fatal charms attracted too much attention from Spike Kennedy, Dog Kelley had him thrown bodily out of the Alhambra, and later that night Kennedy crept up on the sheriff's house and fired two shots into the bed where he supposed the man of law was sleeping. The sheriff wasn't there but Dora was, and died instantly. Her funeral was a sensation and she became one of the few female occupants of Dodge's flourishing boot hill. The minister at her obsequies, which were widely attended by both dance hall girls and the town's "respectable" element, chose for his text: "He that is without sin among you, let him cast a stone at her." Dora's murderer went unscathed but Dora herself achieved a sort of immortality in the folklore of the Southwest where such legends are cherished.

## THE HANDS AT WORK AND PLAY

Frenzeny and Tavernier, classic portrait painters of the Old West, drew the engaging sketches at the top and bottom of this page, the one showing cowboys eating breakfast as the Texas sun, suitably large for a Texas setting, rises over the Texas plains, the other cutting a mustang out of a corral for taming. In the center is a quaint version of cowhands in the big city which appeared in *Leslie's*, showing waddies patently unaccustomed to hard sidewalks smoking twofer cigars and accepting presents of flowers from admiring children. Kansas City was good to the boys: there were fine restaurants where champagne could be commanded in fountains, gorgeous saloons reaching for half a city block of polished mahogany and glittering crystal, and there was a red light district comparing favorably with anything west of Chicago. Never a dull moment in Kaycee, the boys declared, as they headed reluctantly back to the ranges the other side of the Colorado, the Brazos, the Red and the Canadian.

THE BOYS FROM BELOW THE RED RIVER WERE FULL OF BOUNCE

Occasionally in his off-duty hours in Abilene or Newton the playful Texan engaged in playing an innocent but spirited game of mounted pool (*above*) or boarded the cars of the Santa Fe to frighten hell out of the women. The billiard table usually needed a new cover, which was paid for, and the ladies' valuables were returned to them at the end of the run and a good time, more or less, was had by all.

## THE LOOK OF THE KANSAS COW TOWN

Front Street, Dodge City, in the days when Wyatt Earp was city marshal, was a thoroughfare as celebrated in the news of the world as Fifth Avenue or the Strand. The sign at the corner of Bridge Street announced that the carrying of firearms within city limits was forbidden and Earp was agreeable to laying the long barrel of his Buntline Special alongside of the head of anyone who wanted to argue about it. Below is the Long Branch Saloon where Earp, backed by Bat Masterson, called the bluff of Clay Allison, one of the West's most notable psychopathic killers, branded him a coward and drove him out of town. At the right is the origin of a legend that has become part of the language. In the early days of the Kansas Pacific and Santa Fe railroads running through the cow towns of the Kansas frontier, railroaders were younger men and less inhibited than they came to be in a later age. When they sought the pleasures of the bagnio in the evening at Abilene, Wichita or Dodge City they made a practice of hanging a brakeman's red lantern outside the love store of their choice. Thus the dispatcher's call boy could find his man without undue research and the red light district became part of the national lexicon.

"BEAUTIFUL, BIBULOUS BABYLON OF THE PLAINS"

The sodbusters in the rest of Kansas, most of whom were New Englanders imported to combat the border ruffians of Missouri in the days of Bleeding Kansas and who had long perfected the technique of voting dry and drinking wet, began to talk of state prohibition as early as 1878. "Slowly, secretly and noiselessly the Murphy (Temperance) Movement is heading westward," a Dodge City paper announced ominously in that year. The sodbusters hated and feared the wide-open cow towns and easily dominated Topeka, where the politicians, as everywhere, were available to pressure groups. Albert Griffin, a temperance lecturer, was rudely received in Dodge and told Bat Masterson, who was then marshal, that he planned to return to "stay until every viper engaged in the sale of liquor was crushed from existence." Griffin did return, bringing with him state officials, and riots immediately ensued in Front Street. That evening a delegation of wicked men called upon Griffin, as shown here, and demonstrated the fallacy of his ideas by burning his tracts and telling him to leave town. He took the train next morning and the local paper remarked editorially that "it ought to be evident to everybody familiar with the scenes in Dodge City last Monday that the time is not ripe to attempt to suppress the saloons in this place." Prohibition, after a sort, did eventually come to Kansas, but there was never a day in the town's history when it wasn't possible for an accredited person to get himself tanked in Dodge City, the "Beautiful, Bibulous Babylon of the Plains."

## ON THE RANGE WITH REMINGTON

These two sketches of cowboy life were drawn for *Harper's* by Remington in the eighties, the upper called "Roused by a Scout" and the lower, "A Quarrel over Cards." Both were representative of life among the cattle outfits of New Mexico and demonstrated the hold on the public interest and imagination of the West long after the disappearance of the actual frontier. In the lexicon of Americana, the cowboy has been the longest lived of folk heroes, surpassing in longevity the Indian scout, the baseball player, the brave engineer and the aviator who, early in his career, became a mere military functionary and degenerated shortly to "fly boy."

# Folklore And Legend Clustered Thick About The Man On Horseback From Texas

For over twenty years Dan Smith, who drew the above sketch of "Cowboys Heading Off a Break from the Trail," was known to millions for his covers of the Sunday magazine section of Joseph Pulitzer's *New York World.* Earlier in his career Smith was staff artist for *Leslie's Weekly,* where this action picture first appeared. Some idea of the unabated popularity of cowboy subjects and Western art generally can be gathered from the continued appearance of such subjects not only in the internal economy of popular periodicals but as cover subjects right down to the turn of the century. William F. Sparks's "Cattle Herders Indulging in Revolver Practice on Telegraph Insulators" appeared on the outside of *Leslie's* in 1881 and is only one of many similar or parallel themes to receive such prominent display. In many ways sensational drawings of gunfights, horseplay, and rowdy conduct among the cowboys were more popular than the restrained portrayals of more conservative artists. Everyone knew that in the West all cowboys rode their horses into saloons, shot out the lights as soon as they were lit and killed one another wholesale. No magazine artist or editor in his right mind was going to dissipate the notion.

## TWO AGES OF TEXAS INDIVIDUALISTS

No two men represented Texas and the Texas character to the world more effectively than General Sam Houston (*below*), hero of San Jacinto, first President of the Republic and forever first citizen in the Texas heart, and Roy Bean. And although they lived a full generation apart, Sam Houston and Judge Roy Bean achieved an immortality not even approached by other men. Even in a later age of high pressure promotion and publicity no character in the news ever got himself a better press than Judge Bean of Langtry, Texas, where "the law west of the Pecos" was administered from Bean's combined saloon and "hall of justice." A shrewd and spectacularly folksy magistrate, Judge Bean first attracted local hilarity by his courtroom decisions and later achieved the national prints with regularity. Langtry had been named for an engineer of the Southern Pacific who had located the stretch of railroad thereabouts, but Bean allowed it had been

named by him in admiration of Lily Langtry, then a raving stage beauty and the toast of two continents. When a defendant was charged with shooting up his laundryman, Judge Bean threw the case out of court. "I've been through all the Laws of Texas," he roared, "up till last year, anyway, and I'm damned if I can find any saying it's crime to kill a Chinaman." When a body was discovered neatly drilled through the head, the judge's verdict as coroner was that "the deceased came to his death at the hands of some person unknown who was a damned good shot." "Judge Bean's methods of jurisprudence may be unorthodox," said a superior justice sent out to investigate the Hon. Bean, "but I'm not the one who's going to criticize him . . . not in Langtry anyway." The mighty and famous of the world all got off the Espee's cars at Langtry Siding in the hope of meeting Judge Bean and were seldom disappointed, as he had thoughtfully located his court and saloon handy to the tracks. The railroad's dispatchers began to complain that trains were being delayed by passengers who became fascinated by Bean's justice and entangled with his whisky and it all ended with the judge's becoming a national institution comparable, in his way, to Chauncey Depew or Jumbo, the circus elephant.

## EASTERN ARTISTS TOOK A DIM VIEW OF THE NOBLE RED MAN

The East had no monopoly during the nineteenth century fad of spiritism on mediums, soothsayers and communications with the dead. Ever since the time when Eilley Orrum had made herself, as she announced, the first millionaire on Nevada's Comstock Lode through the agency of her crystal ball, the spirits had been consulted in mining affairs. A mining company at Eureka, also in Nevada but apparently feeling that home talent wasn't to be relied upon, kept an open telegraphic circuit night and day for three years to New York where a spirit medium dictated the direction of its every drift and heading. Accompanying the picture above, the *Police News* informed its readers that at Denison, Texas, during the progress of a seance, "a skeptical son of the plains blazed away at an Indian chief's spook and wounded a live white fraud." Indians didn't rate highly with anyone, even Eastern editors, and the sketch below shows enforcement "of a policy of clearing scalawag red brutes out of Texas settlements."

## THE WINDS IN THE COTTONWOODS TELL OF DEATH IN LINCOLN COUNTY

The cattle wars of Lincoln County, New Mexico, would never have emerged from the realm of local history of struggle for baronial supremacy save for the presence in the cast of characters of William Bonney, prototypal dead-end kid of the American West. One of the few who extended his friendship to the undersized psychopath was John Tunstall, a sporting English cattleman who was a partner with Alexander McSween in a general store in Lincoln. Because he was allied by feudal interests to John Chisum, mighty cattle overlord of the Pecos Valley, Tunstall was one day shot from the saddle (*above*) by henchmen of Major L. G. Murphy, archenemy of Chisum and his authority. This was the start of the cattle wars which were to sweep New Mexico for half a generation, invoke the intervention of President Arthur from Washington, cause scores of deaths by violence and elevate Billy the Kid to the role of mad-dog killer of Southwest legend. Billy swore to bring death to all those implicated in Tunstall's murder. Within a matter of weeks, the Kid's guns had accounted for four Murphy deputies and the Lincoln County War was making into the bloodiest feud in the history of the American cattle industry. Shown below is the ranch house where John Chisum bestowed princely hospitality on all comers and a rare cabinet photograph of Billy the Kid. Of the ruins of the Chisum ranch Walter Noble Burns has written: "The past beats against it like a shadowy surge. It stands in monumental vigil over the dead years. Back of it are ghosts. The wind in the cottonwoods above it is like a threnody. . . . Gone are the days."

# Billy the Kid Entered Valhalla Early in the Game

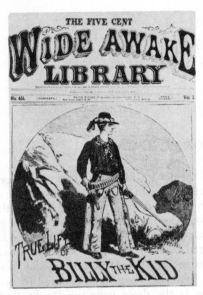

THE FIVE CENT

## WIDE AWAKE LIBRARY

No. 451 COMPLETE.

TRUE LIFE of BILLY THE KID

Not even Buffalo Bill Cody entered the Valhalla of American folk heroes more swiftly than Billy the Kid, and paperback biographies (*left*) were being hawked by news butchers on the trains of the Southern Pacific within six weeks of his death at the hand of Pat Garrett, the resolute sheriff. Below is a painting depicting such gunfights as Billy the Kid survived by the score, executed by Paul Salisbury, a distinguished Western artist in the Remington tradition. Wanted posters (*right*) for the Kid blossomed everywhere in the Southwest in the late seventies.

# REWARD
## ($5,000.00)

Reward for the capture, dead or alive, of one Wm. Wright, better known as

## "BILLY THE KID"

Age, 18. Height, 5 feet, 3 inches. Weight, 125 lbs. Light hair, blue eyes and even features. He is the leader of the worst band of desperadoes the Territory has ever had to deal with. The above reward will be paid for his capture or positive proof of his death.

JIM DALTON, Sheriff.

## DEAD OR ALIVE!
## "BILLY THE KID"

## SHEEP BROUGHT THE WEST TO THE VERGE OF CIVIL WAR

From the beginning sheep were hated by cattlemen. Texas cowboys associated them with Mexicans; beef raisers everywhere feared the way they ate the grazing grass down to the roots and cut up the roots with their sharp hooves. The conflict gradually took on the aspects of civil war. Cowboys established deadlines and ordered the herders not to cross them. In Colorado alone 25,000 sheep and fifty men were killed by night riders who, like those above, cut the fences of the grazers. Sheep were a poor man's property and the great cattle barons felt no compunction about driving them from the land. The fence-cutting wars involving small farmers, sheep grazers and cattlemen raged from the Mexican border to Montana and well into the twentieth century. In some cattle states such as Nevada lamb is not highly regarded to this day as food because of its hostile connotations in the minds of cattle men. Occasionally, too, herds of sheep were menaced by prairie fires and had to be driven to safety by horsemen. This was uncommon practice as the sheep were usually directed by dogs or led by goats.

## BAAAA!

Despite the operational hazards of cowmen and nature, sheepherding continued to be profitable almost everywhere in the West. It flourished in Colorado, Wyoming, Utah, Nevada and Arizona. In Nebraska 'the Southern Nebraska Wool Growers' Association met at Beatrice in the spring for a wool-shearing festival (*right*) at which music and whisky cheered the participants on their way, while the all-embracing Burlington Railroad (*below*) sent ever longer stock trains of lamb stews and chops to the slaughterhouses and processing plants at Omaha, Lincoln and Chicago.

BURLINGTON R.R.

WITTENBERG - SORBER - ST. LOUIS

F. FRENZENY - TAVERNIER

M.K.T. RAILROAD

## THE KATY HAD ITS TROUBLES

As the Missouri-Kansas-Texas Railroad headed for Denison, Texas, in the early seventies, eventually to eliminate the trail drives to Kansas, it hired the famed Western artist team of Frenzeny-Tavernier to execute some promotional art (*left*) showing the joys of the cars. When the rails reached Eufalfa, however, a low person took a shot at Secretary of the Interior J. D. Cox, who was among the dignitaries present, as shown above. Sometimes, too, wrecks strewed the right of way with prematurely slaughtered steers, as in the drawing below.

# Texas Railroading Had Its Informal Aspects

"LET 'EM GO BACK WHERE THEY CAME FROM!"

In a highly informal time and place railroads occasionally carried something other than revenue freight and conventional passengers. When tramps, thieves and drifters congregated in unbearable numbers at Eagle Pass in the eighties a local committee on arrangements commandeered a locomotive of the Mexican Central and sent the greasers packing back where, presumably, they came from. It is improbable that either the I.C.C. or Mexican authorities would sanction such a project today, but things were simpler then.

## AT THE END OF TRAIL WERE THE KANSAS TRACK TOWNS

The trail hands, shown above by Frenzeny and Tavernier in "Calling the Night Guard," in the first years of the cattle trade in Kansas found no trace of the cities that were only the next year or the one thereafter to be "Babylons of the Plains." Abilene, Dodge, Hays and Newton, variously beside the tracks of the Kansas Pacific and the Santa Fe, started as communities of dugouts like so many prairie-dog towns along the single track. A boxcar set out as depot and telegraph station, a water tank, windmill and underground post office and, of course, saloon were all that represented civilization in the beginning. By their return next season, however, the trail riders found everything changed. Magnificent saloons with mahogany bars and crystal fixtures from Kansas City gleamed with coal oil chandeliers, madames paraded their girls after sundown, monte throwers, roulette dealers and keno operators in ratcatcher suits and plug hats dealt in potential fortunes. The presence of the cow hands and their gold pay roll caused the desert to bloom with useful and pleasant things to be had for the buying.

# The Mustangs Were a Heritage from Coronado

Historians of the Southwest, among them J. Frank Dobie, are of the opinion that the wild horses or mustangs which roamed the plains of Texas and New Mexico in uncounted thousands when the first settlers arrived in the early 1800's were descended from the stallions and mares brought to Mexico in the middle of the sixteenth century by the visionary Spanish adventurer Don Francisco Vasquez de Coronado. Breeding with the strays and lost animals from Spanish ranches on both sides of the Rio Grande, the diminutive horses were so abundant that even today, after more than a century and a half of capture, slaughter and elimination by encroaching civilization, a few diminished herds are known to exist in Texas and the central counties of Nevada. The original Spanish steeds were of Arab blood and a high degree of intelligence, and three centuries of precarious existence in the brush evolved an animal ideally suited to the needs of the early stock raisers of the plains. Without the existence of the mustangs, the Indians of the American West would have remained forever the skulking degenerates represented by the Diggers, but once mounted and heirs to a tradition of horsemanship, they became proud and implacable warriors. As is shown in the drawing, the first wagon trains on the plains sometimes saw wild horses pursued and killed by wolves, but until the coming of the white man's civilization the mustangs were able to look out for themselves through countless equine generations.

# Texas Wasn't All Gunfire and Whisky Doings

Although the public concept of Texas in the nineteenth century was one of cattle, cowboys and violence, it also furnished some of the finest hunting anywhere, as is suggested by Frenzeny and Tavernier's "A Deer Drive in the Texas Cross-Timbers" (*above*) and A. R. Waud's "Creasing Mustangs" (*below*). Creasing consisted of stunning a wild horse with a minor gunshot wound to effect its capture.

## TEXAS IN PASTORAL MOOD AND GENTLE

The ubiquitous artist team of Frenzeny and Tavernier found subject material all over the Lone Star State. Above is a pleasant drawing of a ferry across the Red River crowded with passengers and a stagecoach whose horses are being swum across behind the barge. Below is a drawing by the same artists of sugar making, not an industry which instantly suggested itself to readers in connection with the Texas of Sam Houston, the Alamo and the longhorn, but one which had its homely aspects as surely as its counterpart in Vermont, with less likelihood of chilblains.

So well and unfavorably known for its wicked ways was Arizona Territory in the eighties that nobody was surprised when a witness was stabbed to death by the accused in a murder trial at Prescott presided over by Chief Justice French himself.

# XIX

## *Arizona Story*

### As the Century Drew to a Close the Southwest Became the Fast Repository of the Old Ways of the West and the Frontier of Other Times

WHETHER THE PACIFIC NORTHWEST or the Deep Southwest along the Mexican Border from the Big Bend Country of Texas to Fort Yuma on the Colorado retained its character as part of the Old West the longer is a matter for regional dispute. In each case the wilder aspects of the frontier managed to survive well into the twentieth century and there are latent suggestions of them to this day in both Arizona and the deep woods of Oregon.

Last of the great bonanzas of the nineteenth century, save only the Cripple Creek District of Colorado, Tombstone was so individualistic in its philosophy, so productive of violence and so fragrant with exploits of the Western great that its name still kindles the imaginations of men and is magic in factual history, fiction and the cinema. If any names in the record of the Western continent are sure of immortality, and true believers in the American legend know that there are scores of them, then so are those of the Lucky Cuss Mine, of Wyatt Earp, of *The Tombstone Epitaph,* and of Ed Schieffelin who started the whole show and got it thunderingly on the road to immortality.

Ed Schieffelin came to Arizona in 1877 as a scout under the command of a greater scout, Al Sieber, and while on patrol duty near the future but as yet unimagined site of Tombstone, he caught sight of unmistakable traces of silver embedded in the quartz float of a desolate hillside. Schieffelin said nothing of the matter at the time, but shortly thereafter was off on a private prowl which had nothing to do with keeping track of Geronimo's Apaches who were at the moment terrifying the entire Arizona border with their sudden forays from the Dragoon Mountains, their looting and pitiless murder.

At the old Brunckow mine, unproductive for nearly twenty years, Al Sieber came across his former scout sitting on a rock pile and inquired what occupied his time. Prospecting, said Schieffelin good-naturedly.

"All you'll ever find in those hills will be your tombstone," replied Sieber and, all unknown, the future metropolis of Arizona's gunfire age was given a name.

Schieffelin discovered silver in fantastic quantities in the San Pedro Valley. His first mine was named for Sieber's prophetic remark, the Tombstone. Other discoveries followed as Schieffelin cut his brother Al and Richard Gird, a local mine superintendent, in on his incredible secret. The partners uncovered the Lucky Cuss, the Grand Central and the Contention, the last so named for a disagreement of policy among the partners just before its discovery. While Gird and Al Schieffelin were building a cabin at the Lucky Cuss, Ed found the Tough Nut. So many promising locations now belonged to the trio and so rich were their prospects that they hardly knew which one to commence operating.

No mining discovery of consequence was a secret for long in the West and in a short time the valleys of Arizona were crowded with white-topped wagons in numbers suggestive of the rushes in other years to Virginia City, to the Reese, to Alder Gulch and Deadwood. Scores lost their lives to Apaches and others perished from the elements, whisky and assorted mischance, but they kept on coming. The city of Tombstone was organized in 1879 and in the proverbial twinkling of an eye emerged as Metropolis. Stage services were established to all points of the compass: Lordsburg, Benson, Bisbee and Tucson. A town was platted with Allen, Tough Nut and Fremont Streets as its principal thoroughfares. There were radiant saloons, the Alhambra, Crystal Palace and the Oriental. There were strumpets past counting who arrived with their hatboxes and Saratoga trunks on every incoming conveyance. There were gamblers in well-cut frock coats and immaculate linen and, final proof of the advent of civilization, there were no fewer than five newspapers, the *Epitaph, Nugget, Evening Gossip, Prospector* and *Expositor*.

Lady angel of the booming camp—she had her counterpart in Julia Bulette on the Comstock and numberless other venturesome women of various morality as long as the frontier lasted—was Nellie Cashman, proprietress of the Russ House, named for its great original in San Francisco. First clergyman and one who has delighted amateurs of the incongruous ever since was the Rev. Endicott Peabody, destined in later years to be headmaster at ultrafashionable Groton School for the sons of the most proper (and solvent) Bostonians. Counterpart of a thousand French Louis restaurant owners in California, Colorado and Montana, Julius Caesar amazed the miners with flaming deserts and featherweight soufflés at his Maison Dorée, also named for a San Francisco prototype. An enterprising physician, specializing in the occupational sickness of the region, lead poisoning, installed an electric device for the location of gunshot in the human anatomy. The Bird Cage Theater attracted burlesque shows that wouldn't have been permitted in Boston's Scollay Square and its walls bulged with gunfire and inextinguishable laughter as female impersonators followed dog and pony acts, the Swiss bellringers and trained seals.

Incomparably the bloodiest and most celebrated episode in Tombstone's rugged history was the shooting at the O.K. corral in which Wyatt Earp and his brothers and Doc Holliday made an end once and for all of the gang of murderers, cattle rustlers and highwaymen headed by Ike and Billy Clanton and Frank McLowery. Until that time Tombstone had been noted in the outer world for its first millionaire, Ed Schieffelin, and his rich man's eccentricities, and for the wealth of its mines, but with the O.K. corral it became the gunfire capital of the Southwest, heir to the legendary mantle of Abilene, Dodge City and Newton as a vicinity from which the gunsmoke never altogether cleared.

The feud between Wyatt Earp as city marshal and the Clantons was probably the most celebrated in the annals of the American West. Allied with Wyatt Earp were his brothers Morgan and Virgil, Doc Holliday, the enigmatic consumptive, and Marshall Williams, Tombstone agent for Wells Fargo. The Clanton gang included Curly Bill Brocius, Ike and Billy Clanton, John Ringo, Frank and Tom McLowery and Tombstone's crooked sheriff, John Behan. When the smoke at the O.K. cleared Tom and Frank McLowery were dead, as was Billy Clanton. Ike Clanton had ignominiously fled from the scene of battle and Morgan Earp was shot through the shoulder. Doc Holliday had added another chapter to one of the incredible personal sagas of the frontier and, even before Billy Clanton, dying in Doc Goodfellow's office, whispered, "Pull off my boots; I promised my mother I'd never die with them on," folklore was taking substance and history was already made.

Wyatt Earp went on from Tombstone to many places but never to greater moments. After the O.K. corral Tombstone went on to wealthier destinies but never to greater drama. Doc Holliday, "coldest-blooded killer in Tombstone," wit, gambler and lover of Big Nose Kate, lived for fifteen years after his Tombstone days, eventually dying in Colorado of the tuberculosis that had promised death so long.

Together Wyatt Earp and Doc Holliday rode into immortality, sharing Tombstone between them as background for one of the gorgeous interludes which were synonymous with the Old West during the riding years.

The Arizona sands were littered with gruesome remains of prospecting parties wiped out by Apache raiders, but Ed Schieffelin and his brothers were undismayed.

## EVERY TOMBSTONE REQUIRES AN EPITAPH

When Ed Schieffelin, who was just such a whisker'ed desert rat as these, told Scout Al Sieber he was going prospecting in the hills of Arizona close by the Mexican border, Sieber forecast that all he'd ever find would be his tombstone. Ed struck silver rich and named his first mine and the eventual camp that followed it for Sieber's prophetic remark. Tombstone, of course, had to have its epitaph and *The Tombstone Epitaph* soon became one of the celebrated newspapers of the Western frontier, the repository of all the legend that made the community it reported one of the notable properties of the gun-fighting years of the Western continent.

One of the well-known theaters of the golden noontide of the road, Tombstone's still standing Bird Cage, attracted fewer Shakespearean companies than it did burlesque queens, dog and pony shows, Swiss bellringers and vaudeville performers. The tastes of its patrons were low and merry and the management sought to oblige.

## EPICENE DOINGS MARKED THE BIRD CAGE SHOWS

One of the first records of the drag show or performance by female impersonators was, incongruously enough, of a show at Tombstone's supposedly ruggedly virile Bird Cage. An outraged reporter for the *Arizona Star* of Tucson reported in 1884 that "Shortly after midnight the curtain rang up on the can-can in all its glory. As the can-can girls retired three men clad in tights with women's undergarments over them sprang to the stage and vied with each other in the obscenity of their actions. . . . At each repetition they sought to outdo if possible the filthiness of their previous actions and, to cap the climax, both men and women joined in the debasing exhibition together." In the scene below a patron, possibly angered by the performance, threatens the Bird Cage manager while "the girls" look on.

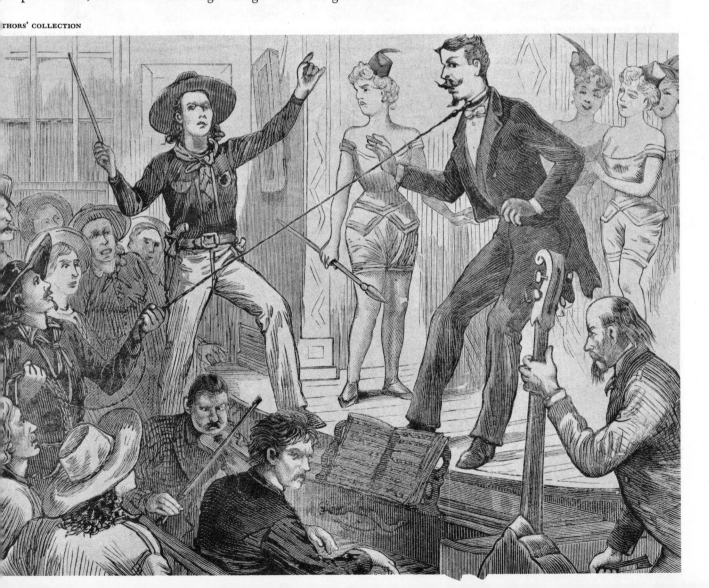

The more sensational aspects of life in the Tombstone eighties are suggested by the manner in which, in the above drawing, train robbers threatened a Southern Pacific express messenger with being blown up with giant powder in a holdup near Tucson, while at Deming a similar gang of desperadoes throw the switch to put the express in a siding where they can plunder it at leisure. The Espee's detective police were busy in those years.

ALL THE VIOLENCE OF THE EARLIER FRONTIER WAS RELIVED IN ARIZONA

When hardhearted bandits held up a wagon train on the El Paso-Fort Yuma crossing and the immigrants stoutly refused to divulge the hiding place of their money, the leader threatened to roast a child alive if the loot were not forthcoming. This sort of thing gave Arizona a bad name in the East and frightened the more timid homesteaders cruelly.

When President Garfield was murdered by an insane assassin in the Baltimore & Ohio depot in Washington, surgeons of national note for the first time attempted the location of the fatal bullet with magnetic coils in an attempt to save the Chief Executive's life. Shortly thereafter, so great was the press of business in gunshot wounds in Tombstone, that an enterprising physician advertised similar facilities at the disposal of Arizona residents who had been so careless as to acquire slugs in their anatomies. "An Electrical Detector Machine Ready to Locate Wounds from Gunfire and Assist in the Extraction of the Foreign Body" ran their advertisement in the *Nugget*. Science was making strides in the Southwest.

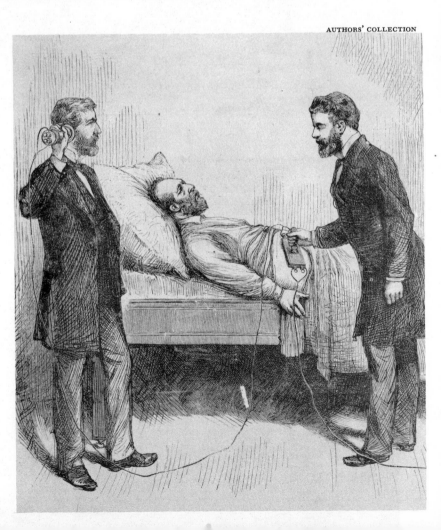

## "YOUR MONEY AND YOUR LIFE"

Most important figure in the pioneer destinies of the Great Southwest in the era immediately before the Civil War was John Butterfield, an old and experienced stager from York State whose Butterfield's Overland Mail & Express Stages swung from Tipton, Missouri, railhead of the Missouri-Pacific Railroad, in a vast half circle through Arizona Territory to California known as the "ox-bow" route. On its initial run the mail arrived in Montgomery Street from St. Louis in twenty-three days, thus effectively breaking the steamship monopoly of fast communications between California and the East via Panama. The scarcity of water, the seemingly interminable stages between coaching stations, the ever-present peril of Apaches all combined to make the El Paso-Tucson-Fort Yuma route one of the most difficult mail runs in the history of American staging and after the Civil War, when the express began carrying valuable consignments of gold, there came the added peril of stage robbers. Most vulnerable point on the Butterfield run between Tucson and Silver City was old Cienega Station, located in a box canyon which made knocking off the drivers and messengers a simple preliminary to seizing the Wells Fargo strongbox. Here a gang of cutthroats committed so many robberies that they maintained a private graveyard later discovered to hold eighteen tenants, but in 1873 the entire gang of Cienega Benders was wiped out by Apaches and for years thereafter hopeful prospectors dug up the surrounding desert in the hope of recovering buried treasure whose secret died with the robbers. None was ever found but records showed that vast sums including a specific $75,000 gold shipment for an Army paymaster disappeared here never again to reach circulation. Old-timers maintain that it is still buried beneath the Arizona cottonwoods that line the canyon. Zogbaum's classic portrayal of a stage robbery is typical of its technique from Tombstone to Alder Gulch and might very well represent a night interlude far away and long ago at Cienega Bend.

# The Road Was a Ribbon of Moonlight

# Over the Purple Moor

# As the Highwayman Came Riding - - -

"Humper Jack Was on the Howl" the *Police News* was happy to caption this lively interlude in a courtroom at Pinto, Arizona. The accompanying news account revealed that, once the shirtsleeved magistrate had disarmed the prisoner, he fined him in the manner of Judge Roy Bean $20 and a round of drinks for all concerned at the Hurry Back Saloon handily located next door to court.

In an unnamed bar in Tombstone a group of the boys brought in the skeleton of an old associate found near his claim in the surrounding desert and demanded a drink for their old comrade. "He Liked Them Filled Right to the Top" they told the bartender.

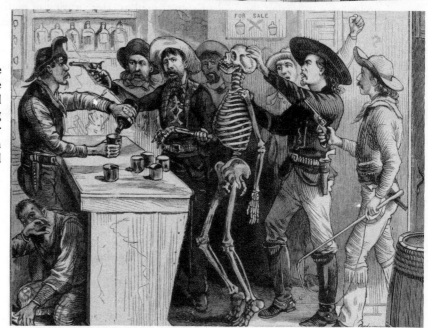

Having perhaps heard of the respectful welcome accorded the Rev. Endicott Peabody when he arrived at Tombstone and was given the loan of the Crystal Palace Saloon of a Sunday morning, "Lampasas Jake, the Cowboy Evangelist," took over less willingly offered premises in neighboring Casa Grande. "Get down on your knees and yell," he exhorted his congregation.

## GREAT SNAKES!

Readers of sensational periodicals liked their reptiles as reported from Arizona and other parts of the Southwest mean, deadly and enormous. At the top, a favorite character of the *Police News*, "an old time prospector and desert rat who was no tenderfoot," gives his quietus to a centipede imprudent enough to awaken him at his own campfire "in the fearful desert waste of Arizona near Fort Yuma." In the center an Indian maiden visits terrible retribution upon her seducer, a United States Cavalryman, at Fort Seldon, New Mexico, while at the bottom "Captain Dade and His Gang Discovered Stung to Death, Wiped Out in Their Lair at Carizozo, N. M."

# The Epic Battle Of the Okay Corral Was the Apotheosis of Gunfighting In Bloody Tombstone

Excepting only the engagement at Northfield in which the embattled Minnesota farmers put an end forever to the organized activities of the James boys, the Battle of the O.K. corral remains the classic massacre of outlaws in the annals of the West. Here, in a matter of moments, Old Man Clanton's gang of stage robbers, cattle rustlers and professional murderers was liquidated as an entity by the forces of law represented by Wyatt Earp, Marshal of Tombstone, his brothers Morgan and Virgil and the quixotic Doc Holliday. Depicted by atmosphere-happy staff artists of *The Illustrated Police News* (*above*), the O.K. battle has little relation to factual reality. Instead of the plainsman's dress of the drawing, the Earps wore the conventional professional attire of the frontier peace officer: slouch hats, single-breasted black frock coats and flowing black ties. None of them wore his hair long and all were clean shaved save for handlebar mustaches. Doc Holliday entered the battle with a double barrel shotgun, the Earps with the conventional single action Colt's peacemaker. The drawing on the dust jacket (*below*) for Stuart Lake's *Wyatt Earp, Frontier Marshal,* is more accurate. When the smoke cleared Tom McLowery, a Clanton henchman, was dead, blown to ribbons by Holliday's shotgun, Billy Clanton, Old Man Clanton's son, was mortally wounded, Frank McLowery was dead and Ike Clanton himself, a coward and traitor to his followers, had fled the field with screams for mercy. Virgil and Morgan Earp were wounded and history had been made and a chapter added to the folklore of the Southwest.

## FROM TOMBSTONE TO GROTON SCHOOL WAS QUITE A STAGE ON THE ROAD

Almost as incongruous a figure in boiling Tombstone as the mysterious Doc Holliday was a youthful Episcopal clergyman who during the eighties was on terms of agreeable acquaintance with such varied Tombstoners as Nellie Cashman, proprietor of the Russ House and everybody's friend, first citizen Ed Schieffelin and Julius Caesar, the camp's leading restaurateur and proprietor of the Maison Dorée. When the Reverend Peabody, educated at Cheltenham and graduated from Cambridge University in England, lacked a church in which to hold services, Nellie Cashman prevailed on the owners of the Crystal Palace to lend him their premises for Sunday morning. There, as depicted above, the good pastor preached salvation among the shrouded barroom nudes and temporarily disused faro layouts. Later the Reverend Peabody goes on to become headmaster of Groton School for scions of the aristocracy back in Massachusetts, a position of fearful responsibilities to the first families of the land. Does the Reverend Peabody, strolling the shaded promenades of Commonwealth Avenue with the thrice-perfumed Shaws, Saltonstalls, Elliots and Cabots, think back to the wooden sidewalks of Tough Nut Street and the miners at the bar of the Palace Saloon? Dining at the Somerset Club with the Very Rev. William Lawrence, Episcopal Bishop of the Diocese of Massachusetts and heir to the brimstone heritage of Cotton Mather, does he recall Wyatt Earp carving a T-bone at the Maison Dorée with his shooting irons before him among the eating tools?

## HOTHEADS WANTED WAR WITH MEXICO, TOO

In the midst of the Apache uprisings there was trouble all along the border with Mexico. Apaches under Victorio who had fled from Arizona raided across the American boundary, their numbers often augmented by renegade Mexicans, killing ranchers and driving off their livestock. As far away as Brownsville Mexican officers ordered cannon trained on the American city across the Rio Grande and full-scale war threatened. All along the Rio Grande smuggling, as shown above, was a problem. Elsewhere American and Mexican authorities cooperated, as shown below, returning wanted criminals to their own countries and attempting to pour oil on troubled waters.

At Brownsville cannon were trained by Mexican gunners on the American shore and patriots of both countries incited others to bravery with oratory compounded with whisky and tequila. The moment was tense, but the trouble of brief duration.

## REAL WOES AND IMAGINARY

Unrest along the Mexican border had its comic repercussions as far away as Brunswick, Georgia, where a regiment of militia (*right*) was thrown into panic when a fictitious general, inspired by practical jokers in the rival city of Savannah, appeared with orders commanding them at once to active duty in Texas. In the sketch below, the U.S. Cavalry gallops out of Fort Brown, Texas, in pursuit of Mexican raiders across the Rio Grande.

## THE ARIZONA COUNTRYSIDE TREMBLED AT GERONIMO'S NAME

The Arizona wars with the Apaches under Cochise and later Geronimo were, like the wars in the Dakotas and Montana, the result of a number of factors all deriving from encroachments by white men in search of precious metals, the declining hunting lands and exploitation by unscrupulous Indian agents, bootleggers and frontier trash generally. The last phase of the Apache wars actually had its beginnings in the sale of liquor to Indians by a stage agent at Sulphur Springs in the Dragoon Mountains. Even less able to contain whisky than most Indians, the Apaches began a small-time war among themselves in which several women and children were killed, and resentment against the whites flared as a result. Soon the dreaded news that Geronimo and his warriors were on the warpath was circulated abroad. One afternoon the stage from Fort Davis arrived at Fort Quitman with a dead driver and a passenger riddled with arrows, and the entire Southwest knew that an Indian war of an undeclared but particularly deadly sort was on. Above is a photograph showing Geronimo (*center*) and his body-guard just before their conference with General Crook in 1886. Below is Remington's drawing for *Harper's,* "The Apaches Are Coming."

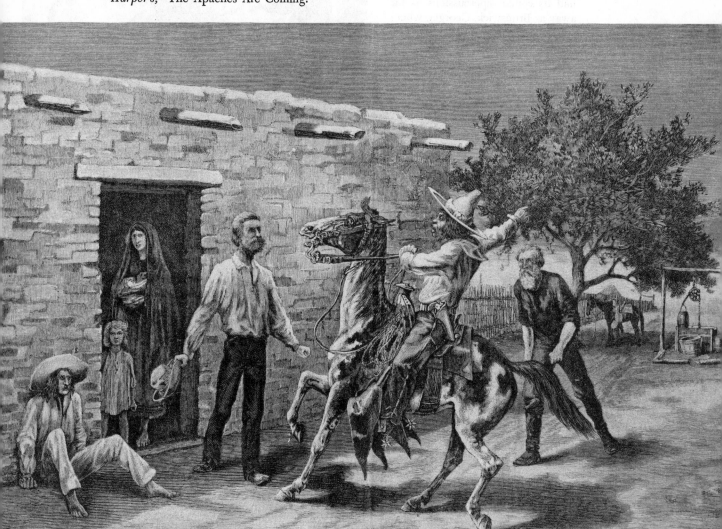

## THE BORDER FLAMED INTO WARFARE

Soon the periodicals of the East, sensational and conservative alike, blossomed with tales of burnings, massacres and atrocities against white settlers in Arizona by Geronimo's Apaches. General Crook was recalled from the Department of the Platte and set about repairing the damage done in his absence. "When you left we were content," one warrior, Alchise, told Crook. "Everything was peace. The officers you had here were taken away and new ones came in—a different kind. . . . We hadn't any confidence in them." Above Paul Frenzeny sketches "An Apache Raid" while below, in the *Police Gazette,* Frank Cody, a New Mexican rancher, is cooked to death by braves over his own stove.

## ACTION IN THE DRAGOONS

Ranking second in reputation for cruelty and atrocities only to the Comanches, the Apaches of Arizona provided lurid reading for the East, as in this contemporary artist's sketch entitled: "The Pima Valley Overrun and Desolated by Red Devils."

TWO PICTURES: AUTHORS' COLLECTION

## THE WORD APACHE WAS SYNONYMOUS WITH MURDER

The sketch above shows a raid upon homesteaders in the Pima Valley in Arizona by followers of Cochise early in the Apache troubles. Below, all the bathos of a sentimental age is captured in "The Little One's Slipper" which occupied a full page to bring tears to the eyes of readers in *Leslie's* for September 25, 1886.

## STUFF OF THE CINEMA

All the folklore of Indian warfare on the frontier, from the Adirondacks to the killing of the Rev. Marcus Whitman in Oregon, was recapitulated in the Apache wars of Arizona. In the contemporary drawing above is shown a captive white boy carried off in some nameless raid and brought up in an Indian camp. His story is as old as warfare between Indians and whites. Below Apache raiders, notably miscostumed by the artist, are shown descending upon a rancher's home in New Mexico and murdering the head of the family while his wife and children cower in concealment. All the clichés of Indian legend became reality again in Arizona.

## MURDER LURKED ON BOTH SIDES OF THE BORDER

More than a decade before the Apache troubles, J. Ross Browne, star reporter for *Harper's*, drew this sketch of the body of a marauding Indian for his "A Tour Through Arizona." Two years later Browne reported the body as still being where he had seen it, "arrows were sticking all over the breast and abdomen; doubtless tokens of barbarous hatred left by some passing Pimo or Maricopa. . . . The sketch is characteristic of life and adventure in Arizona." In the early eighties when he covered the Apache wars, Browne sketched himself, heavily armed as he worked in the theater of war. Below is one of the countless Mexican sheepherders and small ranchers murdered by the renegade Victorio after he fled from Arizona across the national boundary.

When "thieving redskins" burst in upon an unarmed rancher near Globe, Arizona, they were put to flight when the undaunted settler placed a lighted candle in a barrel of black powder and promised to kick it over unless they retired.

These two Arizona scouts with a cabin on the Gila tanned the trophies of their hunting, which was largely devoted to making live Indians into good Indians.

"Pete, did you notice how I dropped the redskin who pit the pizzened arrer in my moccasin?" reminisced one ancient fresh from the services of old John Butterfield in Arizona. "Captin, the varmints lay thick as leaves behind the rocks . . . so Pete and me scrouched down, made a little smoke with some sticks, and then we moved off a few rods where we could get a clar peep. . . . On a sudden I seed the chap that druv the arrer in my hide; I just fetched old Ginger up and drawed a bead on his cratch, and, stranger, I giv him such a winch in the stomach that he dropped straight in his tracks, he did! In five jumps I riz his hair, and Pete and me weren't troubled agin for a week."

## APACHE RAIDERS MADE THE BLOOD RUN COLD

Until Geronimo's final surrender the staff artists of Eastern periodicals had a field day with the treachery and cruelty of the Indians of the Southwest, to whom they compared the Sioux, who had only recently butchered Custer's Seventh Cavalry in Montana, as the pattern of knighthood and chivalry in the field. Certainly the Apaches had no good reputation among the settlers, ranchers, miners and soldiers who encountered them on the warpath in the Arizona eighties.

## WITH REMINGTON IN ARIZONA

It was during the Apache wars in Arizona that Frederic Remington came into his own as the most celebrated portrayer of the types, activities and scenes of the military West. The three sketches here reproduced, all of them typical of the artist's passion for detail of men, horses and equipment, were originally published in *Harper's*. At the top is "Arrival of a Courier," in the center, "Saddle Up," and below, "Dismounted: The Fourth Troopers Moving the Led Horses." The last depicted a classic cavalry maneuver of the period in which three dismounted troopers sought cover while the fourth took charge of their and his own mounts.

## THE BEST OF REMINGTON

Three representative Remingtons of his Arizona period were "Indian Scouts on Geronimo's Trail," drawn for *Harper's* in August 1886, "A Friendly Scout Signaling the Main Column," shown on horseback below, and "Signaling the Main Command," in which a mounted trooper is waving a pennon atop a cavalry spear against the vastness of the Montana desert for background.

Remington was never better than when he depicted the U.S. Cavalry, in this case dismounted, in action against the enemy in the mist-hidden mountain ranges of the Deep Southwest in Arizona and New Mexico.

"The Rescue of Corporal Scott" shows an episode in the Apache campaigns of General Crook in Arizona and was drawn by Remington for the outside cover of *Harper's Weekly* for August 21, 1886.

## DEATH RODE THE ARIZONA NIGHT, AND BURIAL

Very few Remingtons rank "Shot on Picket," which was redrawn for *Harper's* by T. de Thulstrup and published there on a double-truck layout covering two black and white pages. The burial party sketched below was completely drawn by Remington and contains all the pathos, mystery and ghostly qualities of a midnight burial party in an alien land.

Less classic than Remington but still possessed of tremendous interest for readers of their time were the depiction of summary punishment of a thief in camp by cavalrymen in Arizona (*above*) and a battle between old soldier prospectors near Lordsburg, New Mexico, and cowboy claim jumpers, both of which appeared in the *Police News* of the time.

## AN END TO THE APACHES

Inevitably the noose of conquest drew tighter around the last bands of embattled Apaches in Arizona and New Mexico as scouts from General Crook's command drew beads on lonely warriors separated from their friends and troopers of the peerless United States Cavalry rode down and captured stragglers (*above*) on the plains. The end was in sight when Chiefs Nané, Chato and 260 other hostiles sought out General Crook and surrendered, saying they were tired of war at long last. Soon after this Geronimo himself surrendered, together with his lieutenants Nachite and Loco, and the rebellion was at an end. In the lower drawing by W. A. Rogers for *Harper's,* Nané is shown accompanied by a lone gun-bearer, suing for peace with bearded General Crook in the Sierra Madre.

# In the End Whiskey, the Silk Hat and the Motorcar Triumphed

In the fall of 1886 the Apache chiefs Geronimo and Natchez, together with thirty-two of their braves and squaws, were brought into San Antonio aboard the steamcars of the Southern Pacific, whose passengers they had so long and often terrified, on the way to exile in Florida. They had surrendered to General Nelson A. Miles a few weeks previous, appropriately enough, at Skeleton Canyon. Geronimo, terror of the Dragoons and the scourge of the high passes of the Huachucas, was tamed at last. Many years later he posed (*below*) clothed in the properties of the white man who had conquered him, a silk top hat and a motorcar. Civilization and the machine age had completely enslaved the noble red man in the end.

# Bibliography

Asbury, Herbert. *The Barbary Coast*. New York: Alfred A. Knopf, Inc., 1936.

———. *The French Quarter; An Informal History of the New Orleans Underworld*. New York: Garden City Books, 1938.

Ashton, Wendell J. *Voice of The West: Biography of a Pioneer Newspaper*. New York: Duell, Sloan & Pearce, Inc., 1950.

Bancroft, Hubert Howe. *History of California*. San Francisco: The History Company, 1890.

Banning, William, and Hugh George. *Six Horses*. New York: The Century Company, 1930.

Beebe, Lucius. *Comstock Commotion, The Story of The Territorial Enterprise*. California: Stanford University Press, 1954.

——— and Charles Clegg. *U.S. West, the Saga of Wells Fargo*. New York: E. P. Dutton & Co., Inc., 1950.

Breihan, Carl W. *The Complete and Authentic Life of Jesse James*. New York: Frederick Fell, 1953.

Brooks, Juanita. *The Mountain Meadows Massacre*. California: Stanford University Press, 1950.

Brown, Dee and Martin F. Schmitt. *Trail Driving Days*. New York: Charles Scribner's Sons, 1952.

Browne, J. Ross. *A Peep at Washoe*.

Bruce, John. *Gaudy Century: The Story of San Francisco's Hundred Years of Robust Journalism*. New York: Random House, 1948.

Burns, Walter Noble. *Tombstone: An Iliad of the Southwest*. New York: Doubleday, Doran & Co., 1929.

Casey, Robert J. *The Black Hills and Their Incredible Characters*. New York: The Bobbs-Merrill Company, Inc., 1949.

——— *The Texas Border and Some Borderliners*. New York: The Bobbs-Merrill Company, Inc., 1950.

Chalfant, W. A. *Gold, Guns and Ghost Towns*. California: Stanford University Press, 1947.

Chapman, Arthur. *The Pony Express*. New York: G. P. Putnam's Sons, 1932.

Corle, Edwin. *Billy the Kid*. New York: Duell, Sloan & Pearce, Inc., 1953.

Custer, George Armstrong. *My Life on the Plains*. New York: Sheldon and Company, 1874.

Davis, Samuel Post. *The History of Nevada*. The Elms Publishing Co., Inc., 1913.

De Quille, Dan. *The Big Bonanza*. New York: Alfred A. Knopf, Inc., 1947.

De Voto, Bernard. *The Year of Decision.* New York: The Macmillan Co., 1944.

——— *Across the Wide Missouri.* Boston: Houghton Mifflin Co., 1947.

Dimsdale, Thomas J. *The Vigilantes of Montana.* D. W. Tilton & Co., 1866.

Dobie, Charles Cladwell. *San Francisco: A Pageant.* New York: Appleton Century, 1939.

Dodge, Richard Irving. *The Plains of the Great West.* New York: Putnam's Sons, 1877.

Drury, Wells. *An Editor of the Comstock Lode.* New York: Farrar & Rinehart, Inc., 1936.

Fowler, Gene. *Timber Line: A Story of Bonfils and Tammen.* New York: Garden City Books, 1947.

*Frank Leslie's Illustrated Weekly Newspaper.*

Fremont, John C. *The Exploration Expedition to the Rocky Mountains in the Year 1842.*

Gard, Wayne. *Frontier Justice.* Norman: University of Oklahoma Press, 1949.

Glasscock, C. B. *The War of the Copper Kings.* New York: The Bobbs-Merrill Company, Inc., 1935.

Hale, William Harlan. *Horace Greeley: Voice of the People.* New York: Harper & Brothers, 1950.

Harlow, Alvin. *Old Waybills: The Romance of the Express Companies.* New York: Appleton-Century Company, Inc., 1934.

*Harper's Weekly.*

Helper, Hinton. *The Land of Gold.* Baltimore: H. Taylor, 1855.

Hicks, John Edwards. *Adventures of a Tramp Printer 1880–1890.* Kansas City, Mo.: Midamericana Press, 1950.

Holbrook, Stewart. *Holy Old Mackinaw, A Natural History of the American Lumberjack.* New York: The Macmillan Co., 1938.

——— *Far Corner: A Personal View of the Northwest.* New York: The Macmillan Co., 1952.

Holloway, Carroll C. *Texas Gun Lore.* San Antonio, Texas: The Naylor Company, 1951.

Horan, James D. *Desperate Men.* New York: G. P. Putnam's Sons, 1952.

——— *Desperate Women.* New York: G. P. Putnam's Sons, 1952.

Howard, Joseph Kinsey. *Montana: High Wide and Handsome.* New Haven, Conn.: Yale University Press, 1943.

Hunter, Louis C. & Hunter, B. J. *Steamboats on the Western Rivers.* Cambridge, Mass.: Harvard University Press, 1949.

*Illustrated Police News, Law Courts & Weekly Record.*

Inman, Henry. *The Old Santa Fe Trail: The Story of a Great Highway.* New York: The Macmillan Co., 1897.

Jackson, Joseph Henry. *Anybody's Gold: The Story of California's Mining Towns.* New York: Appleton-Century Company, Inc., 1941.

Jannewein, J. Leonard. *Calamity Jane of the Western Trails.* Huron, S. Dak.: Dakota Books, 1953.

Kahn, Edgar M. *Cable Car Days in San Francisco.* California: Stanford University Press, 1944.

Karsner, David. *Silver Dollar: The Story of the Tabors.* New York: Covici, Friede, 1932.

Lake, Stuart N. *Wyatt Earp: Frontier Marshal.* Boston: Houghton Mifflin Co., 1931.

Langford, N. P. *Vigilante Days and Ways.* Chicago: A. C. McClurg & Co., 1912.

Lavender, David. *The Big Divide.* New York: Doubleday & Company, Inc., 1948.

Lewis, Lloyd, and S. M. Pargellis. *Granger Country: A Pictorial Social History of the Burlington Railroad.* Boston: Little, Brown & Co., 1949.

Lewis, Oscar. *The Big Four.* New York: Alfred A. Knopf, Inc., 1938.

—————— *Silver Kings.* New York: Alfred A. Knopf, Inc., 1947.

Lyman, George. *The Saga of the Comstock Lode: Boom Days in Virginia City.* New York: Charles Scribner's Sons, 1934.

Mack, Effie Mona. *Mark Twain in Nevada.* New York: Charles Scribner's Sons, 1947.

Majors, Alexander. *Seventy Years on the Frontier.* Chicago: Rand, McNally & Company, 1893.

Marryat, Francis Samuel. *Mountains and Molehills.* California: Stanford University Press, 1952.

Marshall, James. *Santa Fe, The Railroad That Built an Empire.* New York: Random House, 1945.

Miller, Joseph (ed.). *The Arizona Story.* New York: Hastings House Publishers, Inc., 1952.

Myers, John Myers. *The Last Chance: Tombstone's Early Years.* New York: E. P. Dutton & Co., Inc., 1950.

*National Police Gazette.*

Nickols, Alice. *Bleeding Kansas.*

Parkhill, Forbes. *The Wildest of the West.* New York: Henry Holt & Co., Inc., 1951.

Parkman, Francis. *The Oregon Trail: Sketches of Prairie and Rocky Mountain Life.* New York: Modern Library, 1949.

Peattie, Roderick. *The Black Hills.* New York: Vanguard Press, 1952.

Rathbone, Perry T. (ed.). *Mississippi Panorama.* Missouri: St. Louis City Art Museum, 1950.

Richardson, Albert. *Beyond the Mississippi.* New York: Bliss & Co., 1867.

*Rocky Mountain News.* Denver, Colorado.

Sandoz, Mari. *The Buffalo Hunters: The Story of the Hide Men.* New York: Hastings House Publishers, Inc., 1954.

Settle, Raymond W. & Lund, Mary. *Empire on Wheels.* California: Stanford University Press, 1949.

Shirley, Glenn. *Toughest of Them All.* Albuquerque: University of New Mexico Press, 1953.

Sprague, Marshall. *Money Mountain: The Story of Cripple Creek Gold.* Boston: Little, Brown & Co., 1953.

Taft, Robert. *Photography and the American Scene: A Social History, 1839–1889.* New York: The Macmillan Co., 1938.

—— *Artists and Illustrators of the Old West, 1850–1900.* New York: Charles Scribner's Sons, 1953.

Tallant, Robert. *The Romantic New Orleanians.* New York: E. P. Dutton & Co., Inc., 1950.

*Territorial Enterprise.* Virginia City, Nevada.

*Tombstone Epitaph.* Tombstone, Arizona.

Twain, Mark. *Roughing It.* New York: Harper & Brothers, 1903.

Vestal, Stanley, *Joe Meek, The Merry Mountain Man.* Caldwell, Idaho: Caxton Printers, Ltd., 1952.

—— *Queen of the Cowtowns: Dodge City 1872–1866.* New York: Harper & Brothers, 1952.

Wellman, Paul I. *The Trampling Herd.* New York: Carrick and Evans, Inc., 1939.

Wells, Evelyn and Harry Peterson. *The '49ers.* New York: Doubleday & Company, Inc., 1949.

Willison, George F. *Here They Dug the Gold.* New York: Harcourt, Brace & Co., 1946.

Wilson, Neill C. *Treasure Express: Epic Days of the Wells Fargo.* New York: The Macmillan Co., 1936.

—— *Silver Stampede; The Career of Death Valley's Hell-Camp, Old Panamint.* New York: The Macmillan Co., 1936.

Wilstach, Frank J. *Wild Bill Hickok: The Prince of Pistoleers.* New York: Garden City Publishing Co., Inc., 1926.

Winther, Oscar Osburn. *Via Western Express & Stagecoach.* California: Stanford University Press, 1945.

*Books by Lucius Beebe and Charles Clegg*

U.S. WEST, THE SAGA OF WELLS FARGO

MIXED TRAIN DAILY

HEAR THE TRAIN BLOW

LEGENDS OF THE COMSTOCK LODE

VIRGINIA & TRUCKEE

HIGHBALL, A RAILROAD PAGEANT

THE AMERICAN WEST

*Books by Lucius Beebe*

BOSTON AND THE BOSTON LEGEND

HIGH IRON

HIGHLINERS

TRAINS IN TRANSITION

COMSTOCK COMMOTION, THE STORY OF *The Territorial Enterprise*

SNOOT IF YOU MUST

THE STORK CLUB BAR BOOK